The Encyclopedia of
Collectibles

TIME
LIFE ®
BOOKS

Other Publications:
Planet Earth
Collector's Library of the Civil War
Library of Health
Classics of the Old West
The Epic of Flight
The Good Cook
The Seafarers
The Great Cities
World War II
Home Repair and Improvement
The World's Wild Places
The Time-Life Library of Boating
Human Behavior
The Art of Sewing
The Old West
The Emergence of Man
The American Wilderness
The Time-Life Encyclopedia of Gardening
Life Library of Photography
This Fabulous Century
Foods of the World
Time-Life Library of America
Time-Life Library of Art
Great Ages of Man
Life Science Library
The Life History of the United States
Time Reading Program
Life Nature Library
Life World Library
Family Library:
    How Things Work in Your Home
    The Time-Life Book of the Family Car
    The Time-Life Family Legal Guide
    The Time-Life Book of Family Finance

*This volume is one of a series that offers information
on how to collect objects ranging from advertising giveaways
to war memorabilia.*

The Encyclopedia of
Collectibles

Typewriters to World War Memorabilia

TIME-LIFE BOOKS, ALEXANDRIA, VIRGINIA

TIME-LIFE BOOKS INC.
Managing Editor: Jerry Korn
Text Director: George Constable
Board of Editors: Dale M. Brown, George G. Daniels,
Thomas H. Flaherty Jr., Martin Mann, Philip W.
Payne, Gerry Schremp, Gerald Simons,
Kit van Tulleken
Planning Director: Edward Brash
Art Director: Tom Suzuki
    Assistant: Arnold C. Holeywell
Director of Administration: David L. Harrison
Director of Operations: Gennaro C. Esposito
Director of Research: Carolyn L. Sackett
    Assistant: Phyllis K. Wise
Director of Photography: Dolores A. Littles

Chairman: John D. McSweeney
President: Carl G. Jaeger
Executive Vice Presidents: John Steven Maxwell,
David J. Walsh
Vice Presidents: George Artandi, Stephen L. Bair,
Peter G. Barnes, Nicholas Benton, John L. Canova,
Beatrice T. Dobie, Carol Flaumenhaft,
James L. Mercer, Herbert Sorkin, Paul R. Stewart

The Encyclopedia of Collectibles
Chief Researcher: Katie Hooper McGregor
Researcher: Ann Dusel Kuhns
Copy Coordinators: Diane Ullius Jarrett, Brian Miller
Art Assistant: Mikio Togashi
Editorial Assistant: Dawn Patnode

Editorial Operations
Production Director: Feliciano Madrid
    Assistants: Peter A. Inchauteguiz,
    Karen A. Meyerson
Copy Processing: Gordon E. Buck
Quality Control Director: Robert L. Young
    Assistant: James J. Cox
    Associates: Daniel J. McSweeney,
    Michael G. Wight
Art Coordinator: Anne B. Landry
Copy Room Director: Susan B. Galloway
    Assistants: Celia Beattie, Ricki Tarlow
Correspondents: Elisabeth Kraemer (Bonn); Margot
Hapgood, Dorothy Bacon, Lesley Coleman
(London); Susan Jonas, Lucy T. Voulgaris (New
York); Maria Vincenza Aloisi, Josephine du Brusle
(Paris); Ann Natanson (Rome). Valuable assistance
was also provided by: Judy Aspinall,
Karin B. Pearce (London); Carolyn T. Chubet,
Miriam Hsia, Christina Lieberman (New York);
Mimi Murphy (Rome).

The Encyclopedia of Collectibles
was created under the supervision
of Time-Life Books by
TREE COMMUNICATIONS INC.
President: Rodney Friedman
Publisher: Bruce Michel
Vice President: Ronald Gross
Secretary: Paul Levin

The Encyclopedia of Collectibles
Editor: Andrea DiNoto
Art Director: Sara Burris
Director of Research: Patricia Turbes Mohs
Research Coordinator: Cathy Cashion
Photographers: David Arky, Steven Mays
Assistant Art Director: Christopher Jones
Art Assistant: Sara Bowman
Researchers: Victoria Balfour, Carole Ann Fabian,
Deborah Gale, Carol Gaskin, Amy Gateff,
Linda Heller, Jannika Hurwitt, Kathleen Hushion,
William Logan, Margaret Mooney, Russell
Stockman, Joan Tedeschi, Susan Wasserstein
Writers: Don Earnest, Henry Moscow,
Lyn Stallworth, Jozefa Stuart, Tom Watkins,
Henry Wiencek

Editorial Consultant: David S. Thomson
Consultants for this volume: David Golden
(Typewriters); Elizabeth Baird, Kay Gregory
(Valentines); Kenneth Ames, John Gunsser
(Victorian Furniture); Arnold Kotis (Watches);
Ralph Sessions (Weather Vanes); David Buten,
Byron Born (Wedgwood); Susan Gore, Fred
DiMaio, Katherine Menz (Wicker); Larry Zim
(World's Fair Souvenirs); Mike McAfee (World War
Memorabilia)

The Cover: Lovely cases and precision mechanisms
have long made watches satisfying collectibles. The
14 on the cover are all choice, but the handsome
1810 French timepiece *(top left)*, the seven-faced
watch *(middle right)* that tells the hour in as many
time zones and the Swiss watch with a painted
enamel case *(bottom right)* are among those with
special value.

For information about any Time-Life book, please write:
Reader Information
Time-Life Books
541 North Fairbanks Court
Chicago, Illinois 60611

Library of Congress Cataloguing in Publication Data
Main entry under title:
    The encyclopedia of collectibles.
    Includes bibliographies.
    1. Americana. 2. Antiques—United States.
I. Time-Life Books.
NK805.E63   745.1'09'0973   77-99201
ISBN 0-8094-2764-8
ISBN 0-8094-2763-X lib. bdg.
ISBN 0-8094-2810-5 retail ed.

Acknowledgments: Typewriters, bottom, page 11, bottom,
page 12, bottom, page 13, bottom, page 14, page 15, Don
Sutherland; typewriter, top, page 13, Milwaukee Public
Museum; valentines, page 25, left, page 33, Norcross
Museum; valentine, page 32, Tree Communications, Inc.;
furniture, pages 34-35, 48-49, 50-51, Asa Packer Mansion,
courtesy of the Borough of Jim Thorpe, Pennsylvania;
sofa, pages 40-41, courtesy of the Virginia Museum,
Richmond; rocker, page 52, photograph by Elliott
Kaufman, courtesy Thonet, U.S.A.; chair, top, page 53, the
Charles and Helen Sporn Collection, photo courtesy *Art &
Antiques* magazine; chair, bottom, page 53, the Margaret
Woodbury Strong Museum; watch, page 59, courtesy of
The Time Museum, Rockford, Illinois; watch fob, top left,
page 65, Linda Campbell Franklin; weather vanes, pages
70-71, bottom, page 80, Aarne Anton; lightning rod, top,
page 77, whirligigs, pages 78, 79, Harvey Kahn; weather
vane, top, pages 80-81, David Davies; vase, page 83, stirrup
cup, page 86, vase, page 87, jar, page 88, coffeepot, page
91, Buten Museum of Wedgwood; photograph, page 84, by
courtesy of the Wedgwood Museum Trust; earrings, page
88, creamer, page 90, the Born Collection; pitcher, box,
page 89, Gem Antiques; pot, bowl, bottom, page 94, vase,
page 95, Leo Kaplan Antiques; plates, bottom, page 91,
courtesy the Stradlings; easel, page 99, rocker, page 105,
Inglenook Antiques, photographs by Arthur Vitols; chair,
top left, page 106, stroller, page 107, Inglenook Antiques;
prints, pages 110, 111, The Old Print Shop, Inc.; passport,
page 133, Norma Cardenhead King; jeep, pages 134-135,
Edward Bromage; wings, page 136, J. Duncan Campbell;
insignia, page 137, all items pages 138, 139, uniform, page
140, hats, page 142, silk square, left, page 143, West Point
Museum; posters, pages 144, 145, George Theofiles; shell
casing, bullet, page 148, Dennis Gordon; medal, page 149,
Rochelle Lapidus. The index for this book was prepared by
Barbara L. Klein.

Contents

6 **Typewriters**

17 **Valentines**

35 **Victorian Furniture**

59 **Watches**

68 **Weather Vanes**

82 **Wedgwood**

96 **Wicker**

109 **Wildlife Prints**

120 **World's Fair Souvenirs**

134 **World War Memorabilia**

150 **Index**

The first popular portable, the tiny, nine-inch-deep Blickensderfer (above), prints with a type drum that brushes an ink roller. Although desirable, "Blicks" are quite easy to find.

Typewriters
Machines That Write

The sign on the barn in New York's Catskill Mountains read WE BUY JUNK AND SELL ANTIQUES. It was an irresistible lure. And when I went inside I could not resist the ancient portable above. The tiny, delicate-looking machine bore the unfamiliar name Blickensderfer, had three rows of spindly keys and printed with a type-embossed hard-rubber drum that spun to type the desired letter—much like the type ele-

---

Writer Paul Lippman collects typewriters that are "rare, beautiful or wacky." His apartment is crammed with 150 old machines.

---

ments on modern electric typewriters. I was happy to get such an exotic mechanism for $20.

I soon discovered that there are many far more eccentric typewriters to delight a tinkerer like me. Most are variations of three types, differing mainly in the way letters are printed: from a drum or cylinder, as on the Blickensderfer; from typebars, as on most modern machines; or from a wheel that is positioned—indexed— by hand, as on toy typewriters.

Collectors are most interested in machines made be-

tween 1874, when the first typewriter of note appeared in the United States, and the 1920s, when typewriters became more or less standardized. Some collectors try to find every model made by a certain manufacturer while others focus on machines with unusual features, such as the Oliver *(page 10)*. The more eccentric the mechanism the better, although rarity, historical significance and beauty of design are also considerations.

The most important machine historically—and the most valuable to collectors—is the first that was commercially produced in the United States, the Sholes & Glidden Type Writer of 1874 *(page 8)*. In 1978 one in excellent condition changed hands for $1,200, a stratospheric sum for an old typewriter; most machines can be obtained for less than a tenth that price.

The Sholes & Glidden, manufactured by E. Reming-

Graceful lines, a hand-painted floral motif and mother-of-pearl inlay enhance the value of a Crandall New Model, which prints by means of a tall, skinny type cylinder and has only two rows of keys. Although it dates from 1886, this example is in superb condition and still operates, a fact that makes it even more desirable.

ton & Sons, was not a rousing success. It produced a row of tiny, uneven letters, capitals only. Further, the typist could not see what he was writing, since the typebars, although similar to those still in use, struck paper on the underside of the roller. An early owner, novelist Mark Twain, said he got rid of his machine—they are known as blind Remingtons—because it "was wont to make me swear."

Remington's second try, the 1878 Perfected Type Writer No. 2—later renamed the Standard No. 2—was more efficient and more successful than the original model. So many No. 2s were made, in fact, that 100 years after their introduction collectors were paying less for one than the original $125 price. No collection is really complete without a No. 2, however, because of its significance as the first widely used typewriter.

It is quite easy to identify the early Remingtons: Most are straightforwardly marked "Standard No. 2." In fact, virtually all collectible typewriters are simple to recog-

nize; manufacturers generally displayed their names and model numbers in bold gold letters somewhere on the fronts of their machines.

Determining the age of a machine is not always as easy. Patent dates marked on the frames can be misleading, for some typewriters were manufactured years after the patent was registered. More dependable evidence of age is supplied by old catalogues and advertisements. The serial numbers that appear on machines can also be a clue to age and value.

Among the most desirable machines are the failures, typewriters so bizarre or so poorly constructed that few were manufactured. Almost as valuable as the Sholes & Glidden is one patented by Eugene Fitch and produced—briefly—in 1891 by the Fitch Type Writer Co. of Brooklyn. It had type of vulcanized rubber that loomed behind the roller and struck toward the typist. Another machine that is sought for its strange mechanism is the Williams Number 2 *(right)* of 1892, which

The first typewriter marketed in America, the Sholes & Glidden (left), was awkward to use and typed underneath the roller, out of sight. Rarity makes it valuable. Only some 40 to 60 are known to survive, although those few represent a surprisingly high proportion of the total manufactured: no more than 4,000.

The typebars of the Williams typewriter, which appeared in 1892, fan out both in front and in back of the roller and must make a small grasshopper-like jump to strike the paper—as one typebar in printing position shows in the picture at left. The machine's unusual grasshopper action makes it desirable.

has double sets of typebars, one fore and one aft.

One of my prized machines is an Edland, a jerry-built affair of lightweight metal. It was found on a back shelf in a general store in upstate New York, wrapped in an 1894 *New York Sun.* Evidently the store owner took one disgusted look at it, bundled it up and shoved it aside. I know of only six others that have survived.

Not all eccentric-looking typewriters are rare. A Midwestern minister named Thomas Oliver, looking for a way to speed the preparation of his sermons, designed an unusual machine with typebars that stood vertically on both sides of the roller. Olivers were virtually indestructible and they sold well for years; they are easy to find today. It is said that they were very much in demand among British Army clerks during the North African campaigns of World War II. While the desert sand clogged most machines, it filtered right through the Olivers' vertical typebars, which kept clacking away. Similarly common though odd-looking is the little portable that got me started as a collector, the Blickensderfer; it was manufactured in various models for some 25 years.

Whatever the typewriter, it will be worth little unless it is in good—although not necessarily operating—condition. Nearly all those you find will be loaded with years' accumulations of dust trapped in grease. I clean the inner works with solvent spray and old toothbrushes; if a small but intricate part is very dirty, I strip it in a sonic cleaner, the kind sold for cleaning dentures. Whenever possible, I replace broken parts with parts that have been salvaged from another machine. Since modern screws will not fit in many older machines, I hoard all the old screws I can find. And if I want to use one of my old machines, I replace the rubber roller, which, hardened by age, can damage the type; the roller is often easy to remove, and most typewriter-repair shops can supply a new one to match the old.

If you go looking for typewriters, junk shops are the best places to start—especially in the Northeast and Midwest, where most machines were made and sold. When you are looking, keep your eyes down. The machines are heavy and are more likely to be on the floor than on a shelf. Old typewriter shops are still worth at least a try, although most have probably sold off their early machines.

There will always be unexpected finds. A fellow collector, Don Sutherland, tells about spotting a mint-condition blind Remington in a junk shop. Expecting to pay $40 to $50, he was surprised to find a tag reading $6.50 AS IS. "What do you mean, 'as is'?" he asked. "Well, I don't know how this happened," the shopkeeper responded, "but everything inside has slipped around to the bottom so that it prints underneath the roller instead of on top. But it still types perfectly well." Sutherland paid the $6.50 and left.

With two banks of vertical typebars and its nonstandard keyboard, the Oliver looks like a short-lived eccentric. But it is sturdy and types where you can watch. It was very popular among amateurs and remained in production from 1894 until 1928. Although early models like this are easily found, collectors prize them.

The low-slung Daugherty Visible, introduced in 1890, was the first mass-produced front-stroke visible typewriter, its typebars lying flat in front of the roller—like those on a modern machine—so that the typist was able to see what was being written.

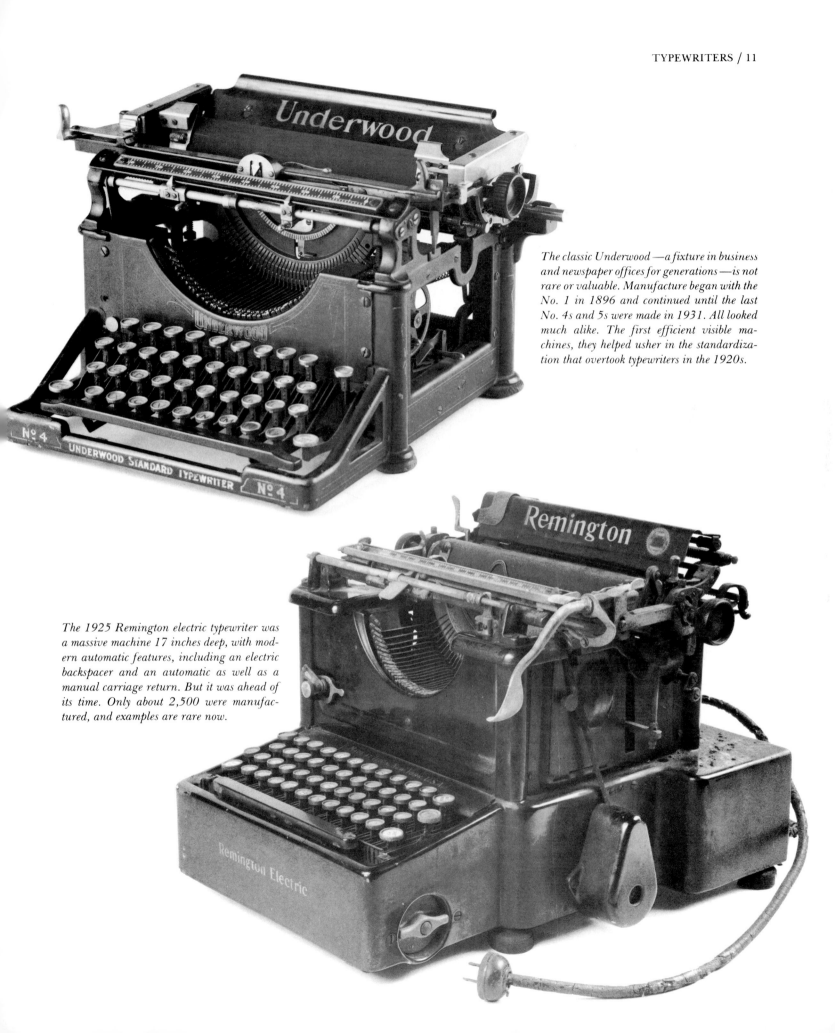

The classic Underwood —a fixture in business and newspaper offices for generations —is not rare or valuable. Manufacture began with the No. 1 in 1896 and continued until the last No. 4s and 5s were made in 1931. All looked much alike. The first efficient visible machines, they helped usher in the standardization that overtook typewriters in the 1920s.

The 1925 Remington electric typewriter was a massive machine 17 inches deep, with modern automatic features, including an electric backspacer and an automatic as well as a manual carriage return. But it was ahead of its time. Only about 2,500 were manufactured, and examples are rare now.

At the center of this Hammond machine, a row of vertical rods precisely controls the rotating type wheel to print in perfect alignment. The mechanism survives in machines that are still used by printers, but the semicircular keyboard was abandoned. Early models, such as this 1884 example, are rare.

The 1892 Duplex has twin keyboards—one for the right hand, one for the left—to speed typing: Two keys could be struck simultaneously without jamming. The idea did not work, however, so Duplexes are understandably difficult to find, and valuable.

The circular typewriter above, invented by J. M. Crary of Jersey City, was produced for only a year. It was designed to print in bound ledgers—the carriage moved not only left to right across the paper, as in other typewriters, but also up and down the page, riding on gear-toothed rails visible in the inset photograph. The ledger page was slipped underneath the carriage, over a flat rectangular platen against which the downward-striking keys printed. The white keys on the circular keyboard are capitals, the black ones small letters.

Pressing down on the disk at the desired letter on the Lambert typewriter causes a plate beneath it to pivot, or index, into printing position. Inventor Frank Lambert spent 17 years devising this index machine, but cheap keyboard typewriters made it obsolete by the time it came out in 1896.

This typewriter—invented in 1894 by Thomas A. Edison to cut sharp stencils for one of his other inventions, the Mimeograph duplicating machine—was slow and cumbersome. The typist had to rotate a disk on the base to select a letter, then press the lever at left to activate a hammer, which struck a plunger that typed on the underside of the roller. To see what he had typed, the operator had to swing the carriage up to the position shown here. An embarrassing failure by a great inventor, the machine is a highly desirable collectible.

Although an uncommon find in the United States, the German-made Mignon was one of the most popular keyboardless typewriters in Europe, where it sold well from 1903 until the 1940s. It was surprisingly easy to operate. With the left hand a typist picked out characters on the letter plate with a pointer that controlled a type cylinder. At the same time the right hand operated the two buttons on the front edge of the machine. One button caused the type cylinder to hit the paper; the other was a space key. The letters AEG and USG are the initials of the manufacturer.

MUSEUMS

Greenfield Village and Henry Ford Museum
Dearborn, Michigan 48121

Milwaukee Public Museum
Milwaukee, Wisconsin 53233

Smithsonian Institution
Washington, D.C. 20560

BOOKS

Adler, Michael H., *The Writing Machine.* George Allen & Unwin Ltd., 1973.

Beeching, Wilfred A., *Century of the Typewriter.* William Heinemann, 1974.

Current, Richard N., *The Typewriter and the Men Who Made It.* University of Illinois Press, 1954.

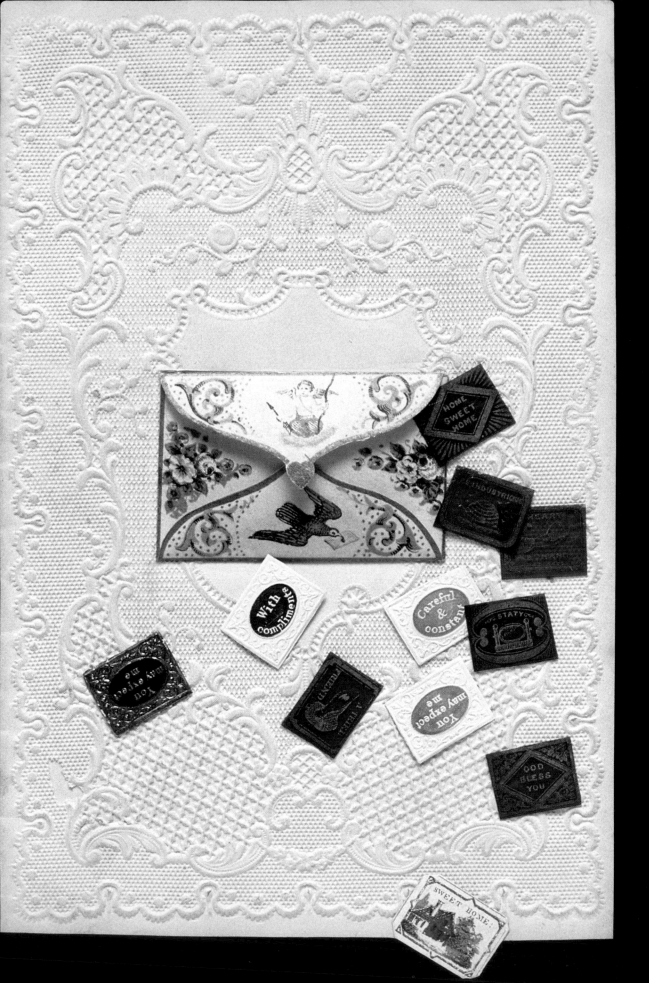

Valentines
Alluring Notes of Romance

For such sweet and sentimental objects, valentines seem to have had a surprisingly violent origin. An early Christian priest named Valentine, it is said, angered pagan Roman authorities by marrying men and maids despite a ban by Emperor Claudius, who wanted men unattached, for military duty. Valentine was sentenced to death for his services to love. On the day of his execution he sent the jailer's daughter, who had befriended him, a note signed "your Valentine." He was then beaten, stoned and beheaded.

The good Valentine's martyrdom was all but forgotten until 496 A.D., when Pope Gelasius exercised the

Suzanne Wylie has searched her native Pennsylvania—and many other areas—for antique valentines since she was a girl.

Church's growing power by converting a gamy Roman fertility ritual into St. Valentine's Day. Eventually this Christianized celebration of love reached France, where it seems to have been observed with Gallic fervor; one young lady was fined 50 sous in 1509 for kissing her valentine so passionately she gave him a nosebleed. In England, the amorous Henry VIII established the holiday by royal charter in 1537, and the custom came to America with the early settlers.

The first valentines were handwritten expressions of affection noting the holiday, such as one given the wife of diarist Samuel Pepys in 1667; it, Pepys noted, was simply "her name writ upon blue paper in gold letters." But by the end of the 18th Century, commercial valentines had appeared. The first were hearts-and-flowers designs with sentimental messages; soon came "comics"—many more insulting than loving or funny—and mechanicals, or trick valentines with moving parts.

Collectors search most for old handmade valentines, understandably rare. Next in value are commercial ones made, principally in England, from around 1810 to 1860, a period notable for lacy valentines that I consider of unsurpassed delicacy and beauty. For several decades

An envelope valentine from the mid-19th Century consists of a tiny envelope—less than two inches wide—that was pasted to a sheet of fine British embossed paper. The envelope contained pieces of paper and transparent chips printed with appropriate sentiments.

afterward, popularity of valentines declined for some reason—more in Europe than in America. Even so, quantities of desirable ones were produced—some are mechanicals of unusual ingenuity, others bear illustrations drawn by artists famed for work in other fields.

Among the old handmade valentines that still occasionally turn up are fine examples painstakingly worked by the Pennsylvania Dutch. Some consist primarily of paper pricked with a pin hundreds of times to resemble lace. Or they are made of paper scissor-cut into intricate openwork designs *(pages 20-21)*. They are folk art and are valued accordingly. Also considered folk art are valentines decorated with theorem painting, a craft young girls learned in the genteel female academies of the early 1800s. The girls cut stencils from oilpaper, usually featuring a rose or heart, following patterns in books. When watercolors were applied through the perforations, the result was a delicate, soft image—and a very ladylike valentine to send a suitor *(page 20)*.

Young ladies—and gentlemen—were cutting, painting and gluing their own love notes into the mid-1800s, but by then commercial manufacturers had ushered in the great age of valentines: layers of embossed and lace papers decorated with hearts, cupids and other traditional symbols of Valentine's Day. Prominent British stationers were H. Dobbs and Co. *(page 24)*, J. T. Wood & Co., John Windsor, Joseph Addenbrooke & Sons, Joseph Mansell, George Kershaw & Son, and George Meek. Their products are particularly desirable and can be identified—the names are embossed in miniature in the paper's border or concealed in the ornamentation.

British firms also exported undecorated embossed and lace blanks to American assemblers of valentines. The first major United States manufacturer was a woman, Esther Howland, who in 1848 set up a production line in her home in Worcester, Massachusetts. Eventually Miss Howland was shipping her ornate, colorful valentines all over the country and taking in $100,000 a year in sales. Most Howland valentines are marked on the back; a small red H was used until the mid-1870s, when the business was reorganized as the New England Valentine Company and its initials were used.

Esther Howland's main competitor, and later her successor, was another New Englander, George C. Whit-

Gold threads, silk and satin, and a hand-painted Virgin make this 18th Century card very valuable. Devotional cards were often exchanged in Europe on St. Valentine's Day. The letters IHS on the Virgin's heart shorten the Greek word for "Jesus."

ney, whose motto was an unromantic "Industry, Punctuality, and Christianity." Setting up his factory near Miss Howland's in Worcester, he aped her business methods and marked his valentines with a red W.

Other American firms—Jotham Taft, T. W. Strong, and Berlin & Jones are names collectors look for—made lacy valentines, but only Miss Howland's approach the best British products in value today. It is easy to tell British lacy valentines from American ones. The United States manufacturers generally pasted brightly colored wafers, or disks, at each corner beneath the lace. The English did not. In addition, the sheets of paper interleaved in American valentines were generally brightly colored, while the English used pastel papers.

Although lacy and handmade valentines are the most valuable, certain other types are of special interest. Civil War valentines depicting soldiers are rare and valuable. Also popular are those that picture sailors with their sweethearts, and stand-up valentines, mostly made in Germany, of honeycomb paper *(page 31)*.

Late in the Victorian period, several popular British illustrators did pictures for valentines; their works are desirable. Especially notable are cards printed by Marcus Ward & Co. with Kate Greenaway's charming drawings of children and Walter Crane's romantic pictures of refined ladies *(page 27)*. Huge numbers of valentines have been made in the 20th Century, principally in the United States. Among those most prized are postcards from the great card craze of the Edwardian years (see the article on Postcards in another volume of this ency-

The truelove knot above, a frequent form of early valentine, has no beginning or end; its message can be started at any point. This one was engraved about 1800 by Francesco Bartolozzi, an Italian artist who was engraver to England's King George III.

clopedia); particularly desirable are the designs of Ellen Clapsaddle and John Winsch, as well as others printed by Meissner and Buch, a German firm. Also valued are valentines from both World Wars showing soldiers in uniform *(page 33)*—an unusual one from World War I pictures a young girl in a Red Cross nurse's uniform.

Since the choicest valentines are generally the most delicate, they must be carefully handled. Do not paste them in a scrapbook; this ruins the back and reduces value. If an especially pretty valentine is to be framed for a wall decoration, it should be matted on acid-free paper in such a way that the old, fragile paper will not touch the glass in the frame. You can repair slightly torn lace paper by pasting thin tissue paper behind the rip; do not use cellophane tape, which causes discoloration.

Valentines may be found in shops specializing in old prints, old books and other paper artifacts. I haunt estate auctions, where old trunks and albums may be for sale; old valentines have such sentimental value that many are stored away for generations. At one auction I spotted a lovely old valentine among the miscellaneous items, but it vanished before bidding began. I climbed on the stage with the auctioneer and, on hands and knees, searched until I located it under a loose plank. It turned out to have been made by Joseph Mansell, one of the best 19th Century British valentine makers, and was very valuable *(page 24)*. But there is more, I think, to collecting old valentines than money: You are preserving things that were precious to people generations ago—and sharing, in a way, their romances.

The exquisite American handmade valentine above, undated but probably done before 1850, is a fine example of theorem painting, in which
watercolors were applied through stencils.

The intricate, shimmering valentine at right
shows how carefully the Pennsylvania Dutch
practiced the cutout technique that makes their
valentines so valuable. The gold paper was
folded in half before cutting, but the two sides
are not exact mirror images because the delicate paper fluttered while being placed on the
blue backing. The date on the back, though not
wholly legible, is either 1801 or 1811.

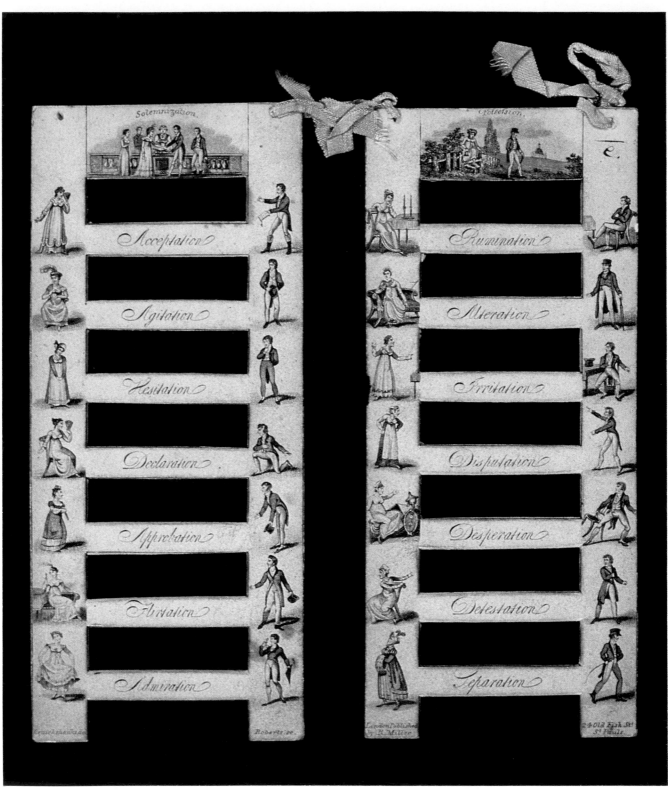

A satirical love token, this courting ladder traces love from meeting through marriage to separation. Created by one of the famed Cruikshank brothers about 1820, it is believed to be a sarcastic reference to the broken marriage of King George IV and Queen Caroline.

Paper Symbols of Affection

Distinguished from valentines are love tokens—cards and paper cutouts that served as expressions of affection on days other than the one honoring Saint Valentine. They were quite common in the 18th and early 19th Centuries but then went out of fashion, and surviving examples are now fairly rare.

Cutout paper gloves are a motif much used in British and American love tokens, probably because gentlemen who could afford it traditionally gave real gloves to their sweethearts. In some, as at right, hand and heart were combined. A more sophisticated, not to say cynical, sort of English love token is the engraved ladder-shaped card at left. Love tokens in Europe often took the form of hand-drawn and hand-lettered cards, called *cartes d'amitiés* in French, *Freundschaftskarten* in German.

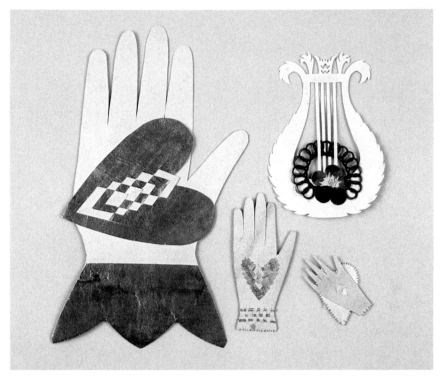

These traditional glove and heart-and-hand love tokens are rarities from the late 1700s; the paper lyre through which an admirer looped a lock of hair is even more unusual.

His sail reading LOVE in Latin, a chunky cupid paddles a gondola across this hand-painted German token. The handwritten verse translates: "*Roses, violets, tulips, carnations, all of spring's flowers fade; steel and iron break, but not our friendship.*"

In the 1860s the American stationery firm of Berlin & Jones offered the lace-paper extravaganza at right for the suitor who wished to propose to his valentine by messenger. A gold ring of embossed paper was attached to the center of the outside sheet of lace paper over the word "Accept." An enclosure (top right) pictured a man proposing on bended knee. The bird-and-foliage flaps folded around the enclosure to form the envelope.

This beautiful and valuable lacy valentine was manufactured about 1850 by Dobbs, a stationery firm that, under several names, produced very desirable valentines through much of the 19th Century.

The unusually elaborate valentine above was made about 1850 by Joseph Mansell of London. It combines lace paper, satin, gold-paper flowers and imitation pearls, and sold new for some $50.

This early-20th Century confection uses several layers of paper and many colors to achieve fragile beauty. The lace paper is coarser, however, than the fine British product that had been used earlier. Valentines of this type are fairly easy to find.

Think not, Oh! think— this trifle vain,
That brings remembrance back again—
When, with a feeling fraught and true,
I wove a fragrant wreath for you.

My Heart I send to the

For 'tis the joyous time of
And blame me not
My heart's own thoughts—where fa   wine
Sweet Type of thee —— My Valentine.

Cobweb valentines, such as the ornate 1840s British example above, are among the most valuable commercially made valentines. The valentine appears to be flat (small picture, top), but a tug on the butterfly lifts a cobweb of cut paper to reveal a scene beneath.

Cupids in the border make a fetching valentine of this illustration of a fashionable lady by Walter Crane. Crane was a leading British popular artist of the late 19th Century who, like children's illustrator Kate Greenaway, created a number of valentines for Marcus Ward & Co. that are desirable.

The pathetic scene above of a despondent lover is one of 14 fine aquatints done in the 1830s that tell a story of a bumpy, but happily resolved, romance. Any aquatint from this Unrequited Love series is valuable; a complete set of 14 of them is a treasure.

Valentines resembling medieval illuminated manuscripts were popular in the 19th Century. This one was printed in Bavaria in the 1880s or 1890s, brought out in England by Ernest Nister and distributed in the United States by publisher E. P. Dutton & Co.

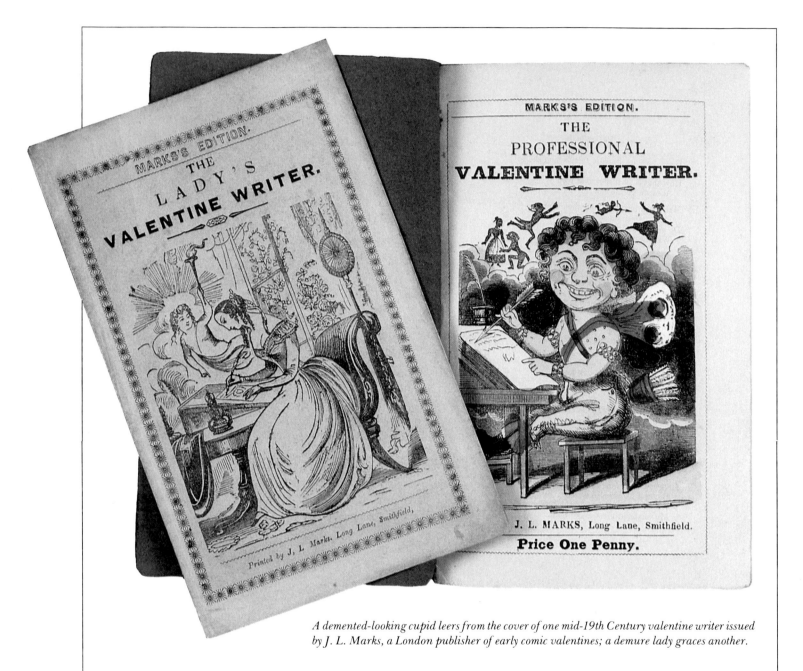

A demented-looking cupid leers from the cover of one mid-19th Century valentine writer issued by J. L. Marks, a London publisher of early comic valentines; a demure lady graces another.

Sentiment Ready-made

Valentine writers were cheap pamphlets of verses that anybody penning a message on a valentine, inspiration flagging, might copy. They flourished when valentines were handmade and handwritten; one appeared in France as early as 1669, and English valentine writers were available in America by 1723. But British and American publishers continued to produce them into the mid-1800s; many commercial valentines, though decorated by the manufacturer, had no message—just an empty space in which the sender could write.

The valentine writer above at right was called "professional" because it contained verses suited to various trades—bakers, butchers, cheesemongers and so on. Many were insulting. The opening lines of one for a baker read, "Bad is your bread, and short of weight,/ And you're a dirty sloven." More genteel pamphlets *(above, left)* included sentimental verses. Collectors value these naïve aids to inspiration, despite their poor printing and dubious doggerel.

Like a knife through my true heart,
Butcher in deed, if not in trade,
How the blood is seen to start,—
From the wound that you have made.

"If I had rule of all below,
Quickly I would do you evil;
All the *Valentine* you'd know,
Would be to send you to the Devil."

T. W. STRONG, N.Y.

A distinctly unfunny comic valentine is the bleeding heart at left, published in New York in 1849 with an equally grisly poem that wishes the recipient sent to the devil. The person who received the missive seems to have been unimpressed, however, writing in the right border, "O! that is to bad."

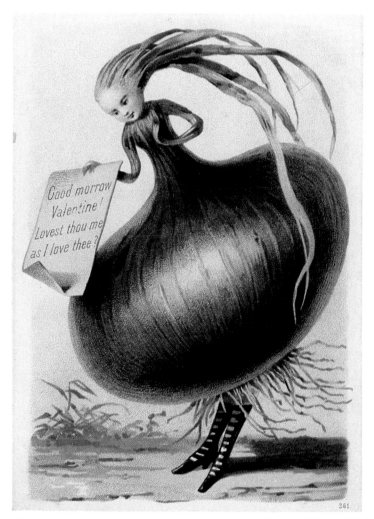

Good morrow Valentine! Lovest thou me as I love thee?

The excesses of a late-19th Century fashion in skirts seem to be the target of this lampooning valentine. The scroll held by the onion girl refers to the ancient tradition that the first person of the opposite sex greeted on February 14 automatically became the greeter's valentine.

Dear Sir I will not deceive,
You are a perfect SPOON.

A gentler comic valentine superimposes a spoon man on fine lace paper marked "Meek," a London stationer of the mid-19th Century. When the valentine is opened, a spoon couple is revealed. The spoon motif derives from an old Welsh custom of a swain carving a wooden spoon for his betrothed.

A DAISY CHAIN

for my Valentine

This daisy-chain novelty opens to a length of about 23 inches; compressed, the chain fits into the little round box at bottom, the top daisy serving as the lid. Similar German-made valentines of the late 19th and early 20th Centuries are fairly easy to find.

An ornate combination of honeycomb paper puffs and flat die-cut pictures creates a three-dimensional balloon. Ballooning was a popular subject on Christmas cards, greeting cards and other items produced (like this valentine) about 1900 and is a specialty of some collectors.

To
The Dearest One—
My Wife

A many-layered triumph of satin ribbons, real lace and cutout flowers (above), produced by Rust Craft Greeting Cards, Inc., in 1936, took four hand operations to make, and it sold at a high price for its time: one dollar. In 1979 it was worth five times that much.

Valentines depicting soldiers or sailors retain a fascination for collectors even when they are neither fancy nor old. This American example was mass-produced by Norcross during World War II.

A flapper with face and pointed hat made of satin glances coquettishly from the valentine at right, made in the 1920s. Valentines from this period are not common, but the recent date makes them inexpensive.

MUSEUMS
Museum of the City of New York
New York, New York 10029

Shelburne Museum, Inc.
Shelburne, Vermont 05482

COLLECTORS ORGANIZATIONS
Antique Valentines Association
P.O. Box 178
Marlboro, New Jersey 07746

National Valentine Collector's Association
111 East Cubbon Street
Santa Ana, California 92701

BOOKS
Lee, Ruth Webb, *A History of Valentines*. Lee Publications, 1952.

Staff, Frank, *The Valentine & Its Origins*. Frederick A. Praeger, 1969.

Victorian Furniture
Fancies of Homes of Yesteryear

When I began collecting Victorian furniture in the 1950s it had not yet been taken up by interior designers. I paid rock-bottom prices for scores of tables, chairs, sofas, beds and desks created not in one style, but in a half-dozen fascinatingly different ones. My collecting enthusiasm swiftly got out of hand. Most Victorian pieces are large, and before long I had filled a barn and several garages. At last I took the ultimate step. My wife and I bought a big old Victorian mansion to house my furniture—and turned it into a museum.

Victorian furniture was long neglected for a number of reasons. It was of too recent manufacture—the peri-

After two decades of collecting Victorian furniture, Bradley Oliver opened his 1874 mansion in Jim Thorpe, Pennsylvania, as a museum.

od extends from roughly 1840 to 1900—to attract purist antique enthusiasts. The pieces' large size made them awkward in 20th Century homes. Some styles were too ornate for contemporary taste. But a reaction against austere modernism in the decades following World War II rekindled interest and led to a rediscovery of the sturdy comfort of this 19th Century furniture.

Like me, most collectors use their acquisitions in everyday living, and durability is a great advantage. Victorian furniture is probably the least fragile made since the Elizabethan era. The strength of many pieces comes partly from their massiveness but also from machine production. Though early-Victorian furniture was largely handmade, by the 1870s factory manufacture had taken over. The new power-driven machines cut more accurately than most craftsmen could, making possible very strong joints. The machines also could work dense and very durable woods, such as rosewood,

The parlor (left) of a mansion built by railroad magnate Asa Packer in 1860, now a museum near the collector's, has a truly Victorian table—a gift from the Queen herself—and overstuffed "Turkish" chairs.

The spool-shaped back supports of this chair—made on power lathes—mark it as an example of the style called Elizabethan Revival. Sections of spool turning were often cut lengthwise for surface decoration.

that are too hard to be worked readily by hand. And the factories produced huge quantities for the growing middle class to buy. Americans stuffed their homes with Victorian pieces, and many survive.

The most valuable is the early handmade furniture, generally adapted from 18th Century French styles: the rococo of the courts of Louis XIV and XV and the later, somewhat simpler fashion of Louis XVI. The most famous of these Victorian versions of 18th Century styles were the Rococo Revival pieces produced by John Henry Belter of New York, who pioneered a technique of steaming layers of laminated rosewood into curved shapes that were then decorated with hand-carved ornaments. Though Belter's technique was borrowed by other manufacturers, such as John and Joseph W. Meeks, Charles A. Baudouine, Alexander Roux, Elijah Galusha and Prudent Mallard, the highest prices are fetched by

furniture that bears Belter's label or that can be attributed to him: A three-piece Belter parlor set sold at a New Orleans auction in 1978 for $42,000.

Style is unreliable evidence in identifying French-style pieces as Victorian. These designs have been made on and off since their introduction. Yet it is possible to tell the Victorian adaptations from the 18th Century originals (which are even more valuable) and, more important, from the innumerable reproductions of the 20th Century. The most obvious clue to a Victorian piece is casters, which are on few 18th Century originals or modern reproductions. Also typically Victorian is the use of steam-bent, laminated wood—you can see the laminations at the edges of pieces. Other characteristics suggest recent manufacture. If you find reddish mahogany rather than rosewood or walnut, or machine-made carving that lacks the intricate detail of fine handwork, the piece is probably a modern reproduction.

Unlike the French-style furniture, the majority of Victorian pieces are fairly easy to identify as Victorian. Some are unique to the period, and others are recognizable as adaptations of old designs. The French-based Louis XVI style was often combined with the simpler Renaissance Revival, rectangular in shape but heavily ornamented with medallions, crests, inlays and moldings. Such pieces are not hard to find.

Two English styles, intermediate in value between Renaissance and Rococo Revival, appeared in America before the Civil War—Gothic Revival and Elizabethan Revival. Gothic Revival furniture, large, heavy and uncomfortable, looks as if it belongs in a castle hall. Elizabethan Revival furniture is perhaps the easiest to recognize, since it features spool turning—lathe-turned parts that resemble stacked spools *(left)*.

Opposite in terms of comfort were the fat, springy, low-slung chairs and sofas called Turkish. No fashionable home was without its Turkish corner, with bulky pieces, fringed at the bottom and covered in rich fabrics, "to enchant," as one historian put it, "the drabness of the industrial day." Little of this overstuffed furniture has survived and what has is often in poor condition.

Unlike the pseudo-Turkish and English styles were several that were uniquely Victorian, some expressions of machine-age mass production and others of reaction to it. One unusual example combined both trends: Eastlake, named after the English artist-critic Sir Charles Lock Eastlake, whose 1868 book *Hints on Household Taste in Furniture, Upholstery and Other Details* had a profound but partly unintended influence on 19th Century décor. Sir Charles decried machine-cut curves and carvings and urged simple, unembellished straight lines. The mass-produced furniture that bears his name is widely available. It is indeed rectilinear—straight pieces are cheaper to cut than curved ones—but that is as far as the manufacturers went in following Eastlake's dictum. To the simple structures they glued on typically Victorian panels, moldings, carvings, knobs and gables.

Among the more imaginative Victorian innovations are two that are types rather than styles. One is known as rustic: chairs and tables made of untrimmed tree branches or the horns of cattle or game. The other, known as patent furniture, includes remarkably contrived folding chairs, as well as diagonally braced chairs that look like little engines with wooden knobs and metal piping; the most desirable were made around the turn of the century by The George Hunzinger Co. of New York City and bear the company name. Much more valuable are intricate folding desks—each a big cabinet that opens to provide an entire office—built by The Wooton Desk Company. One of walnut sold for $7,000 at a New York auction in 1980.

Such exploitations of the machine age as Wooton desks and Hunzinger chairs had gone out of fashion by World War I. But one Victorian innovation has remained popular almost continuously since it appeared in 1842. It is bentwood, invented by Michael Thonet, an Austrian cabinetmaker who steamed strips of beech and molded them into gracefully serpentine shapes. Other firms, such as J. & J. Kohn of Austria and the Sheboygan Chair Co. of Wisconsin, soon copied his technique. Thonet's work, identifiable by a label or his name branded into the chair, is the most valuable. The Thonet company is still making chairs, as are competitors, but the more valuable 19th Century examples can be recognized by their delicacy—the ends of the curlicues, for example, are sharp and come to a real point.

The collector of Victorian furniture is particularly fortunate in two regards: Not only was a great deal of the furniture he wants manufactured but it also frequently comes up for sale. Victorian mansions and public buildings are being torn down and their contents sold off. So, although auctions and antique shows can produce desirable pieces, the avid collector prefers to watch for the sales that precede demolition of the Victorian buildings in his part of the country.

The most desirable finds are made of rosewood or ebony rather than walnut. Inlays add value, as do marble tops, especially if colored. The condition of the wood and frame is important. However, few upholstered pieces survive with original coverings, and collectors expect to reupholster their finds. To learn about Victorian pieces, collectors study old furniture catalogues and 19th Century magazines and books. I was leafing through a book about the 1876 Philadelphia Centennial Exhibition not long after I had bought a Victorian piano, and I was amazed to discover an engraving of my new acquisition. The accompanying article revealed that it was unique, made expressly for that fair.

Gothic Revival pieces like this six-foot armchair are rare because the style was mostly used in formal surroundings such as libraries and churches. This piece was found at a sale of church furnishings.

MANY STYLES, ALL VICTORIAN

Victorian furniture is astonishingly varied because many styles were popular during the Queen's long reign, and manufacturers combined elements of diverse styles in a single piece. Seven of the most important designs produced in America are described below.

EASTLAKE: Sturdy furniture with simple rectangular lines but elaborately overlaid with incised decoration.

ELIZABETHAN REVIVAL: An adaptation of 17th Century English designs that makes extensive use of spool-shaped turnings; it is often called spool furniture.

GOTHIC REVIVAL: Furniture inspired by a renewed interest, during the period 1840 to 1870, in ornate Gothic buildings and characterized by Gothic architectural motifs.

LOUIS XVI REVIVAL: An elegant style originating in the French court, it features straight lines, marquetry surfaces, turned legs, and gilt and ormolu trim. Often combined with Renaissance Revival.

RENAISSANCE REVIVAL: This solid, massive style is characterized by rectangular outlines, plain or inlaid panels, raised molding, medallions, crests and applied floral carvings.

ROCOCO REVIVAL: An adaptation of 18th Century French court furniture, sometimes called Louis XIV or Louis XV. Generally lighter and more delicate than stereotypical Victorian furniture, it has ornate carving, S-curved legs and sinuous balloon-back chairs. An important type of the Rococo Revival style has laminated rosewood backs carved into elaborate lacy patterns. The process was patented by John Henry Belter, a designer active in New York between 1844 and 1863.

TURKISH: A pseudo-Oriental style popular in the last quarter of the 19th Century, this overstuffed furniture has coiled-spring frames upholstered in rich fabrics—plush, velvet, brocade—or leather. The upholstery is generally tufted and fringed.

The balloon back of the chair above—curving out at the top—is characteristic of the Rococo Revival style. This example is especially desirable because it was made of rosewood instead of the more common walnut.

A delicate chair with a high back of ornately carved wood (above) is in the variant of Rococo Revival made famous by John Henry Belter, but it was constructed by one of his foremost competitors: J. and J. W. Meeks.

This 1860 mirror-backed étagère has the delicate look of the best Rococo Revival furniture. Its elaborate carving, like that on most Rococo Revival but unlike the decoration on other Victorian pieces, was done by hand. Such furniture was expensive new, and surviving pieces are very valuable today.

Upholstery of bright red damask and a richly gilded frame combine to make the sofa above the most brilliant of Victorian pieces. The frame, fashioned by Joh

Henry Belter during the 1850s, is delicately carved with Belter's favorite motifs —fruits, flowers and foliage.   This example is the only gilded one now known.

A basket (above), preserved in its original glass dome, was fashioned around 1870 from hundreds of tiny sea shells. The patient but unknown maker of this shade of shells included ceramic and silk roses and two butterflies, one of thread and the other of wire.

The Victorian Lady's Ingenious Handicrafts

To complement their sets of Victorian furniture, many collectors look for Victorian handicrafts—wreaths, baskets and bouquets made from unlikely materials. There are baskets made of goose and swan feathers, fruit and flowers of wax, picture frames of moss, doll gowns of sea shells picked up on holidays, and embroidery utilizing tiny fishbones from the kitchen combined with rose-beetle wings purchased in specialty shops.

These curios were the work of homebound 19th Century ladies who passed their long afternoons painstakingly fash-ioning displays for mantel, étagère or parlor table. Some of their creations were placed under glass domes called shades—collectors refer to handicrafts under such domes as a shade of shells or a shade of fruits. Often collectors can identify the materials used in these objects—a prerequisite for restoration—through research in 19th Century publications such as *Godey's Lady's Book and Magazine, Cassell's Household Guide* and *The Artist: Or Young Ladies Instructor,* which provided detailed instructions for the creators of this now avidly collected folk art.

This floral wreath was painstakingly constructed of seeds, nuts, pine cones, rice and corn kernels. The collector found it in poor condition in a junk shop and restored it after identifying all the grains and seeds, some of which had been dyed.

The handsome rosewood parlor cabinet above is a beautifully preserved example of Renaissance Revival with its boxlike form, raised moldings and contrasting woods. This cabinet is particularly desirable for its fine inlaid front panel of various fruit woods.

The shape of this marble-topped table, its incised decoration and the urn finial at its center identify the piece as an example of Renaissance Revival, although, as with most Victorian furniture, other styles are mixed in. The copper medallions at the corners are Louis XVI-style and the scrolls Empire.

The small size of the table at right, and its curved legs joined around a central column, make it a more characteristic Renaissance Revival piece than the ornate table shown above. Its oval top is unusual.

Renaissance Revival chairs such as the one above, believed to be by the noted American maker John Jelliff of Newark, New Jersey, are much sought after, especially if they are part of a full set, as this one is.

This armchair, like the other pieces on this page, combines elements of Renaissance and Louis XVI Revival styles. The overall shape and inlaying are Renaissance, but the tapering, turned legs are Louis XVI.

The three-sectioned back of this settee, each segment in the shape of a shield, is a mark of Renaissance Revival furniture. Such settees were often made with matching side chairs, and a complete set is difficult to find. Individual Renaissance Revival pieces, however, are common.

Since much Victorian furniture was mass-produced, one-of-a-kind pieces such as the ornate piano above are much prized. It was built *specially for the Philadelphia Centennial Exhibition of 1876 by Hallet, Davis & Co., once noted Boston piano makers.*

The dresser above and the bed, chair and oval table at right are parts of a nine-piece bedroom set in Renaissance Revival style made in the 1860s by the Philadelphia company of George J. Henkels. Such sets, if found complete, are very valuable despite the fact that the massive size of the pieces makes them unsuitable for the average modern home. The bed is more than seven feet long by five feet wide with a headboard six feet tall. The pieces pictured here are of natural walnut with trim of dark-stained, or ebonized, walnut, but such sets were made in a variety of woods.

The chaise at right, part of the same set as the bedroom furniture on the previous pages, is unusual because it was meant to be placed in a bedroom. During the Victorian era, such a day bed was generally a separate addition to a study or even a dining room.

The swirling curves of this rocker are the hallmark of bentwood furniture, developed by the Austrian cabinetmaker Michael Thonet. Nineteenth Century pieces with Thonet's mark are the most valuable, but the work of his competitors, notably J. & J. Kohn, is also desirable.

The brightly colored, diagonally braced chair at right is a choice example of so-called patent furniture. It was made by the premier manufacturer of such pieces, The George Hunzinger Co. of New York.

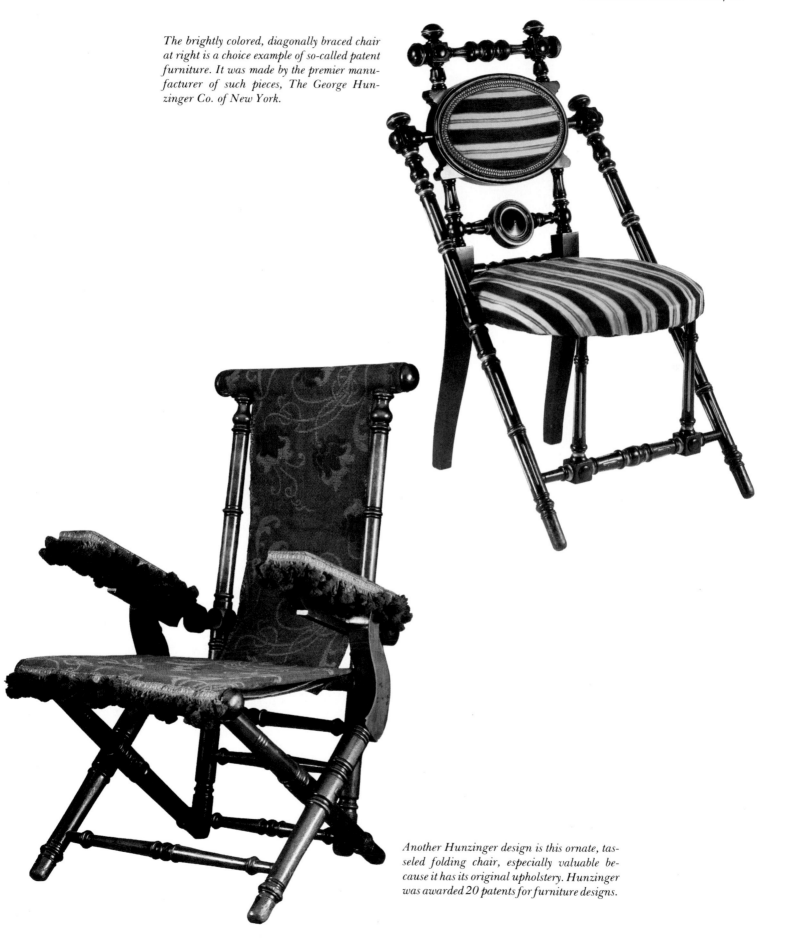

Another Hunzinger design is this ornate, tasseled folding chair, especially valuable because it has its original upholstery. Hunzinger was awarded 20 patents for furniture designs.

A complete office in one piece of furniture, the Wooton patent desk (at right, open for business, and above, its wings folded and locked) is a collector's prize. The desks, boxy Renaissance Revival in style, were produced in small numbers from 1874 to 1880 by William S. Wooton of Indianapolis, a onetime minister. This example, of bleached walnut, contains 61 drawers, 17 shelves, 12 pigeonholes, a mailbox (rectangle in left wing) and, hidden behind the long rectangular panel at top, which flips up, five additional shelves.

Chairs fashioned from the long horns of 19th Century cattle were a novelty for the country retreats of the rich in the 1880s and 1890s — Theodore Roosevelt kept one in the gun room of his estate on New York's Long Island. Such chairs were usually upholstered in leather — the one above has been reupholstered. Modern reproductions can be spotted because they are generally made from short horns.

MUSEUMS
Asa Packer Mansion
Jim Thorpe, Pennsylvania 18229

Association for the Preservation of Tennessee
Antiquities
Nashville, Tennessee 37205

Ballantine House, The Newark Museum
Newark, New Jersey 07101

The Brooklyn Museum
Brooklyn, New York 11238

Campbell House Museum
St. Louis, Missouri 63103

Fountain Elms, Munson-Williams-Proctor Institute
Utica, New York 13502

Gallier House
New Orleans, Louisiana 70116

Galloway House and Village
Fond du Lac, Wisconsin 54935

The Gibson Society, Inc.
Boston, Massachusetts 02116

Greenfield Village and Henry Ford Museum
Dearborn, Michigan 48121

Haas-Lilienthal House
San Francisco, California 94109

Harris County Heritage Society
Houston, Texas 77002

Harry E. Packer Mansion
Jim Thorpe, Pennsylvania 18229

The Henry Clay Home
Lexington, Kentucky 40502

Hillforest Historical Foundation, Inc.
Aurora, Indiana 47001

Historic Mann House
Concord, Michigan 49237

J. F. D. Lanier Memorial
Madison, Indiana 47250

Lawnfield, The Home of President
James A. Garfield
Mentor, Ohio 44060

Lockerbie Street Home of James Whitcomb Riley
Indianapolis, Indiana 46202

Lyndhurst
Tarrytown, New York 10591

Morse-Libby House
Portland, Maine 04101

The Park-McCullough House Association
North Bennington, Vermont 05257

The Preservation Society of Newport County
Newport, Rhode Island 02840

Sagamore Hill National Historic Site
Oyster Bay, New York 11771

Stanton Hall
Natchez, Mississippi 39120

Starrett House
Port Townsend, Washington 98368

Steves Homestead
San Antonio, Texas 78204

Stowe-Day Foundation
Hartford, Connecticut 06105

Sunnyside, Sleepy Hollow Restorations, Inc.
Tarrytown, New York 10591

U. S. Grant's Home State Historic Site
Galena, Illinois 61036

Villa Louis and Museum
Prairie du Chien, Wisconsin 53821

Wickham-Valentine House, Valentine Museum
Richmond, Virginia 23219

BOOKS
Bridgeman, Harriet, and Elizabeth Drury, eds., *The Encyclopedia of Victoriana*. Macmillan Publishing Co., Inc., 1975.

Butler, Joseph T., *American Antiques: 1800-1900*. The Odyssey Press, 1965.

Grotz, George:
The Furniture Doctor. Doubleday & Co., Inc., 1962.
The New Antiques: Knowing and Buying Victorian Furniture. Doubleday & Co., Inc., 1970.

Lichten, Frances, *Decorative Art of Victoria's Era*. Bonanza Books, 1950.

McClinton, Katharine Morrison, *Collecting American Victorian Antiques*. Charles Scribner's Sons, 1966.

The Metropolitan Museum of Art, *19th-Century America: Furniture and Other Decorative Arts*. 1970.

Ormsbee, Thomas H., *Field Guide to American Victorian Furniture*. Bonanza Books, 1952.

Otto, Celia Jackson, *American Furniture of the Nineteenth Century*. The Viking Press, 1965.

Swedberg, Robert W. and Harriett, *Victorian Furniture: Styles and Prices*. Wallace-Homestead Book Co., 1979.

Watches
Timepieces of Times Past

An orthopedic surgeon, Warner D. Bundens has served as president of the National Association of Watch and Clock Collectors, Inc.

During World War II, I was a ship's surgeon on board the U.S.S. *Anne Arundel,* an attack transport with a watch-repair shop but no repairman. I appointed myself the ship's unofficial watchmaker and learned to fix everything from wrist watches to chronometers. Whenever we docked I visited shops, gradually acquiring at rather modest cost dozens of European watches from the 18th, 19th and 20th Centuries.

Even a Navy man with a dealer in every port could not duplicate my collection of antique European watches today unless he spent an enormous sum. One collector spent $2,000 in 1965 for the superb watch at left, made in France by Abraham-Louis Breguet; a similar Breguet sold for $20,000 in 1979. However, the range of value in watches is unusually wide. American-made examples generally are worth less than European ones. Dealers sell prized 100-year-old watches that still work for a hundred times less than a Breguet—and if you are willing to accept a watch that does not run but is reparable, the price is much less yet.

Value in a watch depends only partly on age. More important is the maker—Breguet's few products are valued most—the movement's complexity and accuracy, and the design and material of the case. Especially sought are hunting cases, which have a snap-open cover. Cases of solid gold, enamel or multicolored gold set with precious stones are the most valuable. Next come silver

A close-up of a Breguet watch shows the signature he inscribed on his watch faces as proof of authenticity. One-eighth inch long, it can be seen under the 12 only when lit from the side.

cases. Gold-filled and nickel cases are easily found. In many instances, movement and case were made by different firms, and watches with identical works may differ in value.

The most desirable watches are the ones called complicated. That is, they do more than tell time. For example, some watches also show moon phase, date, day or month—or all four—or have moving figures on the dial *(page 62).* Among the most valuable complicated watches are repeaters, which at the press of a button ring the hour and quarter hour and perhaps even the minute.

Much easier to find, but still popular, are straightforward products of American factories of the late 1800s and early 1900s. Highly valued are railroad watches, made to meet the accuracy requirements of railroad men. The best were produced by the premier American manufacturers— The Elgin National Watch Company, The American Waltham Watch Company, Hamilton Watch Company, Illinois Watch Company, Rockford Watch Co., Hampden Watch Co., and Howard Watch & Clock Company. Women's watches of equal quality—worn on chains as pendants—are also sought.

Railroad watches were costly in their day, but because examples are fairly common now, they seldom bring much more than a good modern watch. Quite different assessments apply to some cheap old timepieces, the so-called dollar watches *(page 61),* which now are worth much more than they were new.

That 20th Century necessity, the wrist watch, is increasingly popular with collectors, who value early women's models made from 1910 to 1920 by Hamilton, Waltham and Elgin, as well as the decorated cases created in the 1920s by Cartier and Tiffany & Co. Men thought wrist watches effeminate until World War I, when soldiers found them easier to use in the trenches than pocket watches. With their new masculine image, men's wrist watches became so popular in the '20s and '30s that production of pocket models almost ceased. Good wrist

Abraham-Louis Breguet of Paris, considered the finest of all watchmakers, fashioned this lovely timepiece in 1815. It is a quarter repeater, chiming the hour and quarter hour just past when the small button atop the stem is pulled out, turned and pushed back in. The ornate gold chain with a carnelian fob was made in the 1890s.

Inexpensive pocket watches from the late 19th Century are favorites of collectors, especially if in their original packing. Many were premiums. The one at right, for Old Honesty tobacco, is a Waterbury Longwind, so called because it took 15 minutes to wind its nine-foot spring. The booklet describes the watch's inventor, Daniel A. A. Buck, who also made the miniature steam engine illustrated.

watches from that era, for either sex, are numerous.

More valuable than most quality wrist watches of the '30s are inexpensive novelties for children. A 1930s Mickey Mouse watch *(page 67)* in pristine condition is as valuable as a fine American timepiece of 100 years ago. Post-World War II American wrist watches are less choice. A lowered tariff brought a flood of Swiss movements, and most United States manufacturers made inexpensive watches that are not sought by collectors.

Assessing the quality of an old watch, European or American, is not hard. Watches made before 1875 were wound by key and many were also set by key; but even this "key-wind, key-set" type is not highly valued unless the case is exceptional. The built-in winding system was introduced in 1875, but for the next decade many firms used both systems; such transitional pieces are more desirable than their predecessors or successors.

The back of a movement reveals much information. Opening the case—they unscrew or snap off—you can quickly tell if a movement is damascened, its steel parts treated so they have a wavy pattern like watered silk. This finish or engraved decorations, such as engine turning, can add value. There may be a serial number, the movement name or inscriptions noting the number of jewels and adjustments. The more jewels—rubies or sapphires used as wear-resistant bearings—the better. Standard-grade American watches had 15, 17 or 21 jewels. Valuable precision watches such as the best railroads have 23 jewels, and a few complicated watches as many as 35. "Adjusted" means the mechanism will not lose or

gain time even if carried on its side or upside down.

Most American manufacturers marked watch movements with serial numbers, which reveal dates of production. For example, an Elgin watch with a serial number between 100,000 and 200,000 was made between 1870 and 1874. Lists of serial numbers by year are compiled in reference books *(box, page 67)*.

Old watches are a staple of antique dealers, and the less expensive examples are common at pawnshops and flea markets. I seldom attend country auctions—the prices are high and the finds scarce—but specialized auctions in the cities are good sources.

Do not pass up inoperative watches. Often, cleaning will get them ticking again. And repairs are not as difficult as they seem. Instruction manuals for amateurs are available *(page 67)* and parts can be ordered by mail.

Collectors often become repairmen by necessity, as happened to a friend of mine after he bought his first pocket watch—for two dollars—on a whim at a New York auction. It was a wretched imitation railroad watch the maker had tried to palm off as genuine by putting a picture of a locomotive on the dial. It did not work. My friend took it to a jeweler, who wanted more to fix it than what it had cost. My friend asked what the problem was. "Needs a new balance staff," he was told. Finding that this meant simply the axle on which the balance wheel turns, my friend located and inserted one himself.

For related material, see the articles on Clocks and Jewelry in separate volumes of this encyclopedia.

Between 1896 and 1921 a firm headed by Robert H. Ingersoll sold more than 70 million dollar watches similar to this Yankee model.

A decorated dial adds value to an old dollar watch: A nautical scene enlivens this New England Watch Company product.

Old Faces to Cherish

Watch faces were made separately from cases and movements, often by companies that specialized in them, and many collectors treasure those in unusual colors—such as the red and lavender examples above—as well as those decorated with flowers, landscapes or ani- *mals. The most valuable of the examples pictured is the one at bottom left; created by the O'Hara Dial Company, it has numerals that seem to be made of tree branches. Dials were often chipped in use, and perfect ones are rarely found.*

Complicated watches with multipurpose mechanisms such as this 1880s Waltham are very valuable. The buttons on the edge of the case activate two separate stop-watch hands for timing two stages of an event, all combined with a regular watch that also chimes the time.

The face of this complicated watch indicates day, date, month and moon phase as well as time; its back has seven dials indicating time in seven cities. Swiss-made, the watch was sold in London to English travelers.

An automaton watch made in Europe about 1900 features on its dial the tiny figure of a butcher who chops at a pig's head with each tick. Despite its dull gun-metal case, the watch is valuable.

Symbols of the Masonic order—including square and compasses, eye and trowel, level and Bible—can be seen in a watch made in the 1920s by the Dudley Watch Company of Lancaster, Pennsylvania, whose founder was a Mason. Five of the 19 ruby bearings are visible.

Unusual damascening—wavy engraved lines—on the plates covering the works of this 1911 Bunn Special make it especially desirable. Such decoration often took longer to make than the mechanism.

Skeleton watches, which have glass back and front to reveal the movements, are favored by collectors. This one, made in 1904 by New England Watch Company, is a relatively inexpensive example.

This 19th Century Swiss watch is valued for its enameled, pearl-rimmed hunting case, which has hinged lids over face and back. The inner back cover, normally closed, has holes to admit the key (right) for winding.

The multicolored flowers and leaves of this woman's hunting case of the 1890s are fashioned of gold alloyed with various metals. The mechanism, less valuable, is a common 15-jewel movement made by Waltham.

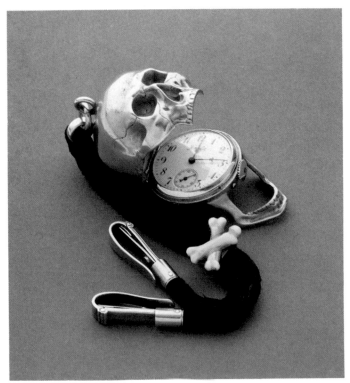

Form watches, made in unusual shapes such as this gold skull, are valuable. The word "Hamlet" on this Swiss-made watch may refer to the "poor Yorick" speech in Shakespeare's play. The chain is made of hair.

The inscription inside the case above reveals that the watch was presented to H. H. Wheeler in 1882. The gold case and the fine movement by Jules Jurgensen, a top Swiss watchmaker, make this piece valuable.

Fob Fancies

To make it easier to fish a watch out of a narrow pocket in waistband or vest, a small dangling tag, or fob, was often attached. These fobs, valued by many collectors, were made in almost infinite variety. Some were sculptured forms, others were emblazoned with club emblems or commemorative inscriptions, and there even are fob silhouettes of political candidates.

Thousands of companies gave fobs away as advertising, commissioning designs in the shapes of their products—for example, plows, paint cans and lanterns. Many men had fobs made specially for themselves.

Most desirable to collectors are the industrial fobs. Reproductions—particularly of those issued by railroads—are common. These less valuable new ones generally do not have an inscription on the back.

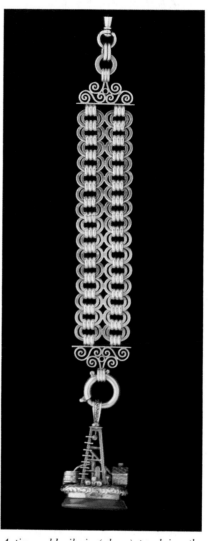

A tiny gold oil rig (above) proclaims the wealth of a Texas oilman of about 1900 who commissioned this fob, which hangs on an even more valuable gold chain.

Among the fobs sold by jewelers are such comic figures as this gold-plated, bowler-hatted man who, seated on a square of agate, seems to grasp the gold chain.

The Greek letters of the Sigma Nu college fraternity adorn the brass fob shown above, which is attached to a leather strap that in turn held the watch.

Red, white and blue beads form a simplified version of the American flag in this fob from the 1920s. Making such beaded fobs was a popular craft early in the century.

A company that made mowing blades gave out the fob at left in the shape of its product. The fob at right attests that its wearer paid $15 for his suit in 1915.

Diamonds and red enamel decorate a ring that contains a tiny watch. A desirable novelty, it was made in Switzerland in the 1830s. The watch is wound by the key to its right, inserted through a hole in the back.

The opulent lapel watch above, a woman's timepiece sold by Cartier about 1920, is more valuable for its case and strap of platinum set with diamonds and pearls than for its Swiss-made works. A platinum pin attaches the strap to a gown or jacket.

This buttonhole watch, popular in the early 1900s, looks small when its face peeks through a buttonhole. But the works, hidden behind the lapel, are normal-sized. Like most such trick timepieces, it is inaccurate.

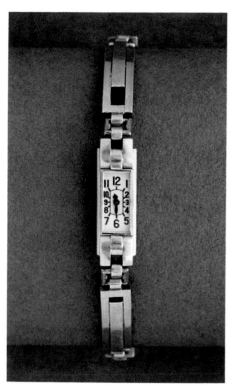

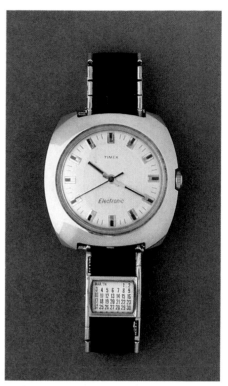

This woman's wrist watch of the 1920s is valuable for the delicacy of its tiny works and for its case and strap of precious platinum.

Mickey Mouse points to the hour and minute on a child's watch of the 1930s, a novelty that became a costly adult fad 40 years later.

Early electric watches, such as this Timex from about 1960, are still fairly easy to find at flea markets and garage sales.

©Walt Disney Productions

MUSEUMS
American Clock and Watch Museum, Inc.
Bristol, Connecticut 06010

American Watchmakers' Institute Museum
Cincinnati, Ohio 45211

The Metropolitan Museum of Art
New York, New York 10028

National Association of Watch and Clock Collectors Museum, Inc.
Columbia, Pennsylvania 17512

Smithsonian Institution
Washington, D.C. 20560

The Time Museum
Rockford, Illinois 61108

COLLECTORS ORGANIZATIONS
International Watch Fob Club
5892 Stow Road
Hudson, Ohio 44236

National Association of Watch and
Clock Collectors, Inc.
514 Poplar Street

Columbia, Pennsylvania 17512

BOOKS
Bailey, Chris H., *Two Hundred Years of American Clocks & Watches.* Prentice-Hall, Inc., 1975.

Clutton, Cecil, and George Daniels, *Watches: A Complete History of the Technical and Decorative Development of the Watch.* Sotheby Parke Bernet, 1979.

Clutton, Cecil, et al., eds., *Britten's Clocks and Watches and Their Makers.* Revised 8th ed. E. P. Dutton, 1973.

Cutmore, M., *The Watch Collector's Handbook.* Charles E. Tuttle Co., Inc., 1976.

Daniels, George, *English and American Watches.* Abelard-Schuman, 1967.

de Carle, Donald, *Watches and Their Value.* N.A.G. Press Ltd., 1978.

Ehrhardt, Roy, *American Pocket Watch Identification and Price Guide,* Book 2. Heart of America Press, 1979.

Fried, Henry B., *The Watch Repairer's Manual.* 3rd ed. Chilton Book Company, 1974.

Weather Vanes
Fine Folk Art in Wind Watchers

When the police of Middletown, New York, came upon a cache of two dozen stolen weather vanes in 1973, the station house was soon besieged by victims of the thieves. There were so many claimants that in one case chemical analysis of the paint on a disputed vane had to be made before the rightful owner could be identified—one collector came forward with the mounting, which bore traces of paint matching that on the vane.

Weather-vane rustling has reached epidemic proportions in recent years—on at least two occasions helicopters have swooped down and snatched vanes off

F. M. Crawford, charmed by a pig-shaped vane, has driven hundreds of back roads searching for other such gems.

rooftops. The thieves have become daring because old weather vanes are increasingly valuable examples of American folk art. As Pablo Picasso exclaimed when he saw a rooster-shaped vane at a Paris show of Americana, "Cocks have always been seen, but never so well as in American weather vanes."

The most valued weather vanes, handmade by local smiths before 1850, are hollow, three-dimensional figures of hammered sheet copper. Carved wooden vanes from this early period can also be quite valuable—few have survived and they are generally fragile. At a 1979 auction in New York I saw the ancient wood of a handsomely carved rooster shattered into fragments when workmen knocked the bird from its perch.

Handmade vanes of this age are so rare that few exist outside museums. Most collectors look for factory-made vanes, about two feet long, produced in the late 19th and early 20th Centuries by hammering copper into iron molds. The parts were trimmed and soldered together and, in some cases, covered with gold leaf.

The value of manufactured copper weather vanes is largely determined—since they are viewed as works of art—by their condition and beauty. But the vanes made by two manufacturers, whose products are identifiable, are much sought after. One was Cushing and White of Waltham, Massachusetts, which stamped the firm name on many vanes made from 1868 to 1872. Vanes from the J. Howard Company of East Bridgewater, Massa-

chusetts, are distinctive because the heads are cast zinc, heavier than hollow copper, for balance.

Other major manufacturers produced catalogues that can be found in large public libraries and sometimes enable a collector to determine a vane's source. The leading manufacturers, whose catalogues—and weather vanes—are eagerly sought, include J. W. Fiske of New York City and E. G. Washburne & Co. of Danvers, Massachusetts. But knowledge of a vane's source by no means determines its value; a record price for a weather vane—$25,000 at a 1979 auction in New York—was for a copper Indian by an unknown maker.

More common than the three-dimensional weather vane is a simpler type, also made during the last century: the silhouette cut from sheet iron. Some were shaped like animals—the ubiquitous rooster (*page 76*) or the even more popular trotting horse—but many were iron arrows or banners (*pages 70-71*). Usually less desirable than these weather vanes, which were intended only to point wind direction, are objects that have other functions. Among them are whirligigs (*pages 78-79*)—wind-driven mechanical toys—and lightning-rod weather vanes. The latter—most are only four or five inches high and nine inches long—were mass-produced up until the 1930s. Originally sold for less than half a dollar, they can cost more than a hundred times that now at antique shops and shows.

Good old examples of all these types have become frustratingly hard to find—and modern copies confusingly numerous. Many reproductions of antique three-dimensional copper vanes have been made in molds surviving from the 19th Century. The iron molds long used by Cushing and White, for example, were salvaged by a junk dealer in 1933 and later were used to turn out limited-edition facsimiles. Similarly, J. W. Fiske made old-style weather vanes until 1978. Such facsimiles, although made with no intention to defraud, turn up in antique shops and are often difficult to distinguish from old ones. To complicate matters, the honest facsimile

Columbia, or the Goddess of Liberty, holds aloft the Stars and Stripes in the rare 32-inch-tall molded copper vane at right. The vane is valuable both because human figures are less common than most animal forms and because the patriotic design indicates an early manufacture date.

makers have been joined by outright counterfeiters.

There are, however, some reliable tests of a vane's authenticity. Old copper vanes have a greenish patina caused by surface oxidation, and it is usually streaky with shades ranging from pale green to near-black. True patina will sometimes reflect the ways wind and rain naturally corrode a figure, as in the ram weather vane on pages 74-75. By contrast, counterfeit vanes, artificially aged with acid, have an even, powdery turquoise coating, or bear drip lines achieved by paint or a chemical wash. Clever fakers also splatter their vanes with black paint to imitate the surface pitting that occurs on some old examples. But painted vanes lack the raised black deposits of copper oxide that have built up on old copper vanes. Traces of gold leaf (often visible on the underside of a vane) are also a good indication of age.

The experienced collector can perceive other telltale signs. The tube that rotates on the supporting rod should be of old copper or brass, and it should show signs of scoring; the pivot hole may be elliptical, de-formed from round by the churning of the vane in seasonal winds. Further, 19th Century craftsmen joined the various sections of copper weather vanes with seams of carefully applied solder, then filed away any excess solder at the joint. File marks on the seams, visible with a magnifying glass, are evidence of an old vane.

Iron silhouette vanes are easier to fake than copper ones. Counterfeiters commonly snip their fakes from well-aged sheet iron that is marked with authentic rust, surface pitting and other corrosion. However, the forgers seldom convincingly age the cut edges. A magnifying glass will usually show that the edges of fake iron vanes do not have the same caked-on rust and pronounced pitting as the sides.

Fake wooden vanes are not much of a problem; even if weathered wood was used, recent cut marks are hard for the counterfeiter to camouflage. A last check for the authenticity of all weather vanes is simply this: Would the figure have swung easily in the wind? An authentic vane has a large rear area to act as a rudder. The front

Banneret weather vanes such as the one above are generally less valuable than three-dimensional copper figures. This yard-long example, however, is prized for the lovely scrollwork of its tail and because its manufacturer is known. The large amount of zinc cast in the arrowhead for balance identifies it as an 1890s product of the J. Howard Company.

therefore must be weighted so the vane balances. The J. Howard Company used zinc, but most other manufacturers poured lead into the heads of their vanes. A figure that does not balance may not be an outright fake—it could be an old flagpole or garden ornament or a tradesman's sign—but it is not a true weather vane.

Bullet holes, incidentally, are no guarantee of age. Weather vanes have served to sharpen the aim of passing marksmen over the years and many fine vanes have a hole or two—they hardly affect value. But the counterfeiters know this and often pepper their fakes to make them look like authentic rooftop targets.

This proliferation of replicas is an indication of the popularity and scarcity of old weather vanes. They are hard to find at affordable prices anywhere. Big city auctions are the last places to look for a bargain. Unpretentious back-country antique barns in New England, northern New York state, Pennsylvania, Ohio and Michigan, where weather vanes were originally made, are the best bets. If you are lucky you may spot a desir-able weather vane still at work atop a barn or farmhouse; lightning-rod vanes are quite often found on site. One collector, detouring on a little-traveled back road in Maine, saw a fine 1890s vane on an isolated farm and talked the farmer's wife into parting with it.

If you really must have a vane and the owner will not sell, you can always buy the building it sits on. At least that is what one determined dealer did. The vane was an astonishing nine-foot-tall copper figure of Chief Tammany, the semimythical leader of the Delaware Indians of colonial times, and it topped an abandoned clubhouse once used by the Improved Order of Red Men in East Branch, New York. Unable to persuade the building's owner to part with the vane, the dealer offered $10,000 for the clubhouse, vane and all. He got them both—and 10 years later another dealer offered him $50,000 for Chief Tammany alone.

For related material, see the articles on Folk Art and Lightning-Rod Ornaments in separate volumes of this encyclopedia.

The angular horse-shaped weather vane above is not as rounded as most molded copper vanes, an indication that it may be a rare handmade example rather than factory-produced. Horse weather vanes with riders are also harder to find than plain horses.

This Grecian-style horse, two feet long, is unusual because it is made of cast iron rather than the more commonly used, and lighter, molded copper. The gold painted finish is often found on cast-iron vanes.

More characteristic of 19th Century horse vanes than the others on these pages is the speeding race horse above. It is modeled on a Civil War-era trotter named Dexter —subject of a notable Currier & Ives print and so famous that most manufacturers made and advertised Dexter vanes.

The molded copper body of this ram weather vane, which once graced a barn in upstate New York, displays authentic weathering in its patina. The greenest oxidation and the greatest evidence of erosion by wind and rain are on the front and top. Further, as the enlarged segment at right shows, the drip lines are natural. The zinc of the separately cast head also shows its characteristically dull patina. These evidences of age and the weather vane's rare design—rams are far less common than horses, eagles or roosters—make it very valuable.

Only the beautifully chased tail plumes of the foot-high weathercock at right are made of copper. The body is cast zinc, identifying the vane, like the banneret on pages 70-71, as a product of the J. Howard Company.

The lordly two-foot-tall fowl at left is a flat silhouette vane cut from sheet iron. Not as widely sought as rounded copper vanes, iron silhouettes are nonetheless valuable.

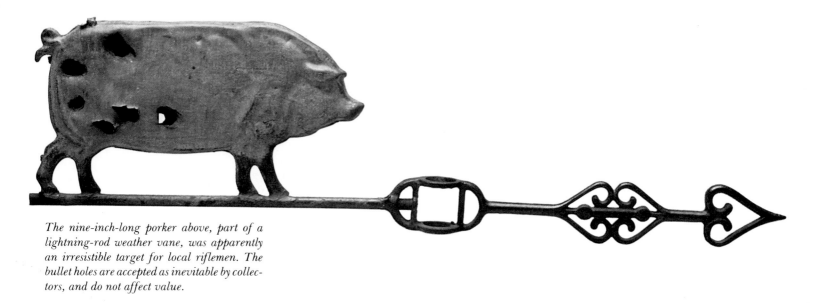

The nine-inch-long porker above, part of a lightning-rod weather vane, was apparently an irresistible target for local riflemen. The bullet holes are accepted as inevitable by collectors, and do not affect value.

A century of weathering has revealed the regular pattern of the squares of gold leaf applied to this stately copper cow.

In the complex whirligig above, the rooster acts as rudder, turning the rotary blades into the wind. They, in turn, activate a hidden mechanism that makes the man rock back and forth as if sawing wood. This imaginative toy is also valued for its careful carving.

Jolly Jack Tar twirls his oars in this simple painted whirligig, cut with a band saw from a plank. Commercially made, the figure has value because it is from the early 1900s.

Toy Variants of Weather Vanes

The wind-driven toys called whirligigs once were common on fence posts and porch rails. These variants of the weather vane are now valued as folk art, their worth largely determined by the skill and originality of the maker, though age and condition can be important.

The earliest and rarest whirligigs, such as the 19th Century schoolmaster at right, are hand-carved figures of solid wood with paddle-like arms that twirl in the wind. Few of these fragile antiques have survived. Most collectors content themselves with whirligigs crafted between the late 1890s and the middle of the 20th Century—they still are manufactured. The most common, which also have flailing arms *(above)*, were simply sawed from planks. More complex devices, such as the man sawing wood at left, are more desirable. Well-preserved whirligigs are the most highly prized, but they should bear some signs of aging—wear on moving parts, cracks in the wood and paint—as proof that they were not made recently.

Hornbooks—oldtime school-exercise slates—form the wind-catching paddles of the two-foot-high figure above of a 19th Century schoolmaster in knee breeches. It was hand-carved from shiny hardwood.

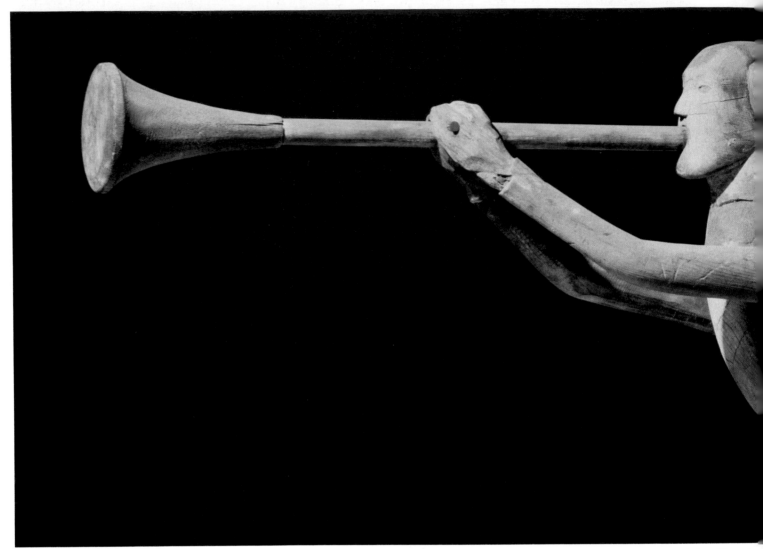

The angel Gabriel trumpets the Second Coming in this wooden vane, 40 inches long, made in the 19th Century. Such figures of the heavenly herald and o

Heavy weathering, wear around the pivot hole and traces of gray paint on its underside all confirm the age of this turn-of-the-century wooden fish vane, two feet long. Such maritime motifs were popular on vanes made on Cape Cod and in other New England coastal areas.

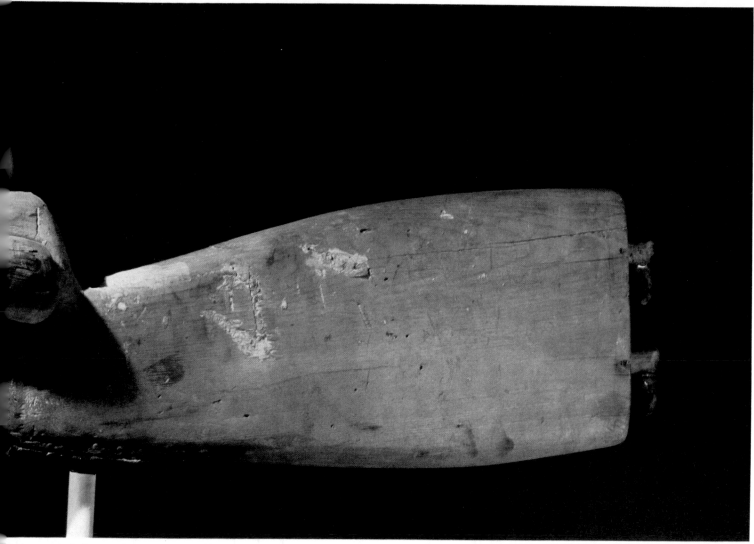

...igious symbols decorated many vanes, reflecting revivalist movements that swept America. The angel's long skirts provide the vane's wind-catching rudder.

MUSEUMS
Abby Aldrich Rockefeller Folk Art Collection
Williamsburg, Virginia 23185

Fenimore House
The New York State Historical Association
Cooperstown, New York 13326

Greenfield Village and Henry Ford Museum
Dearborn, Michigan 48121

Heritage Plantation of Sandwich
Sandwich, Massachusetts 02563

Museum of the Concord Antiquarian Society
Concord, Massachusetts 01742

Pennsylvania Farm Museum of Landis Valley

Lancaster, Pennsylvania 17601

Shelburne Museum, Inc.
Shelburne, Vermont 05482

Smithsonian Institution
Washington, D.C. 20560

BOOKS
Christensen, Erwin O., *Index of American Design.*
The Macmillan Company, 1959.

Fitzgerald, Ken, *Weathervanes and Whirligigs.*
Clarkson N. Potter, Inc., 1967.

Kayne, Myrna, *Yankee Weathervanes.* E. P. Dutton &
Company, Inc., 1975.

Basalt medallions portraying Washington and Franklin are prized because their style dates them to the 1700s. Josiah Wedgwood produced many portraits of America's Founding Fathers.

Wedgwood
Varied Works of a Famous Potter

Most people recognize a cameo or ashtray of mat blue china decorated with a raised white design—it is Wedgwood. But so are many other forms of pottery in a number of other designs and colors. From its founding in 1759, the English company produced dinner services and tea sets, vases and busts, advertising calendar tiles, baby feeders, cigar holders, sword hilts, beer-keg handles, dairy-barn milk crocks, foot-bath basins and even bidets. The vari-

---

Elizabeth Chellis is a charter member and former president of The Wedgwood International Seminar, a collectors' group.

---

ety of ceramic materials is equally staggering: creamy earthenware, fine bone china, the black stoneware called basalt, as well as majolica and Art Nouveau lusterware.

All of this confusing assortment of pottery is collectible. Even valuable old examples can be picked up at bargain prices—despite the fact that Wedgwood has been a preeminent collectible for more than a century—if you have the detailed knowledge that enables you to recognize unusual pieces. One collector tells of an estate sale where he overheard two experienced dealers deride a dessert set, clearly marked, as a fake—Wedgwood, they said, never made any such pink shell-shaped compotes. The collector knew better—the shape honored

old Josiah Wedgwood's interest in sea shells—and got the rare set for a low bid.

The broad desirability of such a conglomeration of wares owes a good deal to the unusual character of the company's venerable founder. Josiah Wedgwood was the fifth generation in a line of potters in Staffordshire, the famed English ceramics center (see the article on Staffordshire in another volume of this encyclopedia). Like many of his equally eminent contemporaries, such as his American friend Benjamin Franklin, Wedgwood developed a passion for experiment and the study of what was at the time known as natural philosophy; it is hardly a coincidence that one of his grandchildren was Charles Darwin.

It was because of his experimentation in pottery that Josiah Wedgwood became famous and established the dynasty of Wedgwood potters (many of whom were also named Josiah). After 10 years of trials he found a composition that used fine kaolin clay from Cornwall and a lead glaze, which produced an ivory-colored, light but strong earthenware—relatively inexpensive but close enough in appearance to fine porcelain so that it won

---

The most valuable Wedgwood works are the first reproductions—at right is one of 20 made in 1790—of the Portland vase, a First Century A.D. Roman glass funerary urn owned by the Duchess of Portland.

At a 1930 celebration of Josiah Wedgwood's 200th birthday, designer Daisy Makeig-Jones—famed for her fanciful lusterwares—is sur- rounded by pottery workers costumed as Josiah's Portland vase. She too is in costume—as the shrouded finial atop some Wedgwood pieces.

wide popularity. Queen Charlotte ordered a tea set and soon afterward a dinner service, providing this pottery its name, queen's ware. Empress Catherine of Russia ordered a service of 952 pieces.

To create jasper, the ceramic most closely associated with the Wedgwood name, Josiah conducted more than 10,000 experiments. "If I had more time, more hands and more heads I could do something," he confided to an associate. "I am almost crazy." He finally found a mixture of stoneware clays and barium sulphate that could be fired thick or translucently thin and could be given almost any color.

The techniques that were developed by Josiah and others introduced by his descendants have been used ever since, and many of the old designs have been put into production repeatedly over the years. Naturally the most valuable of the designs are the oldest, particularly those that were made during Josiah's own lifetime (he died in 1795). Fortunately for collectors, almost all Wedgwood can be dated by marks appearing on the back of each piece (box, opposite).

Pieces from the 18th Century and the early part of the 19th Century are extremely valuable. As long ago as 1875 the rarity of these early articles was bemoaned by the Victorian collector Elizabeth Meteyard in her book *The Wedgwood Handbook.* Nevertheless, good examples continue to turn up. And more recent pieces are quite abundant, their value depending on their distinctiveness and their quality.

A dollar or so will buy some earthenware plates from the 1930s and 1940s, and quite desirable higher-quality pieces from the same period often sell for considerably less than the price that department stores charge for equivalent pieces of Wedgwood brand-new. Even mid-19th Century wares go for bargain prices in thrift or consignment shops, which offer individuals a good way to sell off unwanted family possessions. But you must watch out for fakes. One posh antique store listed a cheap price for what a sign proclaimed a "Wedgwood bowl." On the underside the bowl was marked "J. Wedgwood"—a giveaway, for the Wedgwood firm never used the initial J in its pottery marks.

More valuable than even the genuine mass-produced wares are the limited editions that Wedgwood made at

MARKS THAT DATE WEDGWOOD

All Wedgwood products are marked in such a way that the collector can identify a find and date it to a specific period—in some cases to the day it was made. Some of the details of these markings have changed over the years, and at times several markings have been in use simultaneously, but the name "Wedgwood" is either impressed or printed on the back or the underside of every piece.

This practice dates to 1759, when Josiah impressed his name on his company's first wares, a custom he continued for the next 10 years. From 1769 until 1780 his partner

1769-PRESENT
IMPRESSED OR PRINTED

was Thomas Bentley, a businessman Wedgwood admired for his taste; items made then are marked with both names or both initials. The marking system becomes more complicated thereafter but is detailed in reference books (box, page 95)— representative marks are shown here.

Like all post-1842 British pottery, Wedgwood bears diamond-shaped registry marks. In 1860 Wedgwood added to many of its wares three capital letters indicating the month and year a piece was made—and the potter who made it. Starting in 1930, letters and numerals were used.

wedgwood 1759-1769 IMPRESSED QUEEN'S WARE ONLY	**WEDGWOOD** 1764-1769 IMPRESSED QUEEN'S WARE ONLY FROM BELL WORKS	Wedgwood 1759-1799 IMPRESSED
WEDGWOOD & BENTLEY 1769-1780 IMPRESSED ORNAMENTAL WARES ONLY	 1769-1780 IMPRESSED BASALT, VARIEGATED AND ETRUSCAN VASES ONLY	 WEDGWOOD 1878-PRESENT PRINTED BONE CHINA ONLY
WEDGWOOD 1929-PRESENT IMPRESSED	 **WEDGWOOD** Bone China 1937-PRESENT PRINTED IN BLACK AND GOLD BONE CHINA ONLY	WEDGWOOD 1940-PRESENT PRINTED QUEEN'S WARE ONLY

This silver-rimmed stirrup cup in the shape of a fox's head, of the fine black stoneware called basalt, is prized because it was made in Josiah Wedgwood's lifetime. Similar cups, which were handed to hunters for a final draft before the chase, were made to resemble other animals.

various times over the centuries for various purposes. In 1917, for example, the company made 9,251 dinner-service pieces, each one transfer-decorated with the flags of the 11 American Allies in World War I. The pieces were commissioned by New York socialite Mrs. Robert Coleman Taylor, who insisted that the copper plates from which the designs were made be destroyed. She sold the dinner pieces in order to raise money for her war charities. These Liberty china pieces, as they are known, are difficult to come by, particularly in a complete service.

In other cases, forms or designs are rare because they were discontinued as a result of disappointing sales. In 1812 Josiah II, Wedgwood's son and head of the company, introduced bone china, but he gave up production only 10 years later. Pieces from the 1812-1822 period can be identified by the company name printed in capitals in red, blue or gold on the base. Wedgwood bone china was reintroduced in 1878 and this later porcelain, marked with Wedgwood's Portland-vase symbol and the company's name *(page 85),* is more available. Jasper in a terra-cotta color was produced from 1957 to 1959 and again in 1971, but was discontinued both times because it did not sell well. Sometimes, too, limited runs were brought about by technical failure: The colorants of

crimson and dark olive-green jasper, both introduced in 1910, tended to bleed into the white bas-relief decoration and were discontinued in 1928.

Other valuable finds include queen's ware that was hand-painted and signed between 1858 and 1875 by the French artist Emile Lessore. Also sought after are the bone-china fantasy wares, known as Fairyland lusters *(page 95),* designed by Daisy Makeig-Jones, a woman who worked for the company from 1915 to 1931. A third, less expensive, category includes Wedgwood articles that were intended for unusual purposes: door-knobs, keyhole escutcheons, mantel tiles, cameos for sewing boxes, and even book ends.

Because there is so much Wedgwood, so widely exported, in so many forms, materials, colors and designs, it is fairly easy to find almost everywhere. Prizes turn up even in flea markets. In 1979 a collector saw a sign reading ANY PIECE, 50 CENTS on a table at a New Jersey market—and for that sum bought an original 18th Century blue jasper tea-caddy spoon that was worth a thousand times its price.

For related material, see the articles on Buttons, Majolica and Staffordshire in separate volumes of The Encyclopedia of Collectibles.

A polished basalt vase from Josiah Wedgwood's time gains further value from the unusual paint—a mixture of pigment and wax known as encaustic—used to affix the design. Later basalt pieces were decorated with applied relief in jasper and are more widely available.

Jewelry from the late 1800s, such as these earrings of gold-mounted Wedgwood cameos, is fairly common. Demeter (left), goddess of fertility, and Poseidon, god of the sea, are shown.

The signs of the zodiac encircle an early-19th Century stoneware jar inspired by an Egyptian burial piece. It is a rare find. The lid is decorated with an applied jasper relief. The white stoneware base was dipped in jasper, and the zodiac and Egyptian motifs were added before firing.

A necklace with cut-steel settings can be dated to the 1700s and is very desirable. Missing and replaced beads hardly affect the value.

A four-inch-wide pin box is prized because its terra-cotta jasper, produced only briefly, is hard to find. A mark on the base dates this piece to
1957, the year the color was introduced. The kidney shape is common.

During firing, crimson jasper tended to bleed
into the white jasper relief, as can be seen on
this milk pitcher, notably in the smoke over the
brazier. The color was discontinued and is
therefore hard to find.

The dessert plate at left is especially desirable
because it is lilac, one of the rarest jasper colors
from the 18th Century. The piece can be dated
by its beveled edges and quality of design.

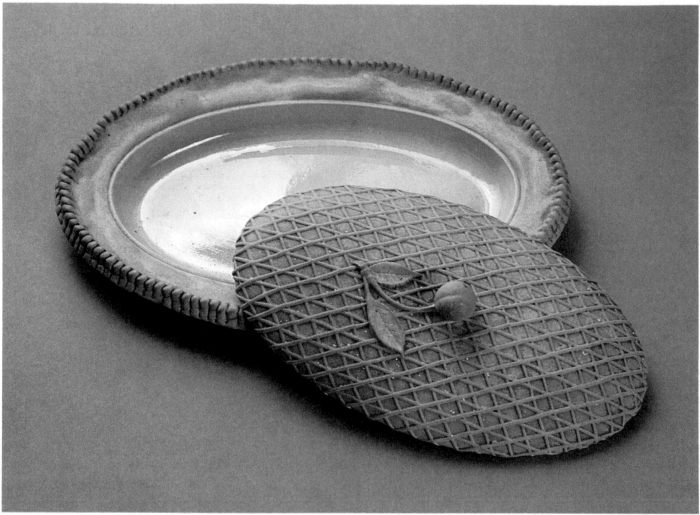

This pie dish, made of the tan ceramic called caneware, has a lid imitating baked crust to give a traditional look to pies baked crustless during a flour shortage in the early 19th Century. The crust design proved so popular that it has been produced ever since.

A creamer of tan caneware from the late 1800s is admired for its hand-painted enamel design but is not rare. Caneware pieces, such as inkstands and teapots, molded to resemble bamboo are difficult to find and desirable.

Rare Pieces from a Special Partnership

When Josiah Wedgwood was 24 years old his opinions about the necessity for better-made, better-designed pottery caught the attention of Thomas Whieldon, who was already recognized as the master potter of Staffordshire and who agreed that their craft was in need of innovation and improvement. Whieldon accepted the young Wedgwood into partnership in 1754.

Their association lasted only until 1759, when Wedgwood left to found his own company. During those five years, however, Wedgwood found ways to increase the variety of colors that could be glazed in tortoise shell (see below), invented a new gleaming green glaze, which has remained popular to the present day, and introduced wares shaped to resemble vegetables and fruit.

The partners produced a large number of wares using these glazes and forms, the most famous of which are pineapple and cauliflower tea sets, but neither man marked his products. Because wares similarly glazed and shaped were soon being made by other Staffordshire potters as well, it is very difficult to be sure that a find, however perfect an example of Staffordshire it may be, is from the Whieldon-Wedgwood kilns.

A coffeepot resembling a cauliflower is unmarked, but the quality of the work and the perfect green glaze suggest it may have been made by Wedgwood and Whieldon in the late 1750s.

These plates are prized for ornate designs and tortoise-shell glazes. The pits on the one at right—caused by a faulty mix or improper firing—are common on such wares and do not affect value. The collector believes both are Wedgwood-Whieldon products.

A queen's ware dinner plate decorated with water lilies is valuable because it dates to 1807, when the design was introduced. The water-lily pattern was jointly conceived by Josiah II, then head of the company, and his brother John, founder of the Royal Horticultural Society.

A two-foot-tall epergne made in the early 19th Century is desirable because of its ornateness, although the loss of six baskets from the top section detracts slightly from the value. The design was introduced in 1790 and reproduced at various times thereafter.

A hand-painted bone-china flower basket (above), three inches across, is sought because it dates to Wedgwood's first venture into bone china, 1812 to 1822. Bone china produced since 1878 is commoner.

A 1930s glazed bone-china coffeepot (left) is admired for its solid color, known as alpine pink, but is not hard to find. The same color was used for tea sets and dinner services, which also are widely available.

Flanked by the flags of World War I Allies, the shield of the United States appears on a porcelain hot-water pot and sugar bowl. The pieces are from the valuable Liberty china sets, which were made in limited numbers for the benefit of war charities.

A glazed trumpet vase (above) illustrates the imagination displayed by designer Daisy Makeig-Jones in her famous Fairyland luster. Bats and elves cavort inside, birds fly around the rim, and on the outside flit butterfly women —buxom Victorians held aloft by gossamer wings.

MUSEUMS
The Art Institute of Chicago
Chicago, Illinois 60603

Birmingham Museum of Art
Birmingham, Alabama 35203

COLLECTORS ORGANIZATIONS
Wedgwood International Seminar
New York, New York 10003

PERIODICALS
The American Wedgwoodian, The Wedgwood
International Seminar, New York, New York 10003

The BMW Bulletin, Buten Museum of Wedgwood,
Merion, Pennsylvania 19066

BOOKS
Barnard, Harry, *Chats on Wedgwood Ware.* Charles River Books, 1977.

Buten, David, *Wedgwood Guide to Marks and Dating.* Buten Museum of Wedgwood, 1976.

Buten, David, and Patricia Pelehach, *Wedgwood and America: Wedgwood Bas-relief Ware.* Buten Museum of Wedgwood, 1977.

Buten, Harry, *Wedgwood Rarities.* Buten Museum of Wedgwood, 1969.

des Fontaines, Una, *Wedgwood Fairyland Lustre.* Born-Hawes, 1975.

Graham, John Meredith, II, and Hensleigh Cecil Wedgwood, *Wedgwood.* Arno Press, 1974.

Kelly, Alison, *Decorative Wedgwood in Architecture and Furniture.* Country Life, 1965.

Kelly, Alison, *The Story of Wedgwood.* Viking Press, 1975.

Kelly, Alison, *Wedgwood Ware.* Ward Lock, 1970.

Klamkin, Marian, *The Collector's Book of Wedgwood.* Dodd, Mead & Company, 1971.

Mankowitz, Wolf, *Wedgwood.* Spring Books, 1966.

Meteyard, Elizabeth, *The Wedgwood Handbook.* Gale Towers, reprinted 1970.

Moore, Hannah H., *Wedgwood and His Imitators.* Ars Ceramica, 1978.

Reilly, Robin, *Wedgwood Jasper.* World Publishing Company, 1972.

Reilly, Robin, and George Savage, *Wedgwood: The Portrait Medallions.* Barrie & Jenkins, 1973.

Wicker
A Craze for Furnishings of Woven Reeds

When William and Susanna White boarded the *Mayflower* in 1620, they took with them a wicker cradle for the baby they were expecting, and in due time it was occupied by Peregrine White, the first child born to the Pilgrim settlers in the New World. Even then there was nothing new about wicker—the Egyptians made baskets and coffins of wickerwork as far back as 4000 B.C. But it was a Boston grocer named Cyrus Wakefield who launched America on a phenomenal buying spree of anything and everything made of wicker—a catchall term for pieces that are woven of rattan, reed, cane, dried grasses, wil-

---

Jerry and Merry Gilbert of New York used a number of their wicker finds in furnishing their vacation home.

---

low and such other pliable materials as twisted paper—and thereby made possible the charming furnishings collectors now prize.

In 1844 Wakefield, walking along the wharves where clipper ships unloaded their cargoes, noticed discarded bundles of rattan that had protected the ships' loads from slipping—an almost free raw material. In 1855 he opened a factory to make furniture. Before wicker went out of fashion in the 1930s, there were wicker stools at lunch counters, wicker pony traps and even, as an option offered in 1915 by the Gadabout Motor Corporation of Newark, New Jersey, a wicker body on two-seater automobiles.

Mostly, however, the American public wanted the furniture that collectors look for today. This was produced in dozens of different forms—some plain, some ornate—which ranged from rocking chairs to planters to beach chairs to music stands. In the last decade of the 19th Century, conversation chairs enjoyed a vogue; these were S-shaped sofas on which a courting couple could sit side by side, facing each other but properly separated by a wicker chaperon.

Wakefield was not the only wicker maker, of course. The most notable among his competitors were the five Heywood brothers of Gardner, Massachusetts, whose firm later merged with Wakefield's. Pieces marked with "Wakefield," "Heywood" or the name of any of the combinations leading to the modern Heywood-Wakefield

Company are the most desirable. Other major manufacturers included American Rattan Company, Lloyd Manufacturing Company and Paine's Furniture Company. Some pieces, however, were not marked at all, and those that were generally bore paper labels that have long since fallen off.

Wicker from the 19th Century is naturally the most valuable, but examples from the 1920s and 1930s also are desirable and are considerably easier to find. The real gauge of wicker is the balance between a rare form and a prized design. The least common and therefore most desirable include such oddities as the posing chairs that late-19th Century photographers used as props in their studios, easels for displaying drawings and paintings, and piano stools. Bedroom furniture of wicker, such as headboards and chests of drawers, is also uncommon, as are bookcases and étagères. However, other living-room pieces—sofas, armchairs and tables—are more widely available; collectors place great value on a matching set, such as the one shown on pages 102-103.

Rocking chairs, though fairly easy to find, are desirable, and collectors especially look for those that are mounted on flat platforms designed to preserve the carpet. Even more common are plant stands, baskets, and porch and lawn chairs and settees, which were the first wicker furniture made and were popular the longest.

Beyond the desirability of various types of furniture, the value of wicker is determined by style. Highly prized and the most difficult to find are settees and chairs made in the 1860s and 1870s, when manufacturers were just beginning to experiment with elaborate designs. The backs of early chairs, for example, have panels of cane woven into spider-web patterns. Others have widely spaced loops of rattan.

The wicker manufactured from the 1880s until about 1910 is more ornate and is the style that is most popular among collectors today—the curvaceous, sprawling designs beloved in the late-Victorian era. Pieces often were given tightly woven skirts and rolled arms and backs;

This armchair is prized for its unpainted reed and its mint condition. Its rolled arms and serpentine back date it to the late 1800s. A label under the seat and a tag on the back identify its maker, the premier manufacturer, Heywood Brothers and Wakefield Company.

Plant pedestals are a type of plant stand that is hard to find, and this one, made about 1900, is especially desirable because it is completely covered in closely woven natural reed.

almost every item burgeoned with curlicues and spools.

In the 20th Century there was a move toward austerity; the new wicker furniture was angular and the woven patterns simple and linear. Then rising labor costs and increases in the tariffs on imported rattan led to yet another change in style. Wicker took on an airier look as a result of economical open weaving. This later style of wicker can most often be found on chaise longues and armchairs that were designed for use by hotels and resorts. The manufacturers named such products after well-known resort areas such as Bar Harbor, Newport and Southampton, but collectors call them all Bar Harbor; they can be identified by thicker reeds, open-weave designs and flat arms. Such pieces are not hard to find.

Less valuable, although still collected, is wicker that was machine-woven in the 1920s and 1930s of a twisted-paper fiber. Because it could be mass-produced economically in popular tight weaves—many of them incorporating Art Deco designs *(page 106)*—it brought

wicker a new gust of popularity that faded in the 1930s but revived in the 1960s.

Some new wicker is made in the old styles and is easily mistaken for antique pieces. Age can be determined in several ways. Old wicker pieces are generally heavier and sturdier than newer ones because they were built on hardwood frames; nowadays, bamboo is used. In the case of pieces made of reed, the material on older finds is substantial and smooth; newer reed is thinner and so fibrous that it even looks slightly fuzzy. One telltale sign of a recent reproduction chair is a seat made of flimsy, circular-woven reed; most old chairs have seats of cane on wooden frames.

Do not pass up old wicker that is in need of repair. Unless it is badly damaged—with a broken leg, for example, or loose joints hidden under the wicker—it can be restored. Simple wrapping of wicker requires only modest skill—this technique and others are described in books *(box, page 107)*—and strips of rattan and reed are sold by hobby shops.

Natural-finish wicker, protected only by varnish, is the most desirable. However, most old pieces have been painted and, because so many were subjected to the weather outdoors, painted repeatedly. You are likely to find chairs with a dozen heavy, blobbed coats. The easiest way to remove the paint is to take the piece to a commercial stripper, who for a modest fee will dip it into his hot tank of powerful chemicals and lift it out freshly bared. Such harsh treatment, however, weakens joints and cannot be applied to wicker of twisted-paper fiber, which is dissolved by the hot-tank chemicals. And even on reed and rattan, the chemicals can raise a fine, fibrous fuzz on the wicker. For these reasons, we prefer not to subject our wicker to tank stripping, but to undertake instead the tedious chore of getting paint off with a toothbrush and a water-soluble chemical remover. After stripping, the wicker must be protected. The most practical method of painting is spraying—aerosol cans work perfectly well. However, we find hand brushing better for a smooth varnish finish.

Not-so-old wicker that needs some fixing up can be found in the usual sources of collectibles—country auctions are a good hunting ground, particularly in the Northeast. For the very old pieces and those that have been restored, you probably have to shop the dealers. One East Coast specialist employs a corps of some 20 pickers to scour the countryside for furniture that he then has stripped and repainted. It pays to shop—prices for similar pieces may differ by 100 per cent or more even among dealers in the same area.

For related material, see the article on Victorian Furniture in this volume, and the articles on Baskets and Oak Furniture in separate volumes of this encyclopedia.

A natural-wicker floor lamp with a square shade and an Eiffel Tower base (above) is unusual; table lamps, particularly those with round shades, are considerably more common.

An easel is very rare, and this one—used to display a painting, not as artist's equipment—is particularly prized because it is in such good condition; the few that were made were fragile and easily broken.

A table from the 1890s (left) is valued for its ornate late-Victorian style —closely woven skirt, curved legs and decorative curlicues and spools. A label under the oak shelf identifies the maker as Heywood Brothers and Wakefield Company, adding to the table's worth.

The curlicue design and pineapple corners make this natural-wicker table desirable. The label under the top identifies it as a product of Heywood Brothers and Company.

This teacart is prized in part because it is covered entirely with wicker; those with glass shelves and metal or wooden wheels are more common.

The pie rack, too, is unusual, as is the wicker material—sea grass, a marshland reed used mainly in the early 1900s.

The straight-backed armchair, settee and corner chair with which the collectors have furnished a room in their country home are exceptionally desirable because they are from a matching parlor suite. The set, which is additionally prized because it has a natural finish, was made about 1885. (The plant pedestal at near right, not part of the set, is from a later period; it can be seen in detail on page 98.)

The open crisscross weave, thick reeds and flat arm identify the chair above as a type of resort wicker known as Bar Harbor. Made about 1910 and painted white, it is unusual because of the magazine rack.

This late-Victorian armchair, desirable for its ornate design, would be more valuable in a natural finish, and its owner has already begun to hand-strip paint off the right arm.

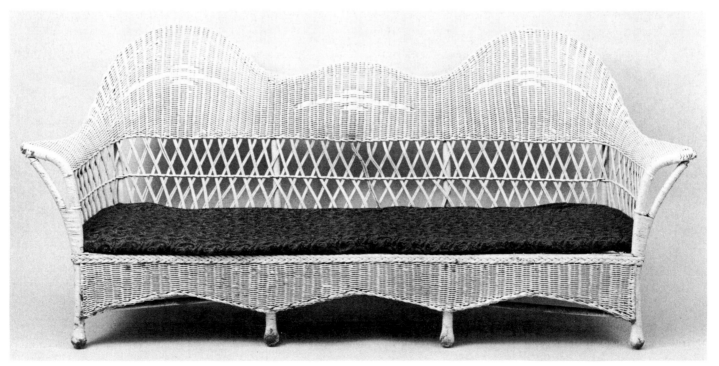

A sofa from the 1920s is prized for its camel back, which has a diamond design of the Art Deco style. The piece, which has been painted white, is

machine-woven of man-made fiber. Wicker furniture that is made of natural material is more sought after.

Strollers such as the one above, once common sights along the board-walks of resorts, are now hard to find. This white-painted example, made about 1900, is in exceptionally good condition. Doubles—wheeled chairs made to accommodate two passengers—are even more desirable.

BOOKS
Corbin, Patricia, *All About Wicker*. E. P. Dutton, 1978.

Hill, Conover, *Antique Wicker Furniture, an Illustrated Value Guide*. Collector Books, 1975.

Saunders, Richard, *Collecting & Restoring Wicker Furniture*. Crown Publishers, Inc., 1976.

Shirley, G. E., *Great Grandmother's Wicker Furniture, 1880's-1920's*. Craftsman Press, 1978.

Thompson, Frances, *The Complete Wicker Book*. Wallace-Homestead Book Co., 1978.

Drawn from Nature by A. Wilson. 1.Cardinal Grosbeak.2.Female & egg.3.Red Tanager.4.Female & egg. Engraved by A. Lawson.

Wildlife Prints
Classic Studies of America's Fauna

Acting on no more than a hunch, I once attended a United States Customs Service auction that was held to dispose of unclaimed or abandoned items. I had been collecting beautifully detailed lithographs and engravings of wildlife since I was 18 years old and knew from experience that they could turn up in unusual places. Why not at a Customs auction? Sure enough, sitting there were four prints from the 1827 first edition of John James Audubon's *Birds of America*—the most valuable series of plates that any wildlife-print collector could ever hope to find. I got all four for $117. In 1980 a single Audubon first-edition print was sold for $2,500.

I do not recommend haunting Customs Service sales just because of my good luck. Nor does a collector of wildlife prints need to search out rarities such as Audubon "firsts." Large numbers of delightful old prints exist. Beginning in the 1700s and continuing throughout the 1800s, both Americans and Europeans were avid for

This tiny print—three by five inches—of a meadow mouse is from a 19th Century study of New York State fauna by James E. DeKay. Such small prints are not very valuable.

William S. Reese, a dealer in fine books and prints, began collecting wildlife prints and Americana when he was a student.

---

pictures of the still-undeveloped continent's unknown birds and beasts. As a result, scores of artists roamed the wilderness, producing thousands of pictures of the creatures that walked, crawled, swam or flew in the American landscape. Teams of half-forgotten artists accompanied such United States government expeditions as the Pacific railroad survey, which mapped a route to the West in the 1850s.

The originals made by all these painter-naturalists were drawn from life—or, in Audubon's case, from animals he shot and had stuffed—and were then copied onto plates by the artists or by talented technicians, and

Male and female cardinals (top) and a pair of tanagers glow with hand-applied colors in this fine 1810 print from American Ornithology, by Scots-born naturalist Alexander Wilson.

were printed from these handmade plates. Most were printed in black and white, then individually colored by hand, but after around 1850, many were reproduced directly in color through the use of multiple lithographic plates. Though intended as scientific studies rather than art, many transcended their original purpose and are outstanding examples of creative artistry. Those that are not hard to find go for modest sums when sold.

Even some small Audubon prints are relatively common, although his greatest work, *Birds of America*, is extremely rare (he also did a volume on mammals). A stupendous four-volume set more than a yard tall, weighing 200 pounds and containing 435 prints, *Birds of America* cost $1,000 when first issued in London in the 1830s (one sold at auction in 1977 for $396,000). Because of the great cost, only some 200 sets were bound, but about 100 additional copies of each print were issued separately and many of the bound volumes have since been cut apart for their individual prints.

Authentic prints from this Audubon first edition bear the names of the three engravers who copied Audubon's original watercolors for printing—William H. Lizars, Robert Havell and his son Robert Havell Jr. Further, each sheet of the paper, 39½ by 26½ inches, bears the watermark of the papermaker, J. Whatman, and a date that may be any year between 1827 and 1838.

More modest editions of *Birds of America* were soon published in the United States, the first a "miniature" (10½ by 6½ inches) lithographed and hand-colored by J. T. Bowen of Philadelphia between 1840 and 1844. Slightly more valuable are the Audubons reproduced by Julius Bien of New York in 1860. Although color-lithographed rather than hand-colored, they are the same size as the first edition.

If Audubon's work is the most desired, prints by other early artists are also sought by collectors. Particularly valuable are those by two early and hardy men, Mark Catesby and Alexander Wilson. Catesby's *The Natural*

History of Carolina, Florida and the Bahama Islands went through three British and at least two German editions. The later British editions are not as sharp and clear as the earlier and are less desirable. The German plates were hand-copied from the English ones with some variations in detail, and prints made from them are accordingly lower in value. Catesby's handsome birds, of whatever edition, are worth considerably more than, say, prints of his lizards and frogs—all wildlife prints of slithery creatures such as reptiles and amphibians are less desirable than prints of mammals or birds.

Alexander Wilson walked from Philadelphia to Niagara Falls, then descended the Ohio and Mississippi Rivers and explored the swamps of Florida to create the nine-volume *American Ornithology*. The first edition was inexplicably printed on wretched paper; the prints are now covered with brown spots. Later editions—recognizable by their better paper—are more desirable.

Establishing which artist did the picture from which a wildlife print was derived is usually easy: The artist's name normally appears in the bottom left-hand corner. The engraver or colorist (if he was not the artist himself) generally signed the right-hand corner. Hand-colored engravings or woodcuts can usually be distinguished from the less valuable prints made by color lithography, which have flatter and less delicate colors. Restrikes,

prints made from the original plates after the first edition, are also less valuable than originals. Many restrikes bear forthright notations such as "2nd Edition." They also tend to be fuzzier in their details than firsts and were often printed on different (usually cheaper) paper. Many of the notable prints—particularly Audubon's—have been repeatedly reproduced by modern methods. Such reproductions can be detected by their pattern of lithographic dots, which can easily be seen with a magnifying glass.

For me, one of the fascinations of collecting prints is in rummaging in antiquarian print shops and bookshops and getting to know other owners, most of whom are steeped in their subject. They are ready to tell the stories of the tireless men who traveled the wild America of 100 or 200 years ago in search of the beasts they delineated. Creating wildlife prints then took courage. Alexander Wilson reported that the water in Southern swamps was "little better than poison," and in Florida he weathered a storm so violent that it tore up trees and flung them at him. "I would," he said, "rather take my chance in a field of battle than in such a tornado again."

For related material, see the articles on Botanical Prints, Currier & Ives and Japanese Prints in separate volumes of The Encyclopedia of Collectibles.

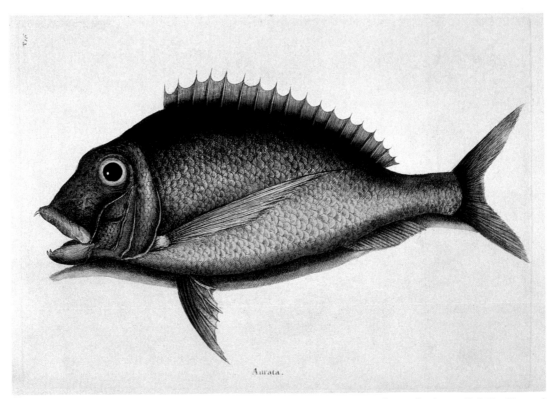

A colorful, lifelike porgy (above) comes from Mark Catesby's 18th Century volume of prints called The Natural History of Carolina, Florida and the Bahama Islands. Catesby's prints are second only to Audubon's in value.

T.73

Phænicopterus.

Keratophiton &c.

Among Catesby's finest prints is this lordly, strutting flamingo. Catesby was a speedy draftsman and usually painted live birds in lifelike postures. Audubon (pages 114-116) shot his specimens, then stuffed and posed them artfully.

Drawn from Nature by A.W.Lion.

1. *Passenger Pigeon.* 2. *Blue-mountain Warbler.* 3.

XENOPICUS ALBOLARVATUS.

This delicately colored print of a pair of rare white-headed woodpeckers comes from a volume titled New and Heretofore Unfigured Species of the Birds of North America by Daniel Giraud Elliot, published by Bowen & Co. of Philadelphia in 1869. Elliot was employed by the American Museum of Natural History in New York City to fill in ornithological gaps left by Audubon, Wilson and other pioneer naturalists.

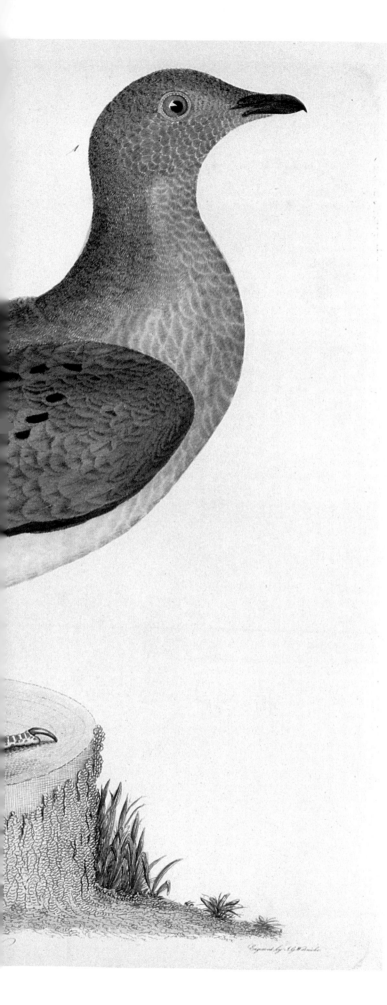

The passenger pigeon (left, foreground) is now extinct, but when Alexander Wilson published this print in the early 1800s, flocks of these birds filled the skies of eastern North America. The two birds clinging to the branch in the background are Blue Mountain warblers.

The Wild Turkey (above) is the most sought-after print by John James Audubon. This version is from the Julius Bien color-lithographed 1860 edition of Birds of America and is valued less than the same plate from the hand-colored first edition.

N°74.

Pl.369.

Great blue Heron.

Male

Drawn from Nature by J.J. Audubon F R S F L.

Lith Printed & Col.d by J T Bowen Phila

With wings half-spread to show its plumage, a great blue heron looks for fish in this superb Audubon print. It is from the lithographed, hand-colored edition produced by J. T. Bowen of Philadelphia from 1840 to 1844.

Two raccoons glower from a tree in this print from Audubon's mammal book, *The Viviparous Quadrupeds of North America. It was lithographed by W. H. Hitchcock and published by Bowen.*

Three deer appear in a setting of New York State hills in this hand-colored lithograph from the 1830s. The original was painted (pinx, in Latin) by Thomas Doughty, a landscapist of the Hudson River School.

COMMON DEER.

Sartain sc.

PAPILIO.

IV.

Drawn by Mary Peart.   L. Bowen. Col.

TURNUS, 1 ♂, 2.3 Var GLAUCUS ♀.

4 ♀ var.,

a. Larva. 1st. stage. magnified.

The sexes of these tiger swallowtail butterflies are indicated by symbols and a numbered code in this 18th Century work by George Edwards, a British naturalist. The bottom of the print reveals that it was copied by Mary Peart, probably Edwards' assistant, and colored by L. Bowen.

Helicops abacurus.

26

This rare mud-snake print is from a massive 19th Century treatise, North American Herpetology, by John Edwards Holbrook. It was copied onto a plate by J. H. Richard and lithographed by P. S. Duval.

MUSEUMS
American Museum of Natural History
New York, New York 10024

PERIODICALS
Print Trader, M. Rainone, Middle Village,
New York 11379

BOOKS
Elbert, John and Catherine, *Old American Prints for Collectors.* Charles Scribner's Sons, 1974.

Zigrosser, Carl, and Christa M. Gaehde, *A Guide to the Collecting and Care of Original Prints.* Crown Publishers Inc., 1965.

This wooden fan from Das Weltausstellung (Universal Exhibition), held in Vienna in 1873, bears a lithograph of the main building, which had a cast-iron dome 354 feet wide. Memorabilia from 19th Century European fairs are rare and valuable.

World's Fair Souvenirs
Mementos of Razzle-Dazzle Exhibitions

When I was eight years old, I ran away from home and walked 10 miles to look through the gates at the 1939 New York World's Fair. (Some kind folk soon put me on a bus for home, and my parents later took me on a real visit.) Ever since, the magnetism of world's fairs has pulled at me and influenced me—my fascination with the fairs'

Larry Zim, an interior designer and authority on world's fairs, has lent parts of his huge collection of memorabilia to several museums.

often daring architecture led me to become a designer.

The 1939 fair, it seems certain, produced a greater number and variety of memorabilia than any other. Many of the 1,500 exhibitors either sold or gave away mementos, 50 booths sold souvenirs to 45 million visitors, and major stores set up branches at the site. As a result of this commercialism, there is an enormous variety of relics, most bearing images of the fair's famous symbols, the 700-foot Trylon tower and the 200-foot

ball called the Perisphere. One collector cherishes 8,000 different items, ranging in value from precious Tiffany dinner plates to plastic lapel badges *(pages 130-131)*. The less costly items—ashtrays, napkin rings, salt and pepper shakers, and glasses—remain widely available.

It is such small household items, in fact, that provide the majority of less expensive collectibles from most fairs. Also widely available are paper items—matchbooks, official guides and programs, photographic views, postcards, and commemorative stamps—plus scarves and pennants decorated with the fair's name and pictures of its notable buildings. Somewhat rarer are medals, commemorative coins, souvenir spoons and such novelties as toys modeled after, say, the buses or trolleys that transported visitors about the grounds.

Most of the 600 souvenirs sold through a New Jersey

The lithograph at right pictures the giant steam engine, built by George H. Corliss of Providence, that was the wonder of the 1876 Centennial Exhibition in Philadelphia; it could have powered the entire fair.

A medal awarded prizewinning exhibitors at London's Great Exhibition of 1851 (above, left) shows Queen Victoria and Prince Albert, who was the main organizer of this first world's fair. The coin purse above at right bears a silver-framed picture of the fair's main building, the Crystal Palace, which also appears on the silver snuffbox at bottom.

In Daumier's sardonic view, a spruce couple enters the 1855 Paris fair, and an exhausted pair departs.

mail-order auction in 1979 were of these relatively common sorts; only a few items went for more than $50 apiece. More costly are such rarities as fine Wedgwood plates, complete china tea services, and some very elaborate and unusual souvenirs—some years ago I found a kitchen set of table and chairs bearing in large designs the insignia of the 1939 New York fair. Valuable, too, are striking posters printed in limited quantities.

Besides the 1939 New York fair, collectors favor the two big Chicago fairs, of 1893 and 1933. The 1893 World's Columbian Exposition, celebrating (a year late) the 400th anniversary of Columbus' discovery of the New World, attracted 27 million visitors—then about one third the entire United States population—and the number of souvenirs it produced is equally staggering. Some two million people passed through the Libbey Glass Company exhibit, for example, and most emerged with a sample of glass made by one of the 150 glass blowers employed there fulltime. Other valued memorabilia from this fair include commemorative coins and stamps and sets of handsome admission tickets *(page 124)*.

The 1933 Chicago fair may be best remembered for its amusement area's controversial attraction, Sally Rand and her seminude fan dance *(page 129)*, but it also offered visitors such mementos as can-banks made in the American Can Company's exhibit, playing cards and souvenir mugs. And there are, literally, pieces of the fair to be found, for the crowd on the last night began to tear the flimsy temporary buildings apart.

The vast St. Louis fair of 1904 is another favorite of collectors. Items made of ruby glass, which became popular there, are much sought, and picture postcards—at least 3,000 different ones were distributed by 50 different exhibitors—are widely available. Other American fairs that threw off a wealth of collectibles include the Centennial Exhibition in Philadelphia in 1876—it attracted almost 10 million people to see 30,720 exhibits, and souvenirs from paperweights to Wedgwood can be found—the Buffalo fair of 1901, the Seattle fair of 1962 and the 1964 fair in New York. The 1915 San Francisco fair featured a 500-foot tower decorated with 120,000 glass jewels, and these relics are choice finds.

The best sources of memorabilia from recent American world's fairs—this sounds obvious, but it is true—are the closets of relatives or friends who visited them. After closets, I recommend flea markets and garage sales, but not necessarily those in or near fair-site cities; most have been combed by collectors. Instead I search out country sales in Vermont or upstate New York or downstate Illinois. World's fairs draw people from all over the country, and the people take mementos home with them. Eventually some come up for sale. Many collectors place advertisements in antiques magazines, but I have had better luck asking dealers and friends who are addicted to antiquing in rural areas to keep an eye out for me as they make their rounds of country shops.

Souvenirs of European world's fairs are, understandably, more difficult to find in the United States than mementos of American fairs. At the 1979 New Jersey auction only one item from the London Crystal Palace exposition of 1851—the first fair of all—was offered for sale (there were 153 items from the New York 1939 fair, 120 from the 1933 Chicago exposition and 54 from the St. Louis fair of 1904). A serious collector of European fair relics should enjoy travel or have a network of friendly fellow collectors around the globe.

For related material, see the articles on Advertising Giveaways, Spoons and Trade Cards in separate volumes of The Encyclopedia of Collectibles.

The Eiffel Tower clock above is especially valuable because it dates from the 1889 Paris exposition, for which the tower was built by Alexandre Gustave Eiffel. At the time it was the tallest structure in the world.

A gilded-brass outer ring frames the world in this lapel pin, sold at the Chicago fair of 1893. It was, as advertised, a worldwide fair, with exhibits from 77 nations.

Tickets like these are much-sought items from the Chicago fair. Manhattan Day was a promotion honoring New York. The Indian appeared on one of four designs used initially for tickets.

A lady's cotton stocking (above), probably a souvenir from the midway of the 1893 fair, is an unusual memento since it is fragile and only a few have survived.

The cotton scarf above bears views of the 1893 fair, including four of its blindingly white exhibit hall. The canals threading the site led one writer to call the fair a "Midwestern Venice."

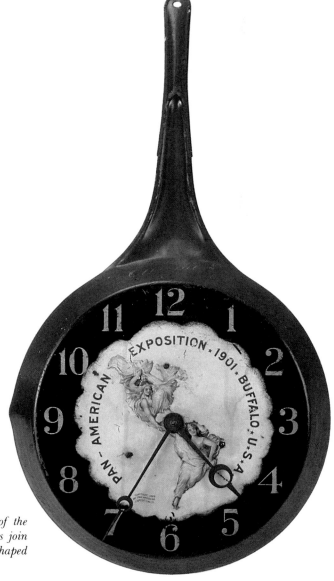

This rare poster of the Buffalo fair of 1901 shows the spirit of Niagara rising from the falls. The ill-fated fair —President McKinley was assassinated while visiting it —was intended in part to celebrate the harnessing of the falls for hydroelectric power.

Two winsome maidens in the shape of the North and South American continents join hands on the face of this frying-pan-shaped clock from the Buffalo fair.

A photograph from a highly valued souvenir booklet that was sold at the 1900 exposition in Paris pictures the main gate, a delirium of Oriental-flavored

The bold typography on the portfolio above, containing prints from the Paris 1925 exposition, exemplifies Art Deco, which dominated the fair and is named for its exhibits of Arts Decoratifs. The prints show department-store displays, such as the one below of perfume in Lalique bottles.

...ouveau design topped by a statue called La Parisienne.

WORLD EXPOSITIONS

The list below includes all of the major world's fairs held in the United States —the main sources of fair memorabilia available to American collectors —and the largest and most influential fairs of Europe and Asia. Since the first world's fair opened in London's Crystal Palace in 1851, international exhibitions have been staged in more than 50 major cities on five continents.

DATE	PLACE	OFFICIAL NAME
1851	London	The Great Exhibition of the Works of Industry of All Nations
1853	New York City	Exhibition of the Industry of All Nations
1855	Paris	Universal Exposition
1862	London	International Exhibition
1873	Vienna	Universal Exhibition
1876	Philadelphia	United States International Centennial Exhibition
1879	Sydney, Australia	Sydney International Exhibition
1883	Boston	Foreign Exhibition
1883	Louisville, Kentucky	Southern Exposition
1884-1885	New Orleans	World's Industrial and Cotton Centennial Exposition
1889	Paris	International Universal Exposition
1893	Chicago	World's Columbian Exposition
1894	San Francisco	California Mid-Winter International Exposition
1895	Atlanta	Cotton States and International Exposition
1898	Omaha	Trans-Mississippi Exposition
1900	Paris	International Universal Exposition
1901	Buffalo	Pan-American Exposition
1901	Charleston, South Carolina	South Carolina Interstate and West Indian Exposition
1904	St. Louis	Louisiana Purchase Exposition
1905	Portland, Oregon	Lewis and Clark Centennial Exposition
1907	Hampton Roads, Virginia	Jamestown Ter-Centennial Exposition
1909	New York City	Hudson-Fulton Celebration
1909	Seattle	Alaska-Yukon Pacific Exposition
1915	San Francisco	Panama-Pacific International Exposition
1915	San Diego	Panama-California Exposition
1924-1925	Wembley, England	British Empire Exhibition
1925	Paris	International Exposition of Decorative Arts and Modern Industries
1926	Philadelphia	Sesquicentennial International Exposition
1929	Barcelona	International Exhibition
1933-1934	Chicago	Century of Progress International Exposition
1935	Brussels	International Exposition
1935	San Diego	California-Pacific International Exposition
1936-1937	Cleveland	Great Lakes Exposition
1936-1937	Dallas	Texas Centennial Central Exposition
1939-1940	San Francisco	Golden Gate International Exposition
1939-1940	New York City	New York World's Fair
1951	London	Festival of Britain
1958	Brussels	Brussels International Fair
1962	Seattle	Century 21 Exposition
1964-1965	New York City	New York World's Fair
1967	Montreal	Universal and International Exposition of 1967 (Expo '67)
1968	San Antonio	Hemisfair '68
1970	Osaka, Japan	Japan World Exposition Osaka 1970
1974	Spokane	International Exposition on the Environment (Expo '74)

TRU-VUE
PRESENTS

BEAUTIFUL · BEWITCHING
SALLY RAND
in her
FAN DANCE
The Most Daring and Sensational
Attraction at
"A Century of Progress".

The movements of the Fan Dance as
originated and presented by Sally Rand
are exquisitely beautiful. Neither camera,
pen nor brush can do justice to her
presentation of this - the most daring,
artistic and spectacular dance ever
attempted in America.

Directed by Jack Bennett
Photography by Francis Dare

These rare strips of film, seen through a stereo viewer, show Sally Rand's fan dance in three dimensions. She was the sensation of the 1933 Chicago fair, where the films were sold as souvenirs. The breathless captions enhance the value. Her Chicago appearances made Miss Rand famous, and she later helped organize an exhibit for the 1939 San Francisco fair.

Her joy is world - she is serene again - alone with the moon, the pool, and her pristine beauty.

The symbols of the 1939 New York World's Fair, the needle-like Trylon and the globular Perisphere —visible on most of the memorabilia shown *on these pages—are combined with banners and the image of a fair guide on this dizzyingly decorated shirt and scarf.*

The entire place setting above consists of souvenirs of the 1939 fair. The plate, distributed by Tiffany & Co., is quite valuable. The silver-plated *utensils are less so, but are nonetheless coveted by collectors. The ashtray and napkin were for sale at stores and the fair's many souvenir booths.*

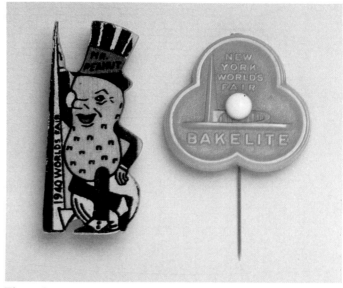

These advertising pins, given away at the 1939 fair, are common collectibles. Bakelite was the earliest synthetic plastic. Mr. Peanut leans against a Trylon marked "1940"; the fair opened again that summer.

Even a carpet sweeper took advantage of fair publicity. Decorated with the ubiquitous Trylon and Perisphere, it follows the fair's color scheme, orange and blue. It was widely sold at the time, but most were long ago discarded.

The watch above, pictured out of its case, is a rare and valuable souvenir of the 1939 fair. Although it was not an expensive timepiece — the maker did not sign either the case or the works — it still keeps time.

The Atomium, the main building of the 1958 Brussels International Fair, is depicted on the plate and in the plastic toy above, both rare in the United States. Atomic energy was the fair's theme, and the Atomium was a model 370 feet high of a crystal of iron atoms.

This model of the symbol of New York's 1964 fair shows its three rings, representing orbits around the earth—to suggest the new space age.

A souvenir (above) of the Florida aquatic show at New York's 1964 fair was tossed into the audience by a porpoise and caught by the collector.

The season ticket in the form of a passport (upper right) is a souvenir of the 1967 Universal and International Exposition —Expo '67 —in Montreal. As visitors entered each national exhibit, their tickets received a stamp, or mock visa. Some were of paper, some rubber-stamped impressions. The inverted pyramid in the Canadian stamp represented its building, one of Expo's many innovations in architecture.

MUSEUMS
Atwater Kent Museum
Philadelphia, Pennsylvania 19106

Buffalo and Erie County Historical Society
Buffalo, New York 14216

Chicago Historical Society
Chicago, Illinois 60614

Missouri Historical Society
St. Louis, Missouri 63112

Presidio Army Museum
San Francisco, California 94129

COLLECTORS ORGANIZATIONS
Expo Collectors and Historians Organization
1436 Killarney Avenue
Los Angeles, California 90065

World's Fair Collectors Society
148 Poplar Street
Garden City, New York 11530

World War Memorabilia
The Many Relics of Global Conflicts

Some collectors buy jeeps *(right)* and tanks. A group of Texans owns and flies more than 100 combat planes from World War II. But I, like most World War collectors, limit my passion for objects linked to the two Wars to things that are easier to store (and generally, to acquire); these include uniforms, helmets, insignia, shoulder patches and the trench art that soldiers fashioned out of military equipment. There is also a variety of ephemera, such as postcards, photographs, sheet music and posters.

Prices for most of these memorabilia are very reasonable, the more common patches and insignia going for

---

Descendant of U.S. Army veterans, and a Specialist 4 in the Vietnam War, Philip Katcher has written several books on uniforms.

---

about a dollar. In general, souvenirs from World War I are the more collectible—they are older and there are fewer of them. In addition, mementos of obscure or seemingly glamorous units or theaters are especially sought after, as are Nazi relics, which have become among the highest priced.

Most American collectors look mainly for memorabilia of the United States Army, Marine Corps and air force. Navy items are not widely collected because they are less varied in design. Highly valued are objects from World War I that evoke the infancy of military aviation. The Army Air Service in that canvas-and-wire era had only 12,000 pilots. (In World War II, America had almost 200,000 pilots.) Early fur-lined flying jackets are valuable, and pilots' and balloonists' wings from 1917 to 1918 are also costly *(page 136)*.

By comparison, souvenirs of the American forces that

Even though it has been almost completely rebuilt, this 1941 Willys jeep is prized because all of the replacement parts, including the tires, are of World War II vintage. The stencils on the bumper identify the owner as a member of the Military Vehicles Collectors Club.

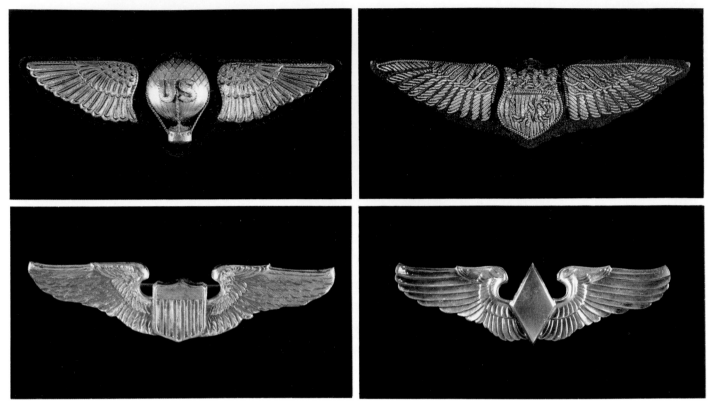

Of these American aviators' wings, the World War I balloonist's (top left) are the most prized. Fewer than 100 were made. The World War II Women's Air Force Service Pilots wings (bottom right) are also difficult to find, for only 1,200 were produced. Early World War I pilots' wings (top right) of embroidered silver thread rather than die-stamped silver are less rare, and pilots' wings from the 1940s (bottom left) are common.

fought on the ground during World War I are still surprisingly easy to find. There are, however, some notable exceptions. Particularly desirable are mementos of the United States Tank Corps. Only a few thousand men served in this new fighting arm, and their insignia—round buttons showing a lumbering tank—are rare.

Also sought are the uniforms and Russian-bear insignia of the Allied expeditionary forces that landed in northern Russia and Siberia in 1918. Russia, in the throes of the Revolution, had pulled out of the war against Germany, and the Allies, among other things, were trying to protect war matériel previously sent to the Russian fronts. One rarity from that campaign is a buffalo-hide coat with muskrat hat and gloves, left over from the 1876 Indian war in the Dakota Territory.

Among other desirable World War I shoulder patches and collar insignia are those worn by soldiers of the U.S. 2nd Infantry Division and by the Marines who fought with them—units that won more Distinguished Service Crosses in France than any others. Also rare are patches and insignia worn by the few Yanks who served in Italy (*page 138*). Patches of the 81st, or Wildcat, Division are popular because the wildcat figure for each of the division's seven brigades is a different color.

Patches from World War II are more numerous than

similar items from World War I (as are airmen's wings). But the rare collar insignia of "the Devil's Brigade"—the American-Canadian 1st Special Service Force, which fought in Italy—are valuable, as are mementos of the hard-fighting 82nd and 101st Airborne Divisions. So are items from the China-Burma-India Theater, where airmen flew a perilous route over the Himalayas to supply forces fighting the Japanese in China.

Souvenirs of enemy forces who fought in similar out-of-the-ordinary campaigns are also sought after. Of all enemy memorabilia, however, none command higher prices than the relics of Nazi Germany. Prices paid for souvenirs of the regular German forces are outstripped by relics of the Schutzstaffel, or SS, the Nazi Party troops. In 1980 a cap worn by a general in the Waffen-SS was listed in a collectors' newsletter at $1,000.

One prized collectible that never became part of a campaign away from home but proved a potent weapon was the poster. Many of America's distinguished early-20th Century illustrators, including James Montgomery Flagg, Howard Chandler Christy and Charles Dana Gibson, helped produce 2,500 different World War I posters, some printed in runs of two million. Their colorful and dramatic designs variously urged civilians to enlist, to produce more and consume less, to purchase Liberty bonds and to keep their mouths shut about military secrets. Flagg painted himself in the much-reproduced poster that shows Uncle Sam demanding, "I want YOU for U.S. Army." A wartime example of this poster sold at a New Jersey auction in 1979 for $850.

Less famous 1917-1918 posters are less valuable and World War II posters are easily found. Other paper memorabilia of both Wars, from training-camp newspapers to military manuals, are readily available.

Most items, rare and not so rare, can be found at collectors' usual haunts—flea markets and garage sales. A few shops specialize. Sometimes antique shops can be fruitful hunting grounds. One collector, stopping at a New England antique barn for directions, asked the proprietor if he had any military items. The shopkeeper said no. But the collector's young daughter opened a cookie jar that was filled with metal disks: The disks proved to be rare collar insignia. The dealer sold the lot at 10 cents apiece, a fraction of what they were worth.

Advertisements also bring results. A collector who specializes in World War I aviation items once advertised in a veterans' newspaper and got a response from two elderly women who lived at a considerable distance. Their response did not sound promising: They had their brother's uniform; he had not gone overseas, so the collector suspected the uniform would lack even a patch. But he made the long trip and in the women's garage, in perfect condition, hung the uniform of a World War I pilot who was an enlisted man rather than an officer; the collector could tell because the wings were not above the left heart pocket, but on the sleeve, where noncommissioned pilots wore them. There were only 50 such pilots, and the uniform has become the collector's most valuable possession.

Wherever you hunt for World War collectibles you must be alert for counterfeits. Many items, from World War I airmen's wings and German imperial spiked helmets to World War II patches, have been reproduced or deliberately faked. A wide range of German World War II objects in particular are of doubtful authenticity only because they were not made for wartime use. Many German factories kept producing military equipment after the conflict was over to supply souvenir-hunting Occupation troops. Telling such productions from the same items made a year or so earlier may be impossible.

Outright fakes of both German and Allied mementos are still being made all over the world but are usually easier to identify. Authentic uniforms, experienced collectors agree, have a telltale smell compounded of good wool and age; after you have sniffed a really old uniform, you can easily recognize copies. The collector of World War I airmen's wings looks at their backs: Genuine ones have a U-shaped safety catch into which a pin dropped, or tiny nut-and-bolt fasteners near the wing tips. Wings with fasteners of the safety-pin type, or those of base metal rather than gold or silver, are suspect.

World War I patches were cut from felt and were usually—and crudely—hand-embroidered; those from World War II were machine-embroidered, mostly of heavier stuff. Most patches made after 1950, either at government order or by counterfeiters, are of material that glows under a black light of the kind mineral collectors use. Even patches worth no more than a dollar can profitably be faked by factories in countries such as Pakistan. Fraudulent medals are often made of cheap metal that, with a little pressure, tends to bend; real medals are of hard, unyielding materials.

Fakes are so abundant, however, that most collectors are taken in eventually. I once bought a Nazi cap by mail that turned out to be made of wool that was too fresh and smooth-looking to be more than 30 years old. But at least I am in good company: In 1845 P. T. Barnum, the American promoter and circus owner remembered for his opinion that "there's a sucker born every minute," purchased a quantity of Napoleonic memorabilia while visiting the scene of the Battle of Waterloo. Barnum planned to display his finds in his museum, but he soon learned that every piece had been faked by English manufacturers long after Napoleon's famous defeat.

For related material, see the articles on Civil War Equipment, Guns, Lindbergh Memorabilia, Medals, Model Soldiers, Posters and Swords in separate volumes of this encyclopedia.

These two sets of Nazi collar insignia include the valuable lightning-bolt marking of the Nazi Waffen-SS (top). The stripe on the facing collar denotes a rank equal to corporal. The oak leaves and wings (bottom) were worn by a Luftwaffe lieutenant.

Among avidly collected handmade American shoulder patches is the Indian head of the 2nd Division (above), which fought in France in World War I. The purple indicates a machine-gun company.

The World War I rattlesnake of the all-black 369th Infantry Regiment (above) is uncommon because the emblem was changed in 1918. The buffalo patch of the other all-black division, the 92nd, is less rare.

This patch with the U.S. Marine Corps emblem can be dated to World War I by its shape and Roman numeral. It was worn by the 5th Marine Brigade, attached to the much-decorated 2nd Division (top left).

The rare patch above bears the Lion of St. Mark, symbol of the city of Venice. It was worn by members of the 332nd Regiment, the only United States infantry regiment on the Italian front during World War I.

Men of the U.S. 1st Ranger Battalion of World War II disdained a diamond-shaped patch issued by the Army and instead wore this non-regulation patch, tailor-made for them in England.

These patches, worn by three legendary American units that served in Asia during World War II, are very desirable. The winged beast above identified the Flying Tigers of the Fourteenth Air Force, stationed inside China. At left is the patch of the U.S. Army engineers who built the 500-mile Ledo Road across northern Burma into India. The patch at right is one of several designs worn by Merrill's Marauders, the commandos led by Brigadier General Frank Merrill in Burma.

A flying rig made for an airman of Britain's Royal Flying Corps during World War I is extremely desirable because it is in perfect condition and includes the padded helmet. The leather coat and gauntlets were made by a noted gentlemen's tailor, Dunhill of London.

On the World War I Army officer's tunic at left, the silver bars, badge, chevron, collar insignia and shoulder patch reveal, respectively, that the owner was a captain, had qualified as an expert shot, had been overseas more than six months, served in the Quartermaster Corps, and was attached to the 7th Division.

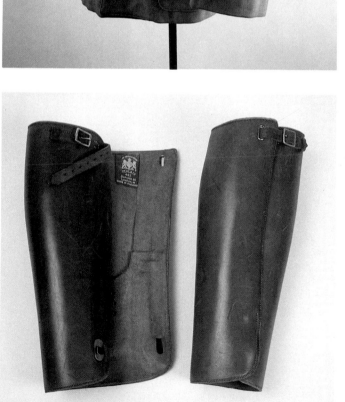

A uniform worn by a woman in Britain's Army Territorial Service in World War II is valued for its completeness and fine condition. The patch and epaulet insignia indicate that it was worn by a second subaltern (second lieutenant) in the Anti-Aircraft Command.

Leather puttees (left) made in London during World War I for an American officer are of unusual quality, produced by Peal & Co., purveyor of leather goods by appointment to the King. Similar puttees are not hard to find.

A World War I American steel helmet is prized for its hand-painted design, added on the way home. The stars, the emblem of New York's 27th Division, show the constellation Orion—a pun on the name of the commander, Major General John Francis O'Ryan.

World War I German Pickelhauben (spiked helmets) such as the one above are desirable but surprisingly easy to find, considering that they were replaced by 1917. The gilded crest shows the Prussian eagle and the legend "With God for king and fatherland."

The Waffen-SS officer's cap above, with its characteristic skull-and-crossbones badge, is an extremely valuable Nazi relic. The other badge, a straight-winged eagle with a wreath and swastika in its talons, was the national emblem of Nazi Germany.

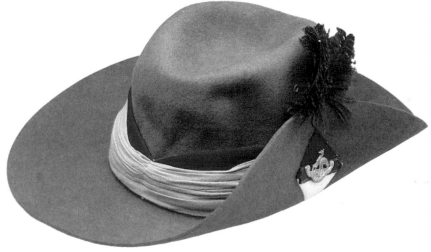

Bush hats worn by troops from British Commonwealth countries during World War II are rare. The regimental colors and the badge showing a large bird with a topknot and two palm trees identify this hat as Rhodesian.

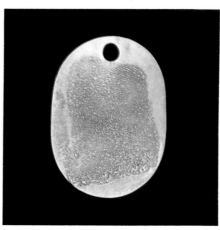

An interesting and fairly rare dog tag, or metal identification disk, used by the U.S. Navy in World War I has the wearer's thumbprint on one side with his name and other service information on the reverse.

American gas masks from World War I are not rare, but this one is unusual because it is part of a complete kit—instructions, spare filters, repair equipment and bag.

The Chinese characters on the silk square above, left, which also shows the Chinese flag, identify the bearer as an American airman and urge that he be helped. American flyers in the Far East during World War II carried such identification in case they were forced down and needed help from Chinese-speaking inhabitants. Another aid for flyers was the silk scarf at right above with its map of Luzon island in the Philippines.

In the dramatically designed poster above by illustrator Fred Strothmann, a menacing German soldier lays Europe waste.

This poster is not rare; several hundred thousand were printed in 1918 and large numbers have survived.

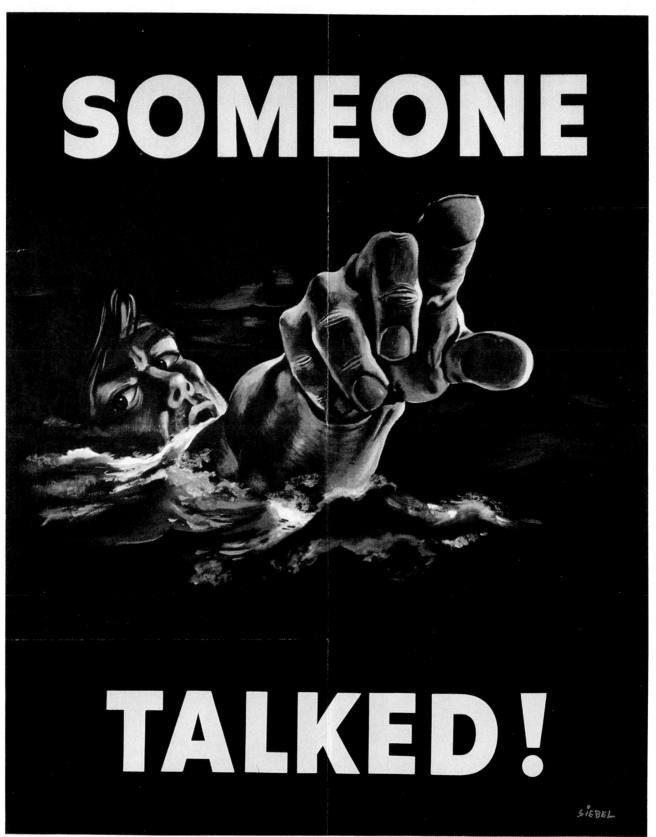

A drowning sailor from a torpedoed ship dramatizes the fear during World War II that loose talk about sailings could be relayed by spies to German submarines. Spy scares inspired many posters that urged increased security; this one is from 1942.

These paper mementos of World War I are in unusually good condition. The photograph above shows American troops in France's Belleau Wood, scene of a fierce 1918 battle. At left, a postcard depicts the age-old sentiment of women who wait. Below, three comically dressed, be-medaled Britishers mug in a studio photograph probably shot in France.

Carrying rifles with fixed bayonets, U.S. Army trainees scramble from a trench in a photograph (left) that appeared on the cover of the Camp McClellan, Alabama, pictorial review in 1917. Many post newspapers from both World Wars have survived.

A songbook published in America in 1942 or 1943 is especially prized. It contains the words to such hits held over from World War I as "Mademoiselle from Armentières" and parodies of popular World War II-era hits, including an impolite version of "A Sleepy Lagoon" dubbed "A Sleepy Latrine."

The most famous British Tommy of the First World War, Ol' Bill (far left), created by cartoonist Bruce Bairnsfather, complains from his "ole" on the French front.

A fine example of the trench art crafted from military gear during World War I is this U.S. Army canteen, laboriously hand-engraved with the American eagle, date and "France."

Shaped and engraved, a 75-millimeter shell casing makes a bizarre flower vase. It was made near Verdun, in northeastern France, where a ferocious battle raged in 1916.

A bullet adorned with a button forms the handle of a letter opener, its blade made of a shell fragment. Château-Thierry was the scene of a 1918 battle.

A mother comforts two infants on this medal, designed by famed French glassmaker René Lalique. It was struck for donors to a center for children left fatherless after World War I.

A satin pillowcase (left) made during World War I is prized for its excellent condition and because two handkerchiefs (not shown) with Navy motifs came tucked inside.

MUSEUMS
The Liberty Memorial Museum
Kansas City, Missouri 64108

National Infantry Museum
Fort Benning, Georgia 31905

Patton Museum of Cavalry and Armor
Fort Knox, Kentucky 40121

United States Air Force Museum
Wright-Patterson Air Force Base, Ohio 45433

United States Marine Corps Museum
Washington, D.C. 20374

United States Navy Memorial Museum
Washington, D.C. 20374

West Point Museum
West Point, New York 10996

Women's Army Corps Museum
Fort McClellan, Alabama 36205

COLLECTORS ORGANIZATIONS
American Society of Military Insignia Collectors

526 Lafayette Avenue
Palmerton, Pennsylvania 18071

Military Vehicles Collectors Club
P.O. Box 33697
Thorton, Colorado 80233

BOOKS
Campbell, J. Duncan, *Aviation Badges and Insignia of the U.S. Army 1913-46.* The Triangle Press, 1977.

Davis, Brian L., *German Army Uniforms and Insignia 1933-45.* Arco Publishing Co., Inc., 1977.

Mollo, Andrew, *Army Uniforms of World War I.* Arco Publishing Co., Inc., 1978.

Schulz, Paul, et al., *World War I Collector's Handbook.* 2 vols. GOS Inc., 1977, 1979.

Theofiles, George, *American Posters of World War I.* Dafran House Publishers, Inc., no date.

Windrow, Martin, and Gerry Embelton, *World War II Combat Uniforms and Insignia.* Squadron/Signal Publications, Inc., 1977.

Index

Virtually all the arts and artifacts, machines and mementos popular among collectors are included in the 16 volumes of The Encyclopedia of Collectibles, arranged alphabetically, of course, so that major subjects are easy to find. The master index that begins below serves as a cross index, enabling you to find quickly not only major articles but also subtopics. For example, the article on Art Glass treats in general the colorful and whimsical wares of Victorian America. Discussion of certain types of art glass—Lalique and Tiffany glass, for example—will be found in several other articles; the index indicates where to look for these discussions. The index also provides quick reference to specific names, such as that of the notorious autograph forger Joseph Cosey.

In each entry, titles of individual volumes are indicated by abbreviations; a key appears at the bottom of the index pages. Page numbers in roman type indicate text references; italicized page numbers refer to illustrations.

A

Aaron, Henry (Hank), AB *144, 147*
Action Comics, CC 151
Acton, Eliza, book by, CD *8*
Adam, Richard and Carl, toy by, TT *93*
Adams, John: autograph, AB *93;* on cigar band, CC *55*
Adams, John Quincy: autograph, AB *92;* document of appointment, AB *93;* on flask, AB *26*, BC *133*
Adams, Maude, TT *34*
Adenauer, Konrad, OP *91*
Advertising: automobiles, AB 110, LM *83;* cartoon, BC *107;* circuses, CC 60-71; garage signs, AB 109, *110;* jukeboxes, IL *114;* in magazines, LM *82, 83;* Shaker, RS *131;* toaster, TT *65. See also* Cigar bands; Posters; Signs; Trade cards
Advertising giveaways, AB 6-19; beer mugs, SS *128;* calendar plates, AB *113*, OP *51;* cigar cutter, SS *67;* comic books, CC 149, 151, CD *119;* corkscrews, CD *25;* knives, IL *142;* paper dolls, OP *81;* paperweights, AB *8, 14*, 114, *115*, OP *103;* pencils, OP *133;* playing cards, PQ *44, 47, 53;* silk pictures, SS *25, 28;* spoons, SS 75, *76;*

watch fobs, TW *65;* world's fair souvenir, TW *131*
Aesop's fables, CC *10*
Agate: button, BC *10;* snuff bottle, SS *69;* watch fob, TW *65*
Agates (marbles), LM 152, *160*
Aikman, George, etching by, FH *67*
Airmail: Lindbergh's role, LM 56; stamps, LM *56*, SS *101, 108, 113, 115*
Airmen, mementos of, TW 134, *136, 137, 139, 140, 143*
Airplanes, LM *52, 53;* on cards, PQ *53, 82;* on stamps, LM *56*, SS *101, 108, 109;* toy, TT *96, 97. See also Spirit of St. Louis*
Airships. *See* Dirigibles
Alabaster: chess set, BC *159;* egg, DF *69*
Aladdin kerosene lamp, LM *27*
Alajalov, Constantin, art by, OP *84*
Albert, Prince (Saxe-Coburg-Gotha), on medal, TW *122*
Album quilts, PQ *146*, 148-149
Alcott, Louisa May, CC *7*
Alden, John: on fruit-crate label, FH *34;* in sculpture, RS *74*
Aldrin, Edwin E., Jr. (Buzz), autograph of, AB *100*
Alexander, James, coverlets woven by, CD 45, *51*
Alexander the Great, coin issued by, CC *122*

Alexander III, Czar (Russia): cartoon of, BC *105;* eggs given by, DF *66*
Alexandra, Queen (England), souvenir of, RS *80*
Alger, Horatio, Jr., book by, CC *18*
Alligators: comic character, CC *156;* on spoon, SS *cover;* stein handle, SS *131*
Almanacs, CC 9, OP *160*, RS *125*
Alvin Manufacturing Company, spoon by, SS *77*
Amazing Stories (magazine), RS *103, 108*
Amber: cigarette holder, SS *66;* pipestem, PQ *35*
Ambrotypes, CC *85*, PQ *18-19, 20*
Americana (books), BB *98, 99, 101-103*, LM *134*
Americana (stamps), SS *98*
American Art China Co., Trenton, N.J., Belleek by, BB *35;* mark, BB *44*
American Automobile Association, badge of, AB *106*
American Ballet Theatre, set design for, CC *122-123*
American Beleek Company, products of, BB 36, *45*
American Cinematographer (magazine), RS *110*
American Clock Co., Bristol, Conn., products of, CC *100*

American Flyer Manufacturing Company, TT 124, *128-129*
American LaFrance fire engines, DF *149-151*
American Magazine, The, LM *73*
American Mutoscope & Biograph Company, product of, OP *111*, 112
American Revolution. *See* Revolutionary War
American Tobacco Company, AB *142;* baseball card, AB *141*
Amethysts: hatpin heads, FH *116, 117;* jewelry, IL *82*
AMI. *See* Automatic Musical Instrument Company
Amulets, African, BB 7, *12, 14, 18*
Analog (magazine), RS 103, *109*
Andy Gump (comic character): Christmas tree light, CC *38;* on marble, LM *157*
Angels: chair ornaments, OP *14, 15;* Christmas tree ornaments, CC *34, 45;* crèches, CD *74, 75;* weather vane, TW *80-81*
Animation film art, AB 32-41
Ansonia Clock Co., products of, CC *100, 101*
Anthony, Susan B.: on button, PQ *70;* on stamp, SS *112*
Apache basket, AB *159*
Apostle spoons, SS 75, 77
Apothecary chest, RS *138*
Apples: corer, IL *cover;* crate

AB *Advertising Giveaways to Baskets;* BB *Beads to Boxes;* BC *Buttons to Chess Sets;* CC *Children's Books to Comics;* CD *Cookbooks to Detective Fiction;* DF *Dogs to Fishing Tackle;* FH *Folk Art to Horse-drawn Carriages;* IL *Inkwells to Lace;*

label, FH *39;* glass, AB *58;* parers, IL *cover,* 116, 119, 121, *124;* redware, RS *49*
Appliqué: mottoes, RS *98;* quilts, PQ 147, *152, 153*
Apron, CC *108*
Aquitania (ship), purser's cap from, OP *32*
Arapaho bag, AB *16*
Arcade Manufacturing Co., toys by, TT *102, 106*
Archuleta, Felipe, sculptures by, FH *19*
Argand, Ami, LM 19
Armorial plates, Chinese porcelain, CC *20, 23-24, 25*
Armour, Tommy, golf clubs signed by, FH *60, 61, 62*
Armstrong, Louis, IL *64, 65;* record labels, IL *70*
Armstrong, Mrs. S. G., watercolor by, FH *9*
Armstrong Manufacturing Co., toaster-stove by, TT *70-71*
Army, United States: buttons, AB *30;* Civil War items, CC *76, 78, 80-82, 84;* stamps honoring, SS *114;* swords, SS 149, *154, 155, 160;* World War memorabilia, TW *138, 139, 141, 142, 147, 148*
Arnold, Benedict, autograph of, AB *94*
Arrowheads, AB *42-53*
Arsinoë I, on coin, CC *124*
Art Deco: camera, BC *28;* candlesticks, BC *40;* cat, BC *131;* cigarette case, SS *66;* costume sketch, TT *27;* fans, DF *96;* handbag, FH *107;* jewelry, IL *76, 95-98;* Lalique glass, LM *6, 7, 12, 13, 16;* lamp, LM *35;* lorgnette, DF *88;* medal, MN *24;* posters, PQ *100, 101;* scarf, LM *87;* sofa, TW *106;* toaster, TT *64;* tramp-art style, TT *145;* world's fair prints, TW *127*
Art glass, AB *cover,* 54-69; bells, BB *50;* candlesticks, BC *35;* egg, DF *68;* imitation *(see* Carnival glass); lamp, LM *26;* lightning-rod balls, LM *39, 42-44;* marbles, LM *150, 153-156;* paperweights, AB *58,* OP *100, 101, 106, 107. See also* Cut glass; Lalique; Tiffany
Arthur, Jean, MN *66*
Art Nouveau: button, BC *16;* candlesticks, BC *40,* TT *47;* cigar label, CC *48;* comb, CC *145;* fans, DF *106;* hatpins, FH *110, 114;* inkwells, IL *7,* TT *46;* jewelry, IL *76, 77, 91-94;* Lalique, René, influence on, IL *94,* LM *6, 10;* lamps, LM 21, *29, 30-32,* TT *42, 43, 44;* match holder, OP *52;* pewter, OP *146;* posters, PQ *95, 97, 98;* pottery, AB *78, 79, 82;* ring

box, BB *156;* silver pieces, IL *91,* SS *47, 54;* world's fair architecture, TW *126-127. See also* Tiffany
Art pottery, AB *70-87;* candleholders, BC 30, *40;* cat, BC *130*
Arts and Crafts Movement: candlesticks, BC *40;* jewelry, IL *90*
Ashendene Press, book, BB *79*
Ashtrays: in radio, RS *18;* from ships, OP *30;* Tiffany glass, TT *46;* world's fair souvenir, TW *130*
Asimov, Isaac, magazine with work by, RS *109*
Asprey & Company, England, flask by, SS *57*
Asquith, Herbert, cartoon of, BC *112*
Aston-Martin (car), toy, TT *108*
Astor, Mary, on poster, MN *59*
Astounding (magazine), RS *103, 109*
Atkins Automaton, DF 110
Atlas, Hazel, Glass Company, Clarksville, W. Va., Depression glass by, CD *145*
Atlases, LM 124, *148;* maps from, LM *127, 138, 139*
Atwater Kent radios, RS *6, 11, 13*
Atwell, Harry, photo by, CC *69*
Auburn Rubber Corp., Indiana, toy by, TT *107*
Audiophone jukebox, IL *107*
Audubon, John James, BB *106;* art by, OP *56,* TW *109, 114-116*
Austen, Jane, book by, BB *110*
Austin (car), toy, TT *108*
Autographs, AB 88-101; ballet dancers, CD *119;* books, AB *92, 94, 96,* BB *93, 96, 99, 112, 113, 116, 117,* CD *154, 156;* jazz, IL *68, 71;* Lindbergh, LM *46, 48, 55-57;* menus, MN *32, 34, 36;* movie stars, MN *56, 65;* operatic, OP *35, 36, 38, 40;* theatrical, TT *38, 39*
Automatic Musical Instrument Company (AMI), jukeboxes by, IL *109*
Automatons, DF *53,* TT *87, 95;* music boxes, MN *69-70, 72-74;* watch, TW *62*
Automobiles, BC *82-97;* advertising, AB 110, LM *83;* board game based on, FH *53;* candy container shaped like, BB *145;* Indianapolis 500 winner, AB *148;* jeep, TW *134-135;* lock for, LM *71;* on matchbook, MN *13;* memorabilia, AB *102-115;* radiator ornaments, AB *104, 106-107,* LM *8, 16;* on shaving mugs, RS *143, 150;* toy, TT *cover,* 86, *104-108*
Autry, Gene: records by, CD 34,

41; songbook, CD *41*
Avalon ware (majolica), LM *120*
Avery Manufacturing Co., thresher by, DF 112
Axes: broadax, TT *80-81;* fireman's, DF *145*
Aztec utensil currency, CC *128*

B

Bab-O cleanser, bank advertising, AB *17*
Baby bottles. *See* Nursing bottles
Baby Snooks doll, DF *54*
Baccarat company, France: door-knob, OP *108;* paperweights, OP *100, 101, 107, 109*
Badges: automobile clubs, AB *106, 107, 109;* Civil War, CC *81;* firemen's, DF *147;* policemen's, PQ *54, 55-56, 58, 59;* political, PQ *cover,* 64, 66, 67; railroaders', RS *26*
Baedeker, Karl, guidebooks, LM *126, 149*
Bags: Indian, MN *117;* salvage, DF *146. See also* Handbags
Bailey, James A., circus, CC *61-62;* posters, CC *60-61, 65*
Bairnsfather, Bruce, character created by, TW *147*
Bakelite: bracelet, IL *97;* pin, TW *131*
Baker, Frank, AB *140*
Baker Street Irregulars, memorabilia of, CD *157*
Bakewell company, Pittsburgh, Pa., pressed glass by, PQ *122*
Bakst, Léon, TT *17;* costumes by, CD *121;* postcard by, PQ *87*
Balanchine, George, CD *119, 124*
Ball, John, Jr., lithograph of, FH *60*
Ball, Tompkins & Black Company, N.Y., goblet by, SS *45*
Ballet dancers: cookbook, CD *16;* lamp base, CD *151;* memorabilia, CD *114-127;* poster, PQ *109;* stamp, SS *122*
Ballet Russe de Monte Carlo memorabilia, CD *116, 117, 124*
Ball jars, manufacturer's guide for, CD *15*
Balloons: on insignia, TW *136;* stein shaped like, SS *131;* toy models, TT *96;* valentine, TW *31*
Balls: for bowls (game), LM *159;* golf, FH 60, *62, 63;* stoneware baseball, SS *147*
Baltimore & Ohio trains: model, TT *128;* plate from, RS *29*
Bamberg, Theo (Okito), magic tricks made by, LM *92, 94, 95*
Bambi (film), scene from, AB *35*
Bamboo: fly rods, DF *154, 155;* majolica design, LM *110*
Bandstand, carved-wood, FH *15*
Banjos, MN *86, 89*
Bank notes, OP *cover, See also*

Paper money
Banks, AB 116-127; advertising giveaways, AB 16, *17;* frog, FH *27;* policeman, PQ *63;* redware, RS *49;* Robinson, Jackie, on, LM *50;* stoneware, SS *143*
Banks, Ernie, AB *147*
Banneret weather vane, TW *70-71*
Barbed wire, AB *128-137*
Barbershop bottles, BB 133, *142*
Barbie dolls, DF 39
Barbotine ware, AB 71, *72*
Barclay Manufacturing Company, Union City, N.J., model soldiers by, MN 43, *52*
Bard, James, paintings by, MN *104,* 105
Bar Harbor furniture, TW 98, *106*
Barkelow, Joel, decoy by, CD *132-133*
Barks, Carl, drawings by, CC 154, *157*
Barling, B., and Sons, England, pipe by, PQ *39*
Barlow knives, IL 133, *141*
Barney Oldfield tires, sign for, AB *110*
Barnum, P. T., TW *137;* circus, CC 61-62; circus posters, CC *60-62, 65*
Barometers, ships', MN 100
Barrelmaker's tool, TT *81*
Barrel organs, MN *82-83*
Barrie, J. M., characters created by, MN *158*
Barthe, Felix, caricature, BC *106*
Bartolozzi, Francesco, valentine by, TW *19*
Barye, Antoine-Louis, BC *127*
Basalt, Wedgwood, TW 82, *86, 87;* mark, TW *85*
Baseball: annuals, BB 106; bank portraying, AB *122;* cards, AB 138-149; majolica pitcher portraying, LM *117;* players' autographs, AB *95;* scorekeeper, AB *14;* stoneware ball, SS *147*
Basie, Count, IL *65;* record label, IL *72*
Basins: pewter, OP *140;* pottery, MN *99*
Basketball cards, AB *148*
Baskets, AB 150-160; Belleek, BB *35;* carriage accessory, FH *157;* glass, AB *57, 67,* CD *102,* PQ *133;* shells, TW *42;* silver-plated, SS *41;* Wedgwood, TW *94*
Basket vis-à-vis (carriage), FH *152-153*
Bassett, Frederick, pewter by, OP *134, 135, 137*
Batman, CC *155*
Bats, as jewelry motif, IL *94, 104*
Batter bowl, glass, CD *146*
Bauer, Ferdinand, print from art

LM *Lalique to Marbles;* MN *Matchsafes to Nursing Bottles;* OP *Oak Furniture to Pharmacist's Equipment;* PQ *Phonographs to Quilts;* RS *Radios to Signs;* SS *Silhouettes to Swords;* TT *Telephones to Trivets;* TW *Typewriters to World War Memorabilia*

151

by, BB *126*

Baum, L. Frank, book by, CC *7, 16*

Bayonets, Civil War, CC *74-75;* candlestick made from, CC *80*

Beach Boys (rock group), record by, RS *61*

Beads, BB *6-21,* IL *99, 100, 103, 104,* TW *88;* on cowboy gloves, CD *69;* egg decorated with, DF *70;* in embroidery, DF *75;* handbags, FH *100, 101-103;* watch fob made of, TW *65*

Beanies. *See* Caps

Bean pots: Flint Enamel, BB *61;* stoneware, SS *146*

Bear, on cigar label, CC *57;* toy, TT *cover. See also* Teddy bears

Beard, James, book by, CD *18*

Beardsley, Aubrey, illustration by, LM *77*

Beaters, IL *117, 121, 122, 123*

Beatles (rock group), AB *35;* memorabilia, RS *53, 58, 59*

Beaton, Cecil, photo by, LM *85*

Beaver Baby Grand radio, RS *8*

Beaver hats, CD *70,* FH *119, 122*

Becker Brewing and Malting Co., Ogden, Utah, mug from, SS *128*

Bedford wreck truck, toy, TT *108*

Beds: dollhouse, DF *28;* oak, in catalogue, OP *10;* painted, OP *70;* Victorian, TW *49*

Bedspreads. *See* Coverlets; Quilts

Beer: bottles, BB *138;* can opener, BB *27;* cans, BB *cover,* 22-33; mugs and pitchers, BB *43, 45,* SS *128. See also* Steins

Beer, John T., art by, BB *76*

Beerbohm, Max, caricatures by, BC *106, 110*

Beer Can Collectors of America, BB *22, 24;* design award winners, BB *30;* insignia, BB *26*

Bees: on birthday card, FH *75;* on cake plate, PQ *126;* in music box, MN *78-79*

Beetles (insects): Egyptian symbols, FH *113, 116,* IL *98;* jewelry motif, IL *94, 98;* toy, TT *93*

Beiderbecke, Bix, IL *70, 71*

Bel Geddes, Norman, medal by, MN *24*

Bell, Alexander Graham, PQ *6,* TT *6*

Bell, Robert Anning, bookplate by, BB *96*

Bellamy, John Haley, eagle carvings by, AB *24, 26*

Belleek porcelain, BB *34-45*

Bellmark Pottery Company, Belleek by, BB *36, 45*

Bells, BB *46-55;* Belleek, BB *41;* cut-glass, CD *110;* fire alarm, DF *146;* in music box, MN *78-79;* pendant, IL *103;*

train's, RS *23*

Bell System, TT *6*

Belt buckles. *See* Buckles

Belter, John Henry, furniture by, TW *36, 38, 40-41*

Belts: firemen's, DF *144;* Navajo, IL *101*

Bench, oak, OP *16*

Benedict, Saint, on medal, MN *18*

Benedict & Burnham, Waterbury, Conn., button by, BC *17*

Benito (Italian artist), work by, LM *85*

Bennett, Edwin, Pottery Company, Baltimore, Md., LM *107;* mark, LM *115*

Bennington pottery, BB *56-67*

Benois, Alexandre, art by, CD *123,* TT *28*

Bentley, Thomas, TW *85*

Bentwood chairs, RS *122, 125,* TW *37, 52*

Bergen, J. D., Company, Meriden, Conn., cut glass by, CD *106;* marks, CD *103*

Bergey, Earle, art by, RS *100*

Bergman foundry, Vienna, Austria, bronzes by, FH *22, 28*

Berkey & Gay Furniture Company, Grand Rapids, Mich., products of, OP *14, 15*

Berlin & Jones, card by, TW *24*

Berliner, Emile, PQ *6, 8*

Bernhardt, Sarah, LM *77;* as Hamlet, TT *34;* headdress, TT *32;* jewelry, IL *91, 93;* posters, PQ *95, 97*

Berra, Larry (Yogi), AB *144*

Berry, Chuck, RS *53*

Bessa, Pancrace, engraving from art by, BB *129*

Bettini, Gianni, PQ *6, 8-9*

Betty Boop (cartoon character), AB *33, 34, 40;* marble, LM *157*

Bibles, BB *68-79;* boxes for, BB *153,* OP *61*

Biblical characters, portrayals of: banks, AB *118, 121;* brooch, IL *80;* doorstop, DF *61;* Lalique, LM *7;* medals, MN *26;* pendant, IL *92;* stamp, SS *98*

Bibliographies, BB *95-96*

Bicentennial: bank, AB *124;* beer cans, BB *32;* license plates, AB *109;* posters, PQ *107*

Bicycle playing cards, PQ *47, 52*

Bicycles, BB *80-91,* PQ *27;* Currier & Ives print, CD *96;* on medal, MN *25;* on shaving mug, RS *146;* on stamp, SS *109;* stein depicting, SS *131;* trade card for, TT *116*

Bien, Julius, prints by, TW *109, 114*

Bigaglia, Pietro, perfume holder by, OP *108*

Bijou Funnies (comic book), CC *160*

Billiards: cue lock, LM *71;* table, miniature, TT *146*

Biloxi Art Pottery, Biloxi, Miss., products of, AB *75, 77*

Bing, Gebrüder, Nuremberg, Germany, toy train by, TT *128*

Binoculars, CC *80*

Bird of paradise, on hat, FH *124*

Birds: on corkscrews, CD *26;* embroidery, DF *73, 78;* engraved glass, CD *107;* on fan, DF *106;* glove stretcher, SS *56;* hemming bird, MN *133;* on Indian pottery, RS *43;* on inro, MN *144;* jewelry motif, IL *86, 94, 100;* on matchsafes, MN *9, 15, 16;* prints, CD *97,* TW *108, 109, 110, 111-115;* on snuffbox, MN *70;* on stamps, SS *98, 120;* stoneware, SS *134, 138, 144, 146;* on trade card, TT *122;* on valentine, TW *24. See also* Decoys; names of individual kinds

Birmingham Age Herald (newspaper), plate honoring, BC *59*

Biro, Lászlo Jozsef, OP *126*

Birthday cards, FH *75, 80, 81;* silk picture on, SS *25*

Biscuit box, silver, SS *40*

Bisque: dolls, DF *34, 35, 36, 47, 48, 49, 50-52, 54, 55;* hatpin holder, FH *115*

Bitters bottles, BB *130, 131, 133, 140, 141*

Black Mask (magazine), CD *155, 158*

Black Patti records, CD *30, 34*

Blacks, music of, CD *29, 30, 31, 39,* IL *62-75, 108*

Blacks, portrayals of, PQ *21, 84;* banks, AB *119, 120-121, 122, 125, 126;* button, PQ *69;* clocks, CC *100;* coin, CC *138;* Currier & Ives print, CD *89;* dolls, DF *40, 55,* OP *80;* folk art, FH *18;* poster, PQ *106;* Rogers groups, RS *72;* stamp, SS *112*

Blacksmiths, PQ *18;* shop, in Currier & Ives print, CD *88*

Blackstone (magician), prop used by, LM *100*

Black Swan record label, IL *66*

Blackton, J. Stuart, megaphone used by, MN *63*

Blair, John, decoy by, CD *130*

Blakey, Art, IL *75*

Blanket chests, OP *65, 73*

Blankets. *See* Coverlets; Navajo: blankets; Quilts

Blickensderfer typewriters, TW *6, 9*

Bliss, R., Manufacturing Co., Pawtucket, R.I., toys by, DF *16, 20-21, 33,* TT *91*

Bloch, Robert, RS *101*

Blocks, picture (toy), TT *cover, 88*

Blondie (comic character), CC

151; on toy, CC *153*

Bloomer Girl chalkware, BC *143*

Blotters: cover, AB *17;* Tiffany, TT *46*

Bluebird records: flier, CD *31;* label, CD *40*

Bluegrass Boys (recording group), CD *42*

Boater (hat), FH *127*

Boats. *See* Ships and boats

Bock, Gustave, CC *47*

Bodices, CC *107, 111*

Bodkins, RS *121*

Boehm, Theobald, flutes by, MN *87, 95*

Bogart, Humphrey, on poster, MN *59*

Bok, Hannes, art by, RS *102*

Boker, Heinrich, Solingen, Germany, knives by, IL *135*

Bollmann, Hermann, map by, LM *143*

Bolm, Adolf, depictions of, CD *118*

Bonaparte, Napoleon. *See* Napoleon

Bone: cane, BC *53;* chess pieces, BC *152, 154, 155;* hatpin, FH *116;* jewelry, IL *92, 99, 100;* knife handle, IL *139;* owl, OP *55;* on pipestem, PQ *41;* scrimshaw, RS, *116, 117, 119-121;* snuff tool, SS *68*

Bone china, Wedgwood, TW *86, 94, 95;* marks, TW *85*

Bonelli, Giorgio, art by, BB *119, 125*

Bonheur, Rosa, BC *127*

Bonnard, Pierre, art by, PQ *97*

Bonnet doll, DF *48*

Bonnets, FH *119, 120-122;* lace ties, IL *156*

Bookbindings, AB *27,* BB *76, 78, 92, 153*

Bookcases, OP *13, 21*

Book end, eagle on, AB *27*

Bookmarks: advertising, AB *15, 16;* silk pictures, SS *26;* silver, SS *57*

Book of Common Prayer, BB *76*

Book of Hours, BB *74*

Bookplates, BB *96-97*

Books, BB *92-117;* almanacs, CC *9,* OP *160,* RS *125;* automobile, AB *107, 110;* botanical, prints from, BB *118-129;* boxes shaped like, BB *154;* choreography, CD *127;* comic books, CC *148, 149, 151, 154-160,* CD *158;* dog illustrations, DF *8;* of exploration, LM *134, 135;* flasks shaped like, BB *67;* golf, FH *66;* on graining, OP *63;* guidebooks, LM *126, 149;* Lindbergh autobiography, LM *48, 57;* magic, LM *93, 102;* movie-related, MN *66,* OP *47, 86;* pincushion shaped like, MN *133;* police blotter, PQ *57;* poster reproductions from, PQ

97; rock group's tour, RS 63; royal souvenir, RS 86; science fiction, RS 101, 103-105; song-books, CD 28, 38, 41, 43 (see also Sheet music); theatrical, TT 18, 38, 39; valentine writers, TW 28; wildlife prints from, TW 108-119. See also Autographs: books; Bibles; Catalogues; Children's books; Cookbooks; Detective fiction

Boone, Daniel, autograph of, AB 96

Booth, Edwin, memorabilia of, SS 79, TT 19, 33, 34

Boots, CC 114; Civil War, CC 83; cowboy, CD 63; sign, RS 155

Bopeep, Little: bookmark, SS 26; cigar label, CC 58; spoon, MN 158

Borden advertising fan, AB 6

Boston & Maine Railroad button, RS 26

Boston & Sandwich Glass Company, Sandwich, Mass., AB 68, BC 12, 30, LM 152; pressed glass, AB 27, PQ 121, 122, 123, 131

Botanical Magazine, print from, BB 127

Botanical prints, BB 118-129

Bottles, BB 130-145; art-glass, AB 64; Civil War, CC 79; lock for, LM 71; openers, AB 15, CD 27, SS 67; pharmacist's, OP 148-150, 150-151, 152, 153, 158; policemen's, PQ 60; pressed-glass, PQ 130, 131; silver accessories for, SS 44, 45; snuff, SS 69; stoneware, SS 140-141. See also Decanters; Flasks; Nursing bottles; Perfume and cologne bottles

Boulton, Matthew, BC 9

Bourke-White, Margaret, photo by, LM 88

Boutet, Nicolas Noël, guns by, FH 90-91

Bowen, J. H., bank by, AB 116

Bowen, J. T., & Co., Philadelphia, Pa., prints from, TW 109, 113, 115, 116

Bowen, L., art by, TW 118

Bowie, James, CC 75, IL 135

Bowie knives, IL 134, 135, 136

Bowls: advertising giveaway, AB 17; art-glass, AB cover, 54, 59, 60, 65; art-pottery, AB 82; Bennington, BB 61, 65; carnival-glass, BC 57, 59-61, 64; Chinese porcelain, CC 22, 31, 32; cut-glass, CD 104, 106, 111, 112; Depression-glass, CD 142, 145-147; Fiesta-ware, DF 128, 130, 131; Indian, RS 42; Lalique, LM 6, 9; mess basin, MN 99; netsuke, MN 142; premium, PQ 116; silver, SS 35; Tiffany, TT 50. See also Compotes; Sugar bowls

Bowls (game), balls for, LM 159

Boxers: on cards, AB 148, PQ 47, 50; on pipe tamper, SS 67

Boxes, BB 146-160; baleen, RS 117; Bible and document, BB 153, OP 61, TT 59; candle, BB 146, 148, BC 32; candy tins, OP 31, 43; cigar, CC 46; collar, FH 15, SS 63; dog-lidded, DF 9; egg-shaped, DF 67, 68, 70; for fan, DF 102-103; hen-shaped, BC 145; inros, MN 144; ivory, CC 26; magic apparatus, LM 95, 100, 101; netsuke, MN 140; pharmaceutical, OP 153, 155; plug-tobacco, SS 63; powder, LM 8; Prince Philip on, LM 50; sewing, MN 90, 125, 128, 133, OP 58; Shaker, RS 123, 130, 138; silver, BB 156, 159, SS 40, 56; Tiffany, TT 46; tinware, TT 54-59; tramp-art, TT 144, 145; Wedgwood, TW 89. See also Chests; Cigarettes: cases and boxes; Jewel boxes; Music boxes; Snuffboxes; Trinket boxes

Boycraft toy dirigible, TT 96-97

Boynton, J., stoneware by, SS 144

Boy Scouts, stamp, SS 98

Bracelets, IL 82, 89, 96, 97, 105; egg-shaped charms, DF 69; Indian ornaments, IL 100

Bradbury, Ray: book by, RS 101, 105; magazine, RS 102

Bradford, T. G., map issued by, LM 124, 139

Bradley, Milton, Co., games by, FH 47, 53, 57

Bradley, Will, poster by, PQ 98

Brady, Mathew, AB 92, CC 85; photo by, PQ 23

Braque, Georges, painting by, on stamp, SS 119

Brass: auto lamps, AB 105; badge, PQ 59; bells, BB 46, 48, 49, 52; boxes, BB 148, 154, 155, 159; buttons, BC 6, 11, PQ 66; candleholders, BC 30, 31, 33-35, 37, 40, 41; cash registers, BC 114, 118, 121; chess set, BC 151; Civil War memorabilia, CC 80, 81, 84; coin, CC 125; dagger, TT 32; door knockers, LM 66, 67; eagle motifs, AB 20, 27, 28, 29, 30, 31, PQ 68; fire-fighting equipment, DF 144, 147; fireplace fender, TT 45; harness ornament, RS 83; hatpins, FH 110, 114; inkwells, IL 11; irons, IL 26, 31; jewelry, IL 97, 99, 105; lamp accessory, LM 23; lock mechanism, LM 70; matchsafes, MN 8, 11; medal, MN 18; owl depictions, OP 52, 53; pharmacist's equipment, OP 154, 156; pipe accessories, SS 67, 70;

railroadiana, RS 23, 25; sewing tools, MN 129, 132, 133; ships' lights, MN 108; sword hilts, SS 150, 154, 155, 159; telescopes, CC 80, MN 103; on tools, TT 75, 78; trivets, TT 158, 160; watch fob, TW 65

Breguet, Abraham-Louis, watches by, TW 58, 59

Brema, Carl, magic tricks by, LM 90, 92, 93, 96

Brenner, Victor, medals by, MN 22, 25

Breweries: bottles, BB 138; mugs, SS 128; steins, SS 131; trays, AB 13, 14. See also Beer cans

Brewster family, carriages made by, FH 146-147, 150-154

Brice, Fanny, doll, DF 54

Bride's boxes, BB 146, 152

Brillat-Savarin, Anthelme, frontispiece from book by, CD 17

Briscoe, Johnson, autograph of, TT 39

Brisé fans, DF 95, 96, 97-100

Britain, William, model soldiers by, MN 40-41, 42-43, 48-51

Britannia metal, OP 136, 145

Broadway record label, CD 36

Brocades, CC 102, 104, 105, 107, 108, 113; bonnet, FH 121

Broiler, IL 118

Brokaw, Isaac, clock by, CC 90

Broken-bank notes, OP 88, 92

Bromo Seltzer dispenser, OP 158

Bronson wagon, FH 150

Bronze: bells, BB 54, 55; candlesticks, BC 40, TT 47; cash registers, BC 116, 118, 121; cats, BC 127-128, 133-135; currency, CC 116, 123, 125-128; dogs, DF 8, 14-15; Duncan, Isadora, figure of, CD 118; frogs, FH 22, 26, 28; hemming bird, MN 133; inkwells, IL 7, 11; lamp, LM 30; Lindbergh bust, LM 49; medals and plaques, MN 18, 21, 23, 24, 26-29, OP 38; opera figures, OP 43; paperweights, AB 115, OP 103; policeman, PQ 62; Rogers group, RS 72; Tiffany artware, TT 42, 46, 47; vessel handles, LM 12

Brooches, AB 22, IL 80, 86, 94, 98, 104

Brookfield Glass Co., New York, N.Y., insulator by, IL 19

Brooklyn Dodgers, AB 146

Broughams (carriages), FH 154; Currier & Ives print, CD 96

Brouwer, Theophilus A., pottery by, AB 75, 77; marks, AB 84

Brown, Clifford, IL 75

Brown, George W., & Co., Forestville, Conn.: sketchbook, TT 87; toys, TT 86, 92

Brown, William Henry,

silhouettes by, SS 8-9, 16

Brown & Williamson Tobacco Corp., cigarette-rolling equipment by, SS 65

Browne, Hablot K., art by, BB 109

Bru, Leon Casimir, and family, dolls made by, DF 34, 36, 51; mark, DF 49

Brunfels, Otto, book by, BB 119

Brunswick records, CD 33, IL 64, 73

Bryan, William Jennings, memorabilia of, PQ 64, 65, 68

Bub, Karl, toy by, TT 104-105

Buck, Daniel A. A., watch invented by, TW 60

Buck, Frank, radio premium, PQ 119

Buck, Pearl, book by, BB 95

Buckets, water, DF 140, 145

Buckles, AB 30, IL 91, 98, 101, 103; Civil War, CC 81; fireman's, DF 147; strait-jacket lock, LM 71

Bucknall, Stephen, LM 59

Buck Rogers premiums, PQ 112, 113, 114-115

Buell, D. C., LM 146

Buffalo, depictions of, BB 102; on stamp, SS 107

Buffalo Bill's Wild West show, poster for, PQ 94

Bugatti Grand Prix Racer (car), BC 86

Buggies: Goddard, FH 149; Jenny Lind, FH 150

Buicks (cars): catalogue, AB 107; Roadmaster, BC 92

Bulldogs: bank, AB 126; bronze, DF 15; cane handle, BC 51

Bull Dog tobacco, match holder advertising, AB 10

Bullets: letter-opener handle, TW 148; molds for, CC 76

Bunker Hill, Battle of: Currier & Ives print, CD 91; map, LM 146; stamp, SS 113

Burdock Blood Bitters trade card, TT 120

Bureaus. See Dressers

Burmese glass, AB 57, 62, 63

Burnette, C. A., Company, Chicago, Ill., paperweight from, AB 8

Burnside, Ambrose, CC 85

Burroughs, Edgar Rice, CC 8, RS 101

Burton, Sir Richard, LM 134, SS 149

Buster Brown: button, AB 8; cigar band, CC 49; doorstop, DF 62; knife, IL 142

Butchers: shaving mugs, RS 148-149; on watch, TW 62

Butler, Benjamin, BC 107

Butter churns, IL 122, SS 144

Butter dishes: carnival-glass, BC 58; Depression-glass, CD 142, 143, 146, 148; individual,

majolica, LM *110;* pressed-glass, PQ *132*
Butterfield, Daniel, CC 76
Butterflies: on carnival glass, BC *61;* on Chinese porcelain, CC *31, 32;* majolica motif, LM *110, 117;* netsuke lid, MN *142;* print of, TW *118;* on valentine, TW *26;* Victorian curio, TW *42;* wings, picture made of, OP *57*
Butter molds, AB *28, 29*
Butter prints, IL *127*
Buttonhooks, AB *15,* MN *125, 135,* OP *55;* in knife, IL *138*
Buttons, BC 6-17; Army uniforms, AB *30;* Civil War, CC *75, 82;* log cabin on, PQ *66;* policemen's, PQ *54, 56-57;* railroaders', RS *26. See also* Pin-back buttons
Byrd, Richard E., LM 52
Byron, Lord, book by, BB *110*

C

Cabinet cards, PQ *23,* TT *34. See also* Photographs
Cabinets: oak, OP *18, 20, 158;* Shaker, RS *129;* Victorian, TW *44*
Cadets (rock group), record by, RS 57
Cadillac, catalogue for, AB *107*
Cadillacs (rock group), record label of, RS *52*
Caille Brothers Company, Detroit, Mich., coin machines by, OP *110, 112, 120, 122*
Cake basket, SS *41*
Cake board, IL *126*
Cake box, tinware, TT *54*
Caldecott, Randolph, art by, CC *13*
Calder, Alexander, poster by, PQ *109*
Calèche (carriage), Currier & Ives print of, CD *96*
Calendars, AB *6, 7;* plates, AB *113,* OP *51;* royal souvenir, RS *82;* silk picture on, SS *25*
California Fruit Growers Exchange, FH 32, 33
Calligraphic drawings, FH *8, 12*
Calligraphic technique, in Japanese prints, IL *37*
Camels: cigarette lighter, SS *71;* on beer mugs, SS *128*
Cameo Doll Company, baby doll by, DF *44*
Cameos: buttons, BC *9;* combs, CC *142, 147;* hatpin holder, FH *115;* jewelry, IL *80-82,* TW *88;* steins, SS 124, *127*
Cameras, BC 18-29; in cane, BC *48;* on shaving mug, RS *150*
Camera Work (magazine), LM *75,* PQ *25*
Campanella, Roy, TT *126*
Campbell, John W., Jr.: book by, RS *105;* as magazine editor, RS

103, *109*
Campbell Brothers circus, program from, CC *66*
Candelabrum, BC *36*
Candle boxes, BB 146, *148,* BC 32
Candleholders, BC 30-41; from bayonet, CC *80;* bell, BB *49;* in canes, BC *48;* Chinese porcelain, CC *33;* Fiesta-ware, DF *129;* lamp made from, LM *21;* Shaker, RS *139;* Tiffany, TT *47*
Candle molds, BC *32*
Candle snuffers, BC 32, *36*
Candlestands, OP *68;* Shaker, RS *133, 137*
Candy containers, BB 133, *145*
Candy dishes, BC *61;* egg-shaped, DF *66*
Candy machine, OP *119*
Candy tins, OP *31, 43*
Cane beads, BB *19*
Canes, BC 42-53, PQ *74*
Caneware (Wedgwood), TW *90*
Canister, tinware, TT *54*
Canning, home: accessories, IL *58, 59;* instruction booklets, CD *15,* IL *58, 59;* jars, IL 52-61
Can openers, IL *116;* in knife, IL *139;* press-type, BB *27*
Canteens: Civil War, CC *75, 78;* World War I, TW *148*
Canton glass beads, BB *15*
Canton ware, CC *22, 24*
Cantor, Eddie, on cigar band, CC *50*
Capadura cigars, advertisement for, BC *107*
Cape Cod lamp, LM *20*
Cap exploders, TT *86*
Capital music box, MN *80*
Capp, Al, OP *151;* toy based on characters of, PQ *152*
Cappiello, Leonetto, posters by, PQ *92, 93, 95*
Caps: beanies, LM *51,* PQ *74;* embroidered, DF *83;* fireman's, DF *144;* Navy, United States, CC *82;* Nazi, TW *142;* policemen's, PQ *57;* purser's, OP *32. See also* Hats
Captain America, CC 154, *155*
Captain Easy, CC *151*
Captain Marvel, CC *155*
Captain Midnight premiums, PQ *113, 117*
Carafe, Fiesta ware, DF *136*
Cards. *See* Baseball cards; *Cartes de visite;* Cigarette premiums; Greeting cards; Playing cards; Postcards; Trade cards; Valentines
Carême, Antonin, cookbook published by, art from, CD *10*
Caretta, Frank, carousel animals by, BC *67, 68, 74*
Caricatures, BC 98-113, LM *85,* OP *84;* TW *122;* brass, BC *114;* corkscrew, CD *27;* eyeglass

wearers, DF *85;* golfer, FH *60;* jazz musicians, IL *69, 70;* menu cover, MN *32-33*
Carmel, Charles, carousel animals by, BC 68, *77, 79*
Carnation milk, bookmark advertising, AB *15*
Carnelian: beads, BB *7, 9, 12;* beads imitating, BB *6, 20;* watch fob, TW *58*
Carnival glass, BC 54-65; hatpin head, FH *113;* insulators, IL *22*
Carousels: animals, BC *cover,* 66-81; bank, AB *119;* toy, TT *96*
Carpet sweeper, TW *131*
Carqueville, Will, poster by, PQ *98*
Carriages. *See* Horse-drawn carriages
Carroll, Lewis, art from book by, CC *7, 16*
Cars. *See* Automobiles
Carson, Fiddlin' John, CD *29, 32;* record label, CD *32*
Carter, Jimmy: autograph, AB *100;* campaign cane, PQ *74*
Carter, Nicholas (pseudonym), book by, CD *159*
Carter Family, CD *37;* recordings, CD *32, 34, 39;* songbook, CD *38*
Cartes de visite, FH *69,* PQ *19, 23;* camera for, BC *20;* Lincoln's, AB *92*
Cartier watch, TW *66*
Cartoons, BC *98-113;* on buttons, PQ *69;* cigar label, CC *59;* movies, AB 32-41; World War I, TW *147. See also* Caricatures; Comics
Cartridges, for guns, CC *77,* FH *84, 92*
Carts: folk-art sculpture, FH *18;* mother-of-pearl egg, DF *68;* teacart, TW *101*
Caruso, Enrico, OP *34, 37;* memorabilia of, BC *99,* OP *36, 37*
Carvalho, D., book published by, CC *18*
Case, J. I., Racine, Wis., implement seat by, DF *120*
Cased glass: bowl, AB *67;* lamp, LM *26;* lightning-rod balls, LM *39, 44*
Case family, knives by, IL 135, *138, 139, 141*
Cash registers, BC 114-125
Casilear, John W., art by, OP *96*
Cass, N. D., Co., Athol, Mass., DF *18, 22*
Cassandre, A. M., posters by, PQ *95, 101*
Cassidy, Butch, painting of, CD *61*
Cassidy, Hopalong: on knife, IL *142;* on pen, OP *132*
Casters (tableware): pewter, OP *141;* silver, RS *29,* SS 35, *37, 42*
Cast iron: banks, AB 116-127,

FH *27,* PQ *63;* clocks, CC *100;* doorstops, DF 56-63; Dutch oven, IL *120;* eagles, AB *27, 29;* egg beater, IL *123;* fruit jars, IL *61;* greyhound, DF *6;* implement seats, DF *120;* inkstand, IL *12;* lamp, LM *20;* lock, LM *59, 64;* matchsafes, MN *15, 16;* mortar and pestle, OP *154;* paperweight, OP *102;* piano-stool legs, TW *104;* sewing-machine base, MN *130;* strength testers, OP *110, 112;* switch stand, railroad's, RS *25;* toys, PQ *63,* TT 86, *87-88, 100-102, 106, 128;* trivets, TT *153, 156, 158;* weather vane, TW *73*
Catalogues: baseball cards, AB *138;* car, AB *107, 112;* cash register, BC *124;* fishing gear, DF *160;* furniture in, OP *7, 10;* keys, LM *63;* magic apparatus, LM *92-93, 102;* police supply, PQ *56;* record, CD *31;* stamp, SS *102;* tool, TT *76;* weather vanes, TW *68*
Catesby, Mark, art by, TW *109-110, 111*
Catlin, George, illustrations by, BB *102, 103*
Cats, BC 126-137; appliqué, RS *98;* carousel, BC *69;* chalkware, BC *145, 146;* Christmas tree ornament, CC *37;* Currier & Ives print, CD *98;* fruit-crate label, FH *32;* inkwell, IL *10;* matchsafe, MN *8*
Cecchetti, Cesare, and family, CD 116, 119
Celadon serving dish, CC *23*
Celebrity cookbooks, CD *16*
Celebrity dolls, DF *54;* paper, LM *50,* OP *75, 82-87*
Célerifère (vehicle), BB *82*
Celestial charts, LM *128-129*
Celluloid: advertising giveaways, AB *6, 8, 9, 10, 14, 15;* boxes, BB *156, 157;* combs, CC 140, *145-147;* film, *41;* hairpin, CC *144;* medal, RS *78;* pencil clip, OP *133;* political buttons, PQ *66, 67, 68, 69;* silhouettes, SS *18;* in valentine, TW *16*
Cels. *See* Animation film art
Centennial Exhibition, Philadelphia, Pa. (1876), TW *123;* ceramics, AB *71, 72;* coffeepot, SS *37;* cut glass, CD *100;* decoys, CD *131;* inkwell, IL *8-9;* iron, miniature, IL *31;* matchsafe, MN *7;* piano, TW 37, *47;* steam engine, TW *121;* trade cards, TT *112*
Centerpieces, glass, BC *60,* CD *145,* LM *14-15*
Central Vermont railroad line, lock from, RS *24*
Ceramic Art Company, Trenton, N.J., Belleek by, BB 36, *39, 43;*

marks, BB *44*

Ceramics. *See* Porcelain; Pottery

Ceresota flour, coloring book issued by, AB *18*

Cernigliaro, Salvatore, carousel animals by, BC *67, 69*

Cézanne, Paul, painting by, on stamp, SS *119*

Chagall, Marc, art by: on poster, PQ *92;* on stamps, SS *98, 120*

Chains: carved-wood, FH *14-15;* watch, TW *58, 64, 65*

Chairs: Civil War camp chair, CC *80;* dog-legged, DF *7;* glass inkwell, IL *10;* miniatures, DF *29;* oak, OP *12-16, 18;* painted, OP *59, 64, 66, 69;* parlor-car, RS *28;* royal, model of, RS *86;* Shaker, RS *122, 123, 124-125, 134-136;* theatrical props, MN *62,* TT *33;* Victorian, TW *34-38, 46, 48, 52, 53, 56, 106;* walnut, OP *6;* wicker, TW *96, 97, 102-107*

Chaise (carriage), FH *146*

Chaise (seat), TW *50-51*

Chalice, pewter, OP *138*

Chalkware, BC *138-147*

Challinor, Edward, pottery, Staffordshire, England, products of, SS *88*

Challinor, Taylor and Company, Pittsburgh, Pa., glass by, OP *50,* PQ *133*

Chalmers (car), paperweight advertising, AB *115*

Chambers, H. C., poster by, PQ *102-103*

Chambers, Thomas, decoys by, CD *135, 137*

Champlevé enamel, BC *15,* IL *11*

Champs (rock group), record by, RS *57*

Chandeliers, BC *34;* Lalique, LM *16*

Chapbooks, CC *18,* OP *75-76, 78*

Chaplin, Charlie: doll, DF *54;* on poster, MN *57*

Chaps, CD *62, 69*

Charity cookbooks, CD *8*

Charleville musket, FH *86-87*

Charlie McCarthy radio, RS *18*

Charpentier, Gustave, poster for opera by, OP *46*

Chase, Salmon, on cigar labels, CC *54*

Chatelaines, IL *90,* MN *126, 135*

Châtillon, Louis de, illustrations by, BB *119, 121*

Chavez, Cesar, cookbook, CD *12;* poster, PQ *106*

Checker, Chubby, record by, RS *56*

Checks, AB *90, 94,* LM *57*

Cheese press, RS *138*

Chelor, Cesar, TT *72*

Chelsea Keramic Art Works, Chelsea, Mass., products of, AB *74-75;* marks, AB *84*

Chemical Bank of New York

City, OP *cover*

Chemise, CC *109*

Chéret, Jules, posters by, PQ *92, 95, 97*

Cherry-Garrard, Apsley, book by, LM *135*

Cherry stoner, IL *125*

Chesapeake Pottery Company, Baltimore, Md., majolica by, LM *107, 110, 120;* mark, LM *115*

Chess sets, BC *148-160*

Chesterfield cigarettes, poster for, PQ *102-103*

Chestnuts: illustration of, BB *128;* matchsafe made from, MN *9*

Chests: apothecary, RS *138;* blanket, OP *65, 73;* medicine, OP *153;* sailor's, MN *109;* spice, OP *63,* RS *139;* tool, TT *73;* tramp-art, TT *144;* trunks, BB *149*

Chevrolets: Bel Air, BC *92;* Corvair, BC *86-87;* Corvette, BC *86, 97;* Deluxe Sport roadster, BC *87*

Chickens: carousel, BC *76;* cookie mold, IL *128;* covered dishes, BC *145,* PQ *133;* and eggs, DF *67, 71,* FH *77,* SS *77;* netsuke, MN *149;* on postcard, PQ *83;* toy, TT *93. See also* Roosters

Chiffonier, oak, OP *11*

Children: advertising giveaways for, AB *16-19, 18;* bookmarks, SS *26;* candy containers, BB *133, 145;* card games, PQ *51;* in Currier & Ives prints, CD *94, 98;* furniture, OP *12, 64,* RS *122;* Indian blanket, MN *120;* inkwell, IL *15;* music boxes, MN *69;* portraits of, PQ *18, 21;* sculptures of, RS *66-72;* tableware, CD *143,* MN *158, 159,* OP *43;* waistcoat, CD *108;* watches for, TW *60, 67. See also* Games; Marbles; Nursing bottles; Premiums; Puppets; Samplers; Toys; Trains

Children's books, CC *6-19;* advertising giveaways, AB *16, 18, 19;* Bible, BB *77;* paper dolls, OP *75-76, 78, 83, 86*

Childs, George A., Company, Brattleboro, Vt., game by, FH *57*

Chilkat shirt, MN *117*

China (earthenware). *See* Pottery

Chinese (people), portrayals of: banks, AB *121, 125;* Belleek, BB *43;* canes, BC *49;* detective story, CD *160;* giant, on circus poster, CC *62;* lock, LM *68*

Chinese Export Porcelain, CC *20-33*

Chinese linking rings, LM *93*

Chippendale style: candlesticks, BC *34;* chairs, miniature,

DF *29*

Choreography systems, CD *127*

Christ depictions of: on chatelaine, IL *90;* on spoon, SS *77*

Christian Science Church, spoon honoring founder of, SS *79*

Christie, Agatha, books by, CD *153, 155*

Christmas cards, FH *68, 69-72, 74-79*

Christmas decorations: chalkware, BC *141, 143;* tree ornaments, CC *34-45. See also* Crèches

Christmas spoon, SS *77*

Christmas tree stands, CC *44*

Christopher, Saint, on medal, MN *26*

Christy, Howard Chandler: art by, CC *50,* LM *77;* caricature of, LM *85*

Chrome: in bracelet, IL *97;* toaster, TT *69*

Chromoliths (steins), SS *124, 125, 129, 131*

Chryslers: catalogue, AB *107;* Firepower V-8, BC *82;* 300-C, BC *86, 96*

Church, of chalkware, BC *141*

Cigarettes: cases and boxes, AB *108,* BB *155,* BC *42, 50, 133,* RS *18,* SS *66;* equipment for rolling, SS *65;* holders, SS *66;* lighters, OP *130,* SS *70-71;* packages, SS *65, 71;* poster for, PQ *102-103;* premiums, AB *138, 140, 141, 142, 143, 145,* RS *85,* SS *62, 64, 65*

Cigars: bands and labels, CC *46-59;* boxes, tramp art from, DF *26,* TT *141, 142, 144;* buncher, SS *72;* cases, CD *118;* cutters, BC *50,* CD *24,* MN *11,* SS *67,* TT *46;* humidor in cane, BC *50;* mold, SS *72;* stand, musical, MN *71;* trade card, BC *107;* vending machine, OP *119*

Cincinnati Limoges pottery, AB *71, 72*

Circus, toy, TT *91*

Circus memorabilia, CC *60-71*

Citizens' Food Committee poster, AB *23*

Citrine necklace, IL *95*

Citroën, toy, TT *108*

City Despatch Post, SS *104*

Civil Rights button, PQ *70*

Civil War equipment, CC *72-87;* books, BB *70, 101;* cornet, MN *84, 97;* cowboys, used by, CD *60;* Currier & Ives prints, CD *91-93;* drums, AB *25,* CC *72;* envelopes, CC *86,* OP *130;* gun accessories, CC *76, 77;* guns, CC *73, 74-75,* FH *84, 86;* insignia, AB *30,* CC *81;* knives, IL *136, 138;* magazine cover, LM *74;* maps, LM *124, 146;*

medal, MN *30;* money, CC *138,* OP *90, 94, 95;* photographs, CC *85,* PQ *22;* playing cards, PQ *51;* Rogers groups, RS *66, 72, 73;* spoons, commemorative, SS *74, 78;* stamps, SS *109, 113;* of surrender, AB *98-99;* swords, CC *74-75,* SS *149, 150-151, 158-159*

Clambroth glass, BC *39;* marbles, LM *154*

Clarion record label, CD *41*

Clark, Gruber & Co., coin minted by, CC *137*

Clark, Hilda, on tray, AB *11*

Clark, M. L. circus, poster for, CC *66*

Clark, T. B., & Company, Honesdale, Pa., glass by, CD *106;* marks, CD *103*

Clark, William, bottle designed by, MN *160*

Clarke, Arthur C., book by, RS *105*

Classic Car Club of America, list published by, BC *85, 93*

Clayton, H. J., book by, CD *9*

Clemente, Roberto, AB *147*

Clements, Vassar, CD *42*

Cleveland, Grover, DF *153;* on cane head, BC *42;* on stamp, SS *107*

Cleveland & Whitehill Co., Newburgh, N.Y., advertising mirror from, AB *9*

Clews, James and Ralph, SS *85*

Clichy company, France, paperweights by, OP *101, 106*

Clifton, Sweetwater, AB *148*

Clipper ships, trade cards for, TT *110*

Clocks, CC *88-101;* advertising giveaways, AB *16;* cash registers, BC *116, 118;* cut glass, CD *104;* frogs on, FH *26;* in music box, MN *77;* theatrical souvenir, TT *18;* world's fair souvenirs, TW *123, 125*

Clodhoppers (recording group), CD *33*

Cloisonné enamel: beads, BB *9, 15, 20;* button, BC *15;* cigarette case, AB *108;* vase, DF *28*

Clothes hangers, Shaker, RS *126*

Clothespins, Shaker, RS *126*

Clothes tree, tramp-art, TT *149*

Clothing and costume, CC *102-115;* ballets, sketches for, CD *116, 120, 121, 123;* Civil War, CC *82-83;* cowboy, CD *61; 62, 63, 68-71;* embroidery, CC *102, 104, 107-109, 111, 114, 115,* DF *78, 79, 81, 83;* Indians, BB *16-17,* MN *117;* lace, IL *147, 148, 150, 154-157;* magazine illustrations, LM *74, 87;* from movies, MN *62, 63;* policemen's, PQ *54, 55, 57;* political, PQ *74;* rock and roll memorabilia, RS 55, 58; theatrical, TT 26, 27, 32, 33; world's fair souvenirs, TW 124, 130; World Wars, TW 137, 140, 141. See also Handbags; Hats; Paper dolls

Clowns: banks, AB 117, 118, 127; on cigarette package, SS 65; circus, CC 68, 71; doorstop, DF 62; inkwell, IL 15; lamp, LM 26; matchsafe, MN 11; on toys, TT cover, 88. See also Pagliacci

Clysmic table water, tray advertising, AB 11

Coach, coronation, miniature, RS 84-85

Coal: paperweight made of, OP 104; ring promoting, PQ 113

Coal and Iron Police badge, PQ 59

Coalport porcelain button, BC 14

Coaster, royal souvenir, RS 87

Coat hook, musical, MN 71

Coats, CC 114, 115; cowboy, CD 68, 71; policeman's, PQ 54; World War I, TW 140, 141

Cobb, Ty, AB 143, 145

Coca-Cola: cigar bands, CC 47, 49; knives, IL 142; trays, AB 11, 14

Cochrane, Gordon (Mickey), AB 142

Cock Robin (character), CC 16

Cocteau, Jean, LM 88

Cody, Buffalo Bill: show poster, PQ 94; silk portrait, SS 20

Coffee bin, oak, OP 21

Coffee canister, tinware, TT 54

Coffeepots: britannia, OP 145; Christmas tree ornament, CC 42; enamel, IL cover; Flint Enamel, BB 60; porcelain, BB 43, CC 22; silver, SS 35-37; Staffordshire, SS 86; tinware, TT 52; Wedgwood, TW 91, 94

Coil baskets, AB 151, 153, 156, 158, 159, 160

Coin machines, LM 50, 51, OP 110-123

Coins, CC 116-139; eagle motif, AB 21, 22, CC 137, 138; in necklaces, BB 18

Coke, Henry J., book by, BB 102

Cole, Henry, greeting card published by, FH 69, 70

Coleman, William and Rebecca, greeting cards by, FH 70, 75

Colette (French writer), OP 101

Colin, Paul, poster by, PQ 100

Collar, lace, IL 148, 158

Collar boxes, FH 15; as tobacco holder, SS 63

Collier's (magazine), AB 109, 111, LM 75, 80

Collins, Eddie, AB 146

Collins, Wilkie, books by, CD 152, 154

Collins & Co., South Canton, Conn., sword by, SS 158-159

Colonna, Edward, pendant by,

IL 92

Coloring books, as advertising giveaways, AB 18, 19

Colt, J. B., Company, N.J., trivets by, TT 153, 155

Colt, Samuel, FH 84

Colt guns, CC 74, CD 67, FH 84, 87, 88-89, 92, 93, 96; derringer, FH 95; Gatling gun, FH 98-99; Peacemaker, FH 82-83, 86, 93

Columbia cycles, BB 88, 90; trade card for, TT 116

Columbian Exposition, bell, BB 41; commemorative coin, CC 138; souvenirs of, TW 123, 124; paperweight, OP 104; pipe, PQ 34; postcards, PQ 78, 79; silk picture, SS 28; spoons, SS cover, 78; stamps, commemorative, SS 105, 110

Columbia Phonograph Company, products of, PQ 6, 8, 13

Columbia records, IL 62, 70, 72

Columbus, Christopher: letter from, BB 95; and tobacco, SS 60

Combs, CC 140-147

Comet Metal Products, MN 43

Comets. See Halley's comet

Comic characters: Christmas tree lights, CC 38; doorstop, DF 62; radio premiums, PQ 110-111, 112, 113, 118; toys, AB 16, CC 152-153, DF 54, LM 157

Comics, CC cover, 148-160, CD 158; advertising giveaways, CC 149, 151, CD 119

Comiskey, Charles, AB 138

Compacts: in cane, BC 47; hat-pin head, FH 114; silver, BC 133

Compass (tool), Shaker, RS 129

Compasses (directional instruments): Lindbergh souvenir, LM 49; nautical, MN 100, 101

Conan the Barbarian (comic character), CC 158

Concord, Battle of, stamps commemorating, SS 115

Conestoga-wagon doorstop, DF 56-57

Conklin, Pete, lithograph of, CC 71

Conklin Company pens, OP 124, 129

Connelly, Marc, autograph of, TT 39

Connoisseur figures (model soldiers), MN 43

Conqueror record label, CD 40

Conrad, Joseph, book by, BB 113

Conroy, Thomas, fishing reel by, DF 156-157

Continental currency, OP 90, 91

Converse, Morton E., & Son, Winchendon, Mass., DF 18, 22; product of, DF 32

Coogan, Jackie: in advertising, AB 17; paper doll of, OP 85

Cookbooks, CD 6-19; preserving guides, CD 15, IL 58, 59

Cookie molds, IL 128

Cookie tin, RS 84-85

Coolidge, Baldwin, photo by, PQ 26-27

Coolidge, Calvin, LM 46, 54

Cooper, Gary, MN 66

Cooper, James Fenimore, book by, CC 18

Co-operative Manufacturing Company, Springfield, Vt., dolls by, DF 39

Copley, John Singleton, IL 80

Copper: badge, PQ 58; boxes, BB 152, 154, 155; canteen, CC 78; currency, CC 116, 124, 125, 127, 128, 134-136; dollhouse furnishings, DF 30-31; iron, IL 28; matchsafe, MN 8; medal, MN 26; pudding mold, IL 128; ships' lights, MN 108; sign, RS 155; token, TT 17; weather vanes, TW 68, 69, 70, 72, 74-77

Coral: jewelry, IL 76, 85, 98, 100; ojime (fastener), BB 14

Corbett, Bertha Louise, characters created by, MN 159

Cord (car), BC 90

Cork press, OP 156

Corkscrews, CD 20-27; in knives, IL 133, 138, 140; for scent bottles, CD 25, MN 125

Corliss, George H., steam engine by, TW 121

Corn: carnival-glass motif, BC 64; husker-shredder, DF 112; majolica motif, LM 117, 120; planter, DF 108-109

Cornell, Ezra, IL 16

Cornucopias, paper, CC 44

Coronation souvenirs, BB 28, RS 77, 78, 80, 81, 83-86

Corrigan, Douglas (Wrong Way), menu honoring, MN 36

Corvair (car), BC 86-87

Corvette (car), BC 86, 97

Cosey, Joseph, forgery by, AB 97

Cosmopolitan (magazine), LM 81

Costume. See Clothing

Cot, Pierre Auguste, silk pictures of art by, SS 27

Cottage furniture, OP 58, 60, 70, 71

Cottolene shortening, trade card for, TT 119

Cotton, William, art by, BC 113

Coty perfume bottles, LM 6, 17

Counterfeit money, OP 88

Country music, CD 28-43

Courtenay, Richard, model soldiers by, MN 43

Courvoisier, Guthrie Sayre, AB 35, 39

Covarrubias, Miguel, caricatures by, BC 110, 113, LM 85

Coverlets, CD 44-59

Covington, U.S.S., life preserver from, OP 32

Cowboys: fruit-crate label, FH 44; gear, CD 60-71

Cowen, Joshua Lionel, TT 126

Cowles, C., & Company, New Haven, Conn., carriage lamps by, FH 156

Cox, Palmer, character, DF 54

Coxon Belleek company, Wooster, Ohio, products of, BB 36, 45; mark, BB 44

Crabtree, Lotta, glass honoring, TT 18

Cracker Jack prizes, AB 16

Crain, Edward L., record by, label from, CD 39

Cram, George F., Co., Indianapolis, Ind., globe by, LM 125

Crandall typewriter, 7

Crane, toy, TT 139

Crane, Walter, art by, CC 10, 15, TW 27

Crary, J. M., typewriter by, TW 13

Craven Art Pottery, East Liverpool, Ohio, vase by, AB 78

Crawdaddy (magazine), RS 60

Crawford, McGregor & Canby Company, golf clubs by, FH 61, 62, 63

Creamers: art-glass, AB 54; Belleek, BB 37; Depression-glass, CD 140, 142-144, 147; majolica, LM 111, 117; owl-shaped, OP 50; pewter, OP 146; pressed-glass, PQ 132, RS 80; silver, SS 35

Cream jar, SS 56

Creasey, John, CD 154

Crèches, CD 72-81

Crewelwork, DF 77, 80

Crisco shortening, cookbook for, CD 14

Crocker, H. S., art by, FH 35

Crockett, Johnny, songbook, CD 28

Crolius, C., flask by, SS 140

Crosby, F. Gordon, AB 109-110

Crosley radios, RS 9, 15, 17

Cross, IL 76, 77

Crow beaded shirt, BB 17

Crowell, Elmer, CD 130, 131

Crown records, CD 39, IL 65

Cruets, art-glass, AB cover; pressed-glass, PQ 130

Cruikshank, George, BC 100; drawing by, BC 98

Cruikshank brothers, card by, TW 22

Crystal: chess set, BC 158-159; egg, DF 68; prisms, BC 37. See also Cut glass; Lalique

Crystal Glass Ltd., Australia, bowl by, BC 61

Crystal Palace exposition, souvenirs of, TW 122, 123

Crystal sets, RS 6, 8

Cuff links, IL 76
Cuffs: cowboy, CD 69; embroidered, DF 78; lace, IL 150
Cunard ship, toast rack from, OP 30
Cunningham, James, & Son Co., Rochester, N.Y., FH 147
Cupboards: Shaker, RS 129, 132, 137; tramp-art, TT 146, 151
Cupids: on booklet, TW 28; on cards, TW 23, 27; carousel carvings, BC 73, 75; engraved platter, CD 108; on medal, MN 27
Cup plates: pressed-glass, AB 27, PQ 122, 125; Staffordshire, SS 84
Cups: advertising giveaways, AB 17; Belleek, BB 35, 37; carnival-glass, BC 60; Depression-glass, CD 143, 145, 147, 151; dining-car, RS 29; Fiesta-ware, DF 127-130; majolica, LM 104, 105, 110; political souvenir, PQ 66; quassia, OP 157; silver, MN 158; SS 42, 45, 57, 58; Staffordshire, SS 88, 92; Wedgwood, TW 86. See also Eggcups; Loving cups; Mugs; Tumblers
Curling iron, TT 68
Currier, Nathaniel, & James M. Ives prints, BC 128, CD 82-99, TW 73; copies from, BC 8, 143, FH 9; trade cards, CD 85, TT 112, 113
Curtis, Cyrus H. K., LM 75
Curtis, Edward S., PQ 16
Curtiss Jenny (airplane), LM 53; on stamp, SS 101
Cushing and White, Waltham, Mass., TW 68
Cuspidors. See Spittoons
Custer, George Armstrong, FH 87, RS 66
Cut glass, CD 100-113; glue holder, IL 13; inkwells, IL 6, 8, 10, 12-13; silver combined with, IL 12-13, SS 56, 57

D

Daggers: in canes, BC 44, 49; as stage props, TT 32, 33
Daguerre, Louis-Jacques-Mandé, BC 21
Daguerreotypes, PQ 16-19; cameras, BC 18, 21
Dagwood (comic character), CC 151; toy based on, CC 153
Dairy wagon, FH 158
Dalbey, R. M., fruit jar, IL 52, 56
Dalhart, Vernon, CD 32
Damascening, TW 60, 63
Damask, CC 108
Dance memorabilia, CD cover, 114-127; posters, CD 116, 117, PQ 109; stamps, SS 122
Darning eggs, MN 132

Darrow, Charles, game by, FH 54
Date nails, railroad, RS 23, 25
Daugherty Visible typewriter, TW 10
Daumier, Honoré, art by, BC 98, 100, 106, 107, TW 122
Daval Manufacturing Company, pinball machine by, OP 116
Dave Clark Five (rock group), record by, RS 61
Davenport, Homer, art by, BC 112
Davis, Jefferson, PQ 23; on stamps, SS 109
Davis, Paul, poster by, PQ 106
Davis, Warren B., art by, AB 111
Deakin, Richard, art from book by, BB 128
Dean, Dizzy, AB 141
Dean, James, on poster, MN 59
Decanters: cut-glass, CD 106, 107, 109; Depression-glass, CD 150; Lalique glass, LM 14; pressed-glass, PQ 131
Declaration of Independence: signers, AB 101, IL 7, SS 23; subscribers' signatures, AB 92
Decoders (radio premiums), PQ 110-111, 117
Decoys, CD 128-139, OP 48
Dedham Pottery, Mass.: mark, AB 84; plate, AB 74
DeDion-Bouton (car), AB 107
Deedboxes, tinware, TT 59
Deer: chalkware, BC 146; on jar, RS 42; print, TW 117 (see also Animals); on trivet, TT 158
Deere & Co.: implement seat, DF 120; plows, DF 110
de Gouy, L. P., book by, CD 18
de Havilland, Olivia, MN 65
DeKay, James E., art by, TW 109
De La Rue & Co., England, greeting cards by, FH 69-70, 75
Delftware, LM 109; cow, LM 109; imitation, inkwell of, IL 14; tile, cat-shaped, BC 131
Delineator, The (magazine), LM 78
Delmonico's (restaurant), N.Y., MN 32
Delmore, Alton and Rabon, CD 43
De Mille, Cecil B., OP 47
Demitasse: set, Fiesta-ware, DF 129; spoon, SS 77
Dentzel, Gustav, carousel animals by, BC 67, 69, 70, 71-73, 75
Depression glass, BC 32, CD 140-151
Deringer, Henry, FH 95
Derringers (pistols), FH 95
Derrydale Press, New York, N.Y., BB 105-106
Desk accessories: inkstands, IL 12-13; silver, IL 12-13, SS 57; Tiffany, TT 43, 45, 46. See also Inkwells
Desks: painted, OP 72; rolltop, OP 8, 19; sewing, RS 122;

Victorian, TW 37, 54-55
de Sperati, Jean, SS 101
Desprès, Jean, ring by, IL 98
Detective cameras, BC 23, 29, 48
Detective fiction, CD 152-160
Devils: on shaving mug, RS 151; on tarot card, PQ 49
Dewey, George, SS 31; spoon honoring, SS 74
Diaghilev, Serge, memorabilia of, CD 115, 117, 119, 121
Diamond-quilted glass, AB 60, 65, 67; bell, BB 50; inkwell, IL 8; lightning-rod ornaments, LM 38, 43
Diamonds: Easter eggs, DF 66; on hatpin, FH 114; jewelry, IL 78, 82, 86, 89, 92-94, 98; Koh-i-noor, IL 85; watches, TW 66
Diary, Civil War soldier's, CC 86
Dice boxes, BB 148, 160, LM 95
Dick, Philip K., book by, RS 104
Dickens, Charles, CD 10; books by, BB 99, 109; card game honoring, PQ 51
Dickens' Ware, AB 83
Dick Tracy premiums, PQ 110-111, 112
Diddie Blitzen Company, lightning-rod balls by, LM 39, 42
Dietrich, Marlene, LM 85; on poster, MN 58
Digges, Dudley, TT 37
DiMaggio, Joe, AB 141
Ding Dong Bell bank, AB 126
Dionne quintuplets radio, RS 18
Dirigibles: cigar label, CC 53; fruit-crate label, FH 45; stamp, SS 108; toy, TT 96-97
Dirks, Rudolph, comic characters by, CC 150
Disfarmer, Mike, PQ 20
Dishes: Belleek, BB 34; carnival-glass, BC 58, 61; Chinese serving pieces, CC 23, 30, 32; cut-glass, CD 106; Harlequin-ware, DF 134; majolica, LM 104-105, 110-112, 121; pressed-glass, covered, PQ 130, 132, 133; scrimshaw, RS 119; silver, SS 39-41, 45; Staffordshire, SS 88; Wedgwood, TW 90. See also Depression glass; Fiesta ware
Disney, Walt: animated films, AB 32-33, 35-37, 39, 41; books, CC 8; comic characters, CC 149, 151, 154, 156, 157; on stamp, SS 112
Ditty boxes, MN 109, RS 117
Doat, Taxile, AB 83
Dobbs, J., barbed wire by, AB 130
Dobbs firm, valentine by, TW 24
Dodge, Geraldine Rockefeller, DF 8
Dogpatch Band toy, CC 152
Dogs, DF 6-15; banks, AB 126, 127; cane heads, BC 44, 45, 49,

51; carousel, BC 67, chalkware, BC 145; Christmas tree ornaments, CC 37, 41; on corkscrew, CD 26; doorstops, DF 57, 59, 61, 62; fruit-crate label, FH 33; on hooked rugs, FH 132-133, 135; matchsafe, MN 11; medals honoring, MN 29, 31; pitcher, LM 118-119; pitcher handles, BB 57, 58; puppet, PQ 137; toy, TT cover, 93; treadmill powered by, DF 122; Victor trademark, DF 8, PQ 8, 12
Dog tag, TW 143
Doilies, lace, details of, IL 159
Dollars: bills, OP 97; silver, AB 21, 22
Dollhouses, DF 16-33
Dolls, DF cover, 34-55; comic characters, CC 152, 153, DF 54; owl Kachinas, OP 48; paper, LM 50, OP 74-87; scrimshaw dishes for, RS 119; wooden eggs, DF 71
Dolphins: bell mount, BB 48; candlesticks, BC 30, 39; cash register, BC 121; compote feet, BC 60; majolica, LM 116
Dominion Glass Co., Canada, insulator by, IL 19
Domino, Fats, record by, RS 56
Donaldson, Lou, IL 75
Donizetti, Gaetano, opera score by, OP 39
Doorknob, OP 108
Door knockers, LM 66, 67
Doorstops, DF 56-63, OP 52
Dormouse, bone, IL 92
Douay Bible, BB 69, 70, 72
Double Dealer, The (magazine), LM 75
Doughty, Thomas, art by, TW 117
Doulton and Company, England: cat by, BC 131. See also Royal Doulton
Down Beat (magazine), IL 62, 75
Doyle, Sir Arthur Conan, character created by, CD 152, 156, 157
Dragonflies: in brooch design, IL 94; in Lalique glass, LM 8; on sword guard, SS 157; Tiffany glass, TT 43
Dragons: bead, BB 15; comb, CC 144; hatpin head, FH 112; matchsafes, MN 6, 8; netsuke, MN 148; pendant, IL 103; sword guard, SS 157
Draisienne (vehicle), BB 82-83
Draper, Eban, caricature, BC 109
Drawer pulls, AB 30, OP 53
Dresden Christmas tree ornaments, CC 35-36, 35-37
Dressers: oak, OP 10, 11; tramp-art, TT 146, 148; Victorian, TW 48

Dresses. *See* Clothing
Dressing tables, OP *67;*
    accessories, BB *159,* SS *54, 56*
Drew, John, TT *34*
Drills, Indian, AB *48, 52, 53*
Driscoll, Clara, TT *43*
Drouet, Louis, flute by, MN *95*
Drums, Civil War, AB *25,* CC *72;*
    toy, TT *cover*
Dry sink, RS *138*
Dubroni camera, BC *20*
Duces of Rhythm & Tempo
    Toppers (rock group), record
    by, RS *52*
Ducks: on Belleek dish, BB *34;*
    decoys, CD *128-130,* 131, *134-138;* magic trick, LM *96*
Dudley Watch Company, Pa.,
    product of, TW *63*
Duesenberg brothers, car by, BC *90*
Dulac, Edmund, art by, CC *17*
DuMaurier, Georges, spoon, SS *cover*
Dumbo (film), scene from, AB *39*
Dump truck, toy, TT *102*
Dunand, Jean, jewelry by, IL *98*
Duncan, Isadora, CD *119;*
    figurine of, CD *118*
Dunham's Cocoanut Doll House,
    DF *19*
Dunhill, Alfred, of London, Inc.,
    pipes by, PQ *36, 38*
Dunhill of London, clothing by,
    TW *140*
Duo-Art mechanical piano, MN *82*
Duplex typewriter, TW *12*
Durbin, Deanna, doll, DF *54*
Durham-Duplex razor, RS *144*
Duster, Shaker, RS *127*
Dutch boy, on paint sign, RS *156*
Dutch oven, IL *120*
Dutton, E. P., & Co., valentine
    from, TW *27*
Duval, P. S., print by, TW *119*
Duvelleroy, House of, fans by,
    DF *105*
Dylan, Bob, on magazine, RS *60*

E

Eagle Lock Co., Terryville,
    Conn., keys by, LM *63*
Eagles, AB 20-31; board game,
    FH *49;* cane heads, BC *42, 51;*
    on canteen, TW *148;* Chinese
    porcelain, AB 22, 26, CC *20;*
    clocks, CC *94;* on coins, AB *21,*
    22, CC *137, 138;* cookie mold,
    IL *128;* corkscrew, CD *24;* in
    coverlet designs, CD *50, 51, 55;*
    on cup plates, AB *27,* PQ *125;*
    on currency, OP *cover, 95, 97;*
    door knocker, LM *67;* on
    headgear, DF *143,* TW *142;* on
    inkwell, IL *8;* on knife sheath,
    IL *134;* Lalique, LM *16;* on
    medal, MN *28;* on parade flier,
    BB *53;* political pin, PQ *68;* on
    sampler, RS *94-95;* on shaving

mug, RS *147;* silk picture, SS
    28; on Staffordshire, SS *82;* on
    stoneware, SS *144;* sword
    decorations, SS 148, 149, *154,*
    155; on toy train, TT *129;* on
    trivet, TT *158*
Eagles (coins), AB 22, CC *137*
Earl, Maud, painting by, DF *11*
Earrings, IL *82, 89, 98, 105;*
    Wedgwood, TW *88*
Earthenware. *See* Pottery
Easel, wicker, TW *99*
Easter eggs, CC *152,* DF *66,* 67,
    69, 70; spoon, SS *77*
Eastlake furniture, TW 36-37, 38
Eastman, Emily, art by, FH *9*
Eastman, George, BC 22
Eaves & Sons, Wolcottville,
    Conn., button by, BC *17*
Ebony: cane, BC *51;* chess pieces,
    BC *149;* flute, MN *95;* netsuke,
    MN *142;* on sewing box, MN
    125; tobacco container, MN
    140
Ecology buttons, PQ *70*
Eddy, Mary Baker, spoon
    honoring, SS *79*
Eden, Anthony, drawing of, BC
    112
Eden Roc (car), BC *87*
Edgar nutmeg grater, IL *119,*
    125
Edison, Thomas A., MN *63,* TT
    6; light bulb, LM *33;*
    phonographs, PQ 6, 7, *9;*
    typewriter, TW *14*
Edison record label, CD *36*
Edland typewriter, TW *9*
Edmilton Corporation,
    Milwaukee, Wis., iron by, IL *33*
Edouart, Auguste, silhouettes by,
    SS 8, *16-17*
Edward VII, King (England),
    memorabilia of, OP *82,* RS *76,*
    77, *80*
Edward VIII, King (England),
    souvenirs of, RS 76, 77, *82, 83*
Edwards, Eddie, IL *63*
Edwards, George, art by, TW *118*
Edwards, Sydenham, DF 6
Egg beaters. *See* Beaters
Eggcups: Fiesta-ware, DF *128;*
    pressed-glass, PQ *120;* royal
    souvenirs, RS *81;* silver-plated,
    SS *42*
Egginton, O. F., Company,
    punch bowl by, CD *106*
Eggs, DF *64-71;* darning eggs,
    MN *132;* doll on, CC *152;* on
    Easter card, FH *77;* on Easter
    spoon, SS *77;* hand coolers, DF
    69, MN *124;* kitchen
    equipment for, IL *121, 123,*
    130, 131
Ehret, Georg Dionysius, art by,
    BB *120;* print from, BB *118*
Ehret, George, on stein, SS *131*
Eiffel Tower, Paris, France, PQ
    24; as clock, TW *123*
Einfalt, Gebrüder, Nuremberg,

Germany, toy by, TT *93*
Einstein, Albert, paper doll, OP
    84
Eisen (Japanese artist), prints by,
    IL *38, 40*
Eisenhower, Dwight D.,
    memorabilia of, PQ *cover,* 69,
    74
Electra company, Albany, N.Y.,
    lightning-rod ball by, LM *41*
Electrical appliances, TT *68;*
    irons, IL *27, 31, 33,* TT 63. *See
    also* Toasters
Electric Cutlery Company,
    Newark, N.J., razor by, OP *55*
Electric Pen machine, OP *114*
Elephants: bells for, BB *52;*
    Chinese porcelain, CC *33;*
    Christmas tree ornaments, CC
    37, *40;* circus memorabilia, CC
    66, 67; on corkscrew, CD *26;*
    fruit-crate label, FH *33;*
    hatpin, FH *116;* on mugs, RS
    83; strength tester shaped like,
    OP *112;* on trade card, TT *118*
Eliot, Charles, caricature, BC *109*
Eliot, George Fielding, map by,
    LM *147*
Elizabeth I, Queen, on coin, CC
    120
Elizabeth II, Queen, memorabilia
    of, OP *83,* RS *86, 87*
Elizabethan Revival furniture,
    TW 36, 38
Ellington, Duke, IL *65, 73;*
    record labels, IL *73*
Elliot, Daniel Giraud, art by, TW
    113
Elliott Hickory Safety Bicycle, BB
    90
Elliston, Robert, CD *131*
Elman, Ziggy, IL *72*
Elssler, Fanny, CD *116*
Embroidery, DF *72-83;* Chinese,
    CC *26, 104, 115,* DF *78, 79, 82,*
    83; on clothing, CC *102, 104,*
    107-109, 111, 114, 115, DF *78,*
    79, 81, 83; handbags, FH *104,*
    105. See also Lace; Samplers
Emerald jewelry, IL *83, 88, 94*
Emeralite lamp, LM 20, *34*
Empire style: dollhouse sofa, DF
    28; dress, CC *103;* pitcher
    ornamentation, SS *46;* table
    adornment, TW *45*
Enamel: buttons, BC 6, *10-12,*
    15; champlevé, BC *15,* IL *11;*
    cigarette cases, AB *108,* SS *66;*
    cloisonné, AB *108,* BB 9, *15,*
    20, BC 15, DF *28;* eggs, DF *66,*
    69; hatpins, FH *112;* inkwells,
    IL *11, 14;* jewelry, IL *76, 78,*
    83, 90, 92-94, 98, 105, TZ *66;*
    matchsafes, MN *6;* medals, MN
    30; pencil, OP *126;* plique-à-
    jour, BC *15,* FH *112;* sewing
    tools, MN *127;* spoons, SS *74;*
    vases, DF *28,* LM *13;* on
    Wedgwood, TW *90*
Enamelware, IL *cover*

Encaustic painting, TW *87*
Enchanted Drawing, The (film), AB
    38-39
Enfield rifled musket, CC *73;*
    tool for, CC *76*
Engines, gasoline, DF *111;*
    tractor driven by, DF *114-115*
Engines, steam, DF 110, TW *121*
England, George Allan, RS *101*
Entertaining Comics, CC *159*
Envelopes, CC *86,* OP *130;*
    stamps on, LM *56,* SS *100, 114,*
    115
Epaulets, Civil War, CC *82*
Epergne, TW *93*
Erector set, TT *89*
Ericsson, L. M., Telephone Co.,
    Sweden, product of, TT *10*
Erie Canal, N.Y., book about, BB
    99
Erikson, Carl, art by, LM *87*
Ernst Louis, Grand Duke
    (Germany), on stein, SS *130*
Erté. *See* Tirtoff, Romain de
Eskimo art: cane, BC *52;* chess
    set, BC *155*
Esquire (magazine), IL *62;*
    automobile art, AB *110*
Étagère, TW *39*
Etaix, Pierre, art by, PQ *109*
Etruscan majolica. *See* Griffen,
    Smith and Hill
Etuis, MN 126, *135*
Evans, Henry, art by, BB *129*
Everly Brothers record, RS *56*
Eversharp pencils, OP *128, 130*
Every Day tobacco tin, SS *62*
Ewer, glass, AB *66*
Exhibit Supply Company,
    Chicago, Ill., coin machine by,
    OP *115*
Expo camera, BC *29*
Expositions. *See* World's fair
    souvenirs
Expo '67 souvenirs, TW *133*
Eye dazzlers (blankets), MN *cover,*
    113, *120, 121*
Eyeglasses, DF 84-93; cases, DF
    91
Eyes: cigar label, CC *56;* sign, RS
    152-153
E. Z. Wolf (comic book), CC *160*

F

Fabergé, Peter Carl: eggs, DF *66,*
    69; hatpins, FH 111, *112;*
    matchsafes, MN 7
Fahrner, Theodore, necklace by,
    IL *95*
Faïence: Egyptian, BB *8,* 9, 11,
    14; European, BB 46, *51,* LM
    109
Fairbanks, Charles, PQ *69*
Fairbanks, Douglas, menu
    honoring, OP *28*
Fairy-book series, CC *14*
Fairyland lusters, TZ 86, *95*
Falkenberg, Fred, AB *143*
Fallows, James, & Son,

Philadelphia, Pa., TT 86, 99
Famous Funnies comic books, CC 151
Fancher, John L., wood carving by, FH *14-15*
Fans, DF 94-107; in cane, BC *47;* electric, TT *68;* giveaways, AB 6, 8; from world's fair, TZ *120*
Fantasia (film), scene from, AB *36*
Fantastic Four (comic characters), CC *158*
Farley, James, SS 105
Farmer, Fannie, books by, CD 6, 9
Farm machinery, DF 108-125; on medal, MN *24;* toy, TT *102*
Farragut, David, rigging used by, MN 100, *106*
Farrar, Geraldine, OP 34, 36, *37, 47*
Father Christmas: chalkware, BC *143;* tree ornaments, CC *34.* See also Santa Claus
Faulkner, William, BB 100, LM 75
Favrile: glass, TT *49, 50;* pottery, AB *78, 82*
Feathers. See Ostrich feathers
Federal-style teapot, SS *32*
Federal Theatre Project: poster, TT *22;* puppet, PQ *145*
Felix the Cat (comic character), CC *151;* toy based on, CC *153*
Feller, Bob, AB *141*
Fencing: barbed-wire, AB 128-137; tools, AB *134;* trivet advertising, TT *159*
Fenton, Christopher Webber, pottery by, BB 56-67
Fenton Art Glass Company, Williamstown, W. Va., carnival glass by, BC 55, *61*
Ferris wheel, toy, TT *89*
Fey, Charles, OP 112
Fey, Jacques, brooch by, IL *94*
Fiat (car), BC 87
Field glasses, Civil War, CC *80*
Fields, W. C., caricature, BC *113*
Fiesta ware, CC 126-137
Fife, Civil War, CC *72*
Figurehead, eagle, AB *24,* 26
Filigree: chess pieces, BC *150, 151;* fan, DF *100;* hairpins, CC *144*
Filing cabinet, oak, OP *18*
Films. See Movies
Film strips, TW *129*
Finger bowl, glass, AB *54*
Finials: barbed-wire fences, AB *137;* birds, FH *14,* IL *8,* LM *9;* cat, BC *135;* clock-shaped, SS *152;* hearses, FH *14, 159;* lion, SS *37;* pipe-shaped, BC *62;* Shaker chairs, RS *136;* soldier, SS *130;* urn-shaped, TW *45*
Finlay, John and Hugh, OP 58
Finlay, Virgil, art by, RS *106*
Fire alarms, DF *146*
Fire Association of Philadelphia,

mark of, DF *148*
Fire engines, DF *138-139,* 140-141, *149-151;* on insignia, DF *147;* toy, TT *100*
Fire extinguishers, glass, BB 133, *144*
Fire-fighting equipment, DF 138-151; toys, TT *100, 139*
Fireman's balls, memorabilia of, DF *141*
Fire marks, DF 139, *148*
Firemen, DF *140;* chalkware, BC *143;* cigar band, CC *50;* Currier & Ives print, CD *85*
Fireplace fender, TT *45*
First-day covers, SS *114, 115*
First editions, AB *96;* BB 92-117; Bibles, BB 69, *72, 77;* bird prints, TW 109; cookbooks, CD 6, *11,* 13; detective fiction, CD 152, 155, *156;* exploration books, LM *134, 135;* modern American, BB *92-93, 112, 114-117;* science fiction, RS *104, 150;* term explained, BB 94-95, 108
First Ladies paper dolls, OP 75, *83*
Fischer, Gustav, pipe by, PQ *36*
Fish: in Belleek designs, BB 37, *39;* carnival-glass, BC *59;* Christmas tree ornaments, CC *36;* decoys, CD *134;* on matchsafe, MN *8;* menu shaped like, MN *34;* needlecase shaped like, MN *126;* pitcher, LM *118;* print of, TW *110;* snuff rasp, SS *68;* on trade card, TT *123;* weather vane, TW *80*
Fisher, M. F. K., cookbook by, CD *17*
Fishing books, BB 105, *106*
Fishing tackle, DF 152-160; in cane, BC *48*
Fish slice (server), SS *53*
Fish trap, willow, AB *153*
Fiske, J. W., New York, TW 68
Fitch, Eugene, TW 8
Fitch, Walter Hood, art by, BB *127*
Fitzgerald, F. Scott, magazine stories by, LM 75, *81*
Fitzgerald Manufacturing Company, product of, TT *71*
Fitzhugh pattern of Chinese porcelain, CC *23,* 24
"5" Royals (rock group), label from record by, RS *52*
Flaccus, E. C., jars by, IL *60*
Flagg, James Montgomery, art by, BC *99,* LM *84,* PQ *95,* TW 137
Flagpole ornament, AB *20*
Flags: Chinese, TW 143; political souvenir, PQ *cover,* 64; ship's, OP *33;* watch fob, TW *65;* on weather vane, TW 69
Flair (magazine), LM *88*
Flamingos (rock group), label

from record by, RS *52*
Flashlight cane, BC *48*
Flasks, BB 131, *132,* 133, *134, 135;* book-shaped, BB *67;* Civil War, CC *79;* cut-glass and sterling, SS *57;* eagles on, AB 26, *28;* motorist's, AB *108;* royal souvenir, RS *78;* stoneware, SS *140*
Flatiron Building, New York, N.Y., on postcard, PQ *80*
Flatware, silver, SS 48-53,
Fleischer, Max, studio, cartoons from, AB 34, 39, *40*
Flint Enamel ware, BB 57, 58, *59-61,* 65, *66, 67*
Florence sewing machine, MN *130*
Flossie Fisher's Funnies, figures from, SS *18*
Flow-blue Staffordshire china, SS 83, *88*
Flower basket, Wedgwood, TW *94*
Flower books (florilegia), BB 119
Flower bowls, AB *65,* BC *64*
Flowers. See Botanical prints
Fly fishing, tackle for, BC *48,* DF *152,* 153, *154-155, 157, 158*
Foch, Ferdinand, LM *55*
Fokine, Michel, *114,* 121
Folk art, AB 24, FH 6-21; butter prints, AB *28,* IL *127;* canes, BC *53;* cats, BC *128, 129;* owls, OP *49, 52, 57;* puppets, PQ *138, 139;* decoys, CD *138;* signs, RS *154-155;* valentines, TW 17, *20-21;* Victorian, TW *42, 43.* See also Carousel animals; Chalkware; Crèches; Pennsylvania Dutch; Scrimshaw; Tramp art; Weather vanes
Font, holy-water, LM *121*
Fontanne, Lynn, TT *35*
Fonteyn, Margot: poster for, CD *116;* recipe from, CD *16*
Football: bank portraying, AB *122;* game based on, FH *57;* coach, AB *148;* medal for, MN *25;* in sculpture, RS *75*
Footstools, OP *60,* RS *134*
Foot warmer, FH *156*
Forain, Jean-Louis, cartoon by, BC *105*
Ford, Henry, II, BC 87
Fords (cars): Fairlane 500 Skyliner, BC *96;* Model A, BC *82, 85, 87;* Model T, AB 106, BC *84,* DF 110; Thunderbird, BC *95;* toy, TT *108;* V-8 station wagon, BC 87
Ford tractors, DF 110
Ford Tri-motor airplane, LM *52*
Forepaugh, Adam, circus, CC 62, 64; memorabilia of, CC *67, 70*
Forks, IL *119;* child's, MN *158;* in pocketknife, IL *139;* silver-plated, SS *49,* TW *130*
Fortune magazine, fake cigar

band from, CC *47*
Fortunetelling devices: dial, BB *160;* fan DF *101;* machines, OP *114;* tarot cards, PQ *49*
Fouquet, Georges, jewelry by, IL *91, 93, 94*
Fox, Henry, caricature of, BC *101*
Foxes: on ale can, BB *30;* in children's book, CC *10;* hatpin head, FH *114;* hunting, books about, BB *104,* 106; musical coat hook, MN *71;* stirrup cup, TW *86*
Fox Talbot, William Henry, BC 21
Fractures, FH 8, *13*
France (ship), on medal, OP *31*
Francis, Anne, RS *110*
Francis, Field & Francis, Philadelphia, Pa., TT 86
Franklin, Benjamin, AB 30; autograph, AB *97;* book, BB *98;* eyeglass style, DF 85, *90;* on medallion, TW *82;* money printed by, OP *90;* portrayed in doorknob, OP *108;* on stamps, SS *104, 106, 107*
Franklin Insurance Co. fire mark, DF *148*
Franklins (cars), BC *83, 88*
Fraser, Claude Lovat, art by, TT *27*
Freed, Alan, RS *50;* poster, RS *51*
Freeman, James, pistols, FH *91*
Freeman & Taylor, spoons by, SS *78, 79*
Frémiet, Emmanuel, cat by, BC *134*
Frémont, John Charles, books by, LM *134*
French Carriage Company, Boston, Mass., sleigh by, FH *160*
French Society for the Manufacture of Dolls and Toys (S.F.B.J.), products of, DF 36, *52;* mark, DF *49*
Frisbie, Russel, drawings by, AB *120*
Fritchie, Barbara, autograph of, AB 90, 92, *96*
Fritsche, William, goblet by, CD *109*
Frogs, FH 22-29; on Lalique decanter, LM *14;* netsuke, MN *146;* song about, illustrated, CC *12,* TT *56;* in toy, TT *93*
Frost, A. B., cartoon by, BC *105*
Frost, Edward Sands, FH 131
Fruit bowls: Chinese porcelain, CC *22;* Tiffany, TT *50.* See also Compotes
Fruit-crate labels, FH *cover,* 30-45
Fruit jars, IL 52-61
Fuchs, Leonhart, art from book by, BB *120*
Fuller, Paul, jukeboxes by. See Wurlitzer
Fuller, S. and J., London, books

from, OP 76, 78
Fulper Pottery, Flemington, N. J.: cat, BC 130; lamp, AB 86
Fu Manchu book, CD 160
Funnies on Parade (comic books), CC 151
Furniture: dollhouse, DF 18, 19, 20, 23, 25, 28-32; eagle ornamentation, AB 26, 27; oak, OP 6-21, TW 100; painted, OP 58-73; Shaker, RS 122, 123, 124-125, 129, 131-139; tramp-art, TT 146, 148-151; Victorian, TW 34-57; wicker, TW 96-107. See also Chairs
Futuria Fantasia (magazine), RS 102

G

Gaines, William M., comic series by, CC 154, 159
Gale, William, & Son, New York, N.Y., ice tongs by, SS 52
Gallé, Emile, lamp by, LM 31
Galloway spreader, DF 124
Galsworthy, John, BB 99
Galt, M.W., Bro. & Company, spoons by, SS 79
Gambler's canes, BC 47
Games, FH 46-59; giveaways, AB 16; played with baseball cards, AB 146. See also Playing cards; Toys
Garagiola, Joe, AB 144
Garbo, Greta, LM 85; on posters, MN 54, 56
Garfield, James A., AB 89; on stamps, SS 106, 107
Garland, Judy, record album by, MN 67
Garner, John Nance, memorabilia of, PQ 72, 74
Garnet jewelry, IL 76, 88
Gas lamps, LM 29; valve adjuster, LM 23
Gas mask, TW 143
Gasoline Alley (comic strip), CC 149
Gasoline engines, DF 111; tractor driven by, DF 114-115
Gates, John Warne, AB 129, 132, 135
Gatto, Victor Joseph, painting by, FH 17
Gaudy Dutch (Staffordshire china), SS 92
Gauntlets: Civil War, CC 83; World War I, TW 140
Gems: cuts and settings, IL 84. See also individual names
General Electric: iron, IL 33; light bulb, LM 33; toasters, TT 63, 64
General Motors anniversary medal, MN 24
Gennett records, CD 32, 34, 35, IL 65
George V, King (England): souvenirs of, RS 76, 81; stamp

collection, SS 101
George VI, King (England), souvenirs of, RS 77, 84-85
Georgia Yellowhammers (recording group), CD 37
Gerard, John, lock by, LM 69
Gernsback, Hugo, magazine edited by, RS 103, 108
Gershwin, George, MN 82; on stamp, SS 112
Gertie the Dinosaur (film), memorabilia of, AB 38
Ghezzi, Pier Leone, caricatures by, BC 98, 100, 106
Gibson, Charles Dana, illustrations by, LM 80
Gibson musical instruments, MN 86, 88, 89
GI Joe (cartoon character), PQ 69
Gilbert, John, on poster, MN 56
Gilbert, W. S., memorabilia of, OP 43
Gillespie, John Birks (Dizzy), IL 75
Gillette razors, RS 143, 145
Gillray, James, caricatures by, BC 100, 102, 107
Giraffes: carousel, BC 69; toy train car for, TT 138
Girandoles, BC 37
Gish, Lillian, MN 60
Glass: actress glass, TT 18; beads, BB 6, 7, 9-11, 13, 15, 18-20; bells, BB 50; buttons, BC 6, 9, 10, 12; candleholders, BC 30, 32, 35, 39, 40; chess sets, BC 158-159; Christmas tree ornaments, CC 36, 39-43; eggs, DF 68; flute, MN 95; hatpin heads, FH 112, 113; inkwells, AB 54, IL 6, 7, 8-10, 12, 13, TT 46; jewel box, BB 156; jewelry, IL 80, 82, 90, 104; lamp shades, BB 60, BC 63, CD 110, 151, LM 16, 20, 26-32, 34, 35, TT 42, 43, 44; marbles, LM 150, 152, 153-157; needlecase, MN 126; nursing bottles, MN 151-152, 154-157, 160; owl depictions, OP 50; pharmacist's equipment, OP 148-154, 157, 158; prisms, BB 60, BC 37; sign, RS 152-153; snuff bottle, SS 69; steins, SS 126; Tiffany, LM 30, TT 40-51. See also Art glass; Bottles; Carnival glass; Cut glass; Depression glass; Fruit jars; Insulators; Lalique; Lightning-rod ornaments; Paperweights; Pressed glass
Glasses: art-glass, AB 54, 64; cut-glass, CD 101, 109, 112, 113; Depression-glass, CD 146, 150; Tiffany, TT 50, 51. See also Goblets; Tumblers
Glidden, Joseph F., barbed wires, AB 132, 133; advertisement, AB 135
Glidden Tour, BC 90

Globes, LM 125
Glove darner, MN 132
Gloves: Civil War, CC 83; cowboy, CD 69; paper love tokens, TW 23; World War I, TW 140
Glove stick, BC 45
Glove stretcher, silver, SS 56
Goat, chalkware, BC 146
Gobelin stitch, DF 74
Goblets: actress-glass, TT 18; pressed-glass, OP 50, PQ 128-129; rock crystal, CD 109; silver, SS 45
Goddard, Robert, BB 107
Goddard, Thomas, coachworks, Boston, Mass., buggies by, FH 147, 149
Godey's Lady's Book (magazine), LM 74
Godiva, Lady, silk picture of, SS 25
Goebel, W., Porzellanfabrik, Rodental, Germany, figurines by, RS 68, 69
Goethe, Johann Wolfgang von, SS 7; art from book by, CC 10
Goetz, James F., Company, Wis., LM 39
Goetz, Karl, medals by, MN 29
Gold: assaying, IL 77; chess pieces, BC 150; cigarette accessories, SS 66; coins, AB 22, CC 121, 124-126, 129, 132, 136, 137; egg charm, DF 69; eyeglass, DF 87; gun decorations, FH 90-91; hatpin heads, FH 112, 114, 116; jewelry, IL 78, 82, 83, 85, 86, 88, 89, 92, 94, 103, 104; matchsafe, MN 8; medals, MN 22, 27; on pens, OP 128, 131; on sword guards, SS 157; thimbles, MN 126, 127; watch chains, TW 58, 65; watches, DF 147, TW 64; watch fobs, MN 70, TW 65. See also Gilt
Golden Legend (book), BB 78
Golden Novelty Company, Chicago, Ill., clock by, FH 26
Goldsmith, Charles, PQ 79
Goldstein, Harry, carousel animals by, BC 68, 78-81
Goldstones (marbles), LM 152, 154-156
Golf-related items, FH 60-67; board game, FH 56; doorstop, DF 61
Golliwog, MN 158
Gone with the Wind (film): lamp style, LM 20, 28; paper dolls, OP 86; program, MN 61
Gontcharova, Natalia, drawings by, CD 120
Goodall, Charles, & Son, London, cards published by, FH 69, 71
Good Housekeeping (magazine), LM 79
Goodman, Benny, IL 65;

memorabilia of, IL 72
Goodwin & Company, baseball cards from, AB 140, 142
Goodyear, Amasa J., buttons by, BC 8, 17
Gorges, Sir Ferdinando, book by, BB 101
Gorham Manufacturing Company, BB 38; matchsafe, MN 8; spoons, SS 74, 75, 77, 78; tableware, SS 35, 43, 47
Gorilla: folk-art, FH 19; matchholder, MN 17
Gothic Revival: furniture, TW 36, 37, 38; jewelry, IL 89
Gottfredson, Floyd, CC 151
Gottlieb, D., and Company, pinball machines by, OP 117
Goudey Gum Co., Boston, Mass., baseball cards from, AB 141, 145
Gourd items: netsuke, MN 140; pipe, PQ 43
Goursat, George (Sem), illustration by, MN 32-33
Goya, Francisco de, art by, on stamp, SS 120
Goyo (Japanese artist), print by, IL 35
Grable, Betty, doll, OP 87
Graflex camera, BC 22, 26
Graf Zeppelin. See Dirigibles
Graham, Martha, poster for, CD 116
Grain grinder, DF 121
Graining, of furniture, OP 58, 62-68
Gramophone and Typewriter, records made by, OP 36, 37
Gramophone Company of Great Britain, product of, PQ 15
Graniteware, BB 59, 62
Grant, Ulysses S., AB 99, LM 146; cartoon of, BC 107; on lantern, PQ 67; menu honoring, MN 34, 36; on playing card, PQ 51; sculpture, RS 73; on stamps, SS 106, 107
Graphophones, PQ 6, 8
Grass baskets, AB 150, 151, 153, 156, 158, 159
Grasshoppers: on birthday card, FH 75; on Lalique vase, LM 10; on sword guard, SS 157
Gratacap, Henry T., fireman's helmet by, DF 143
Gravely, B. F., & Sons, tobacco box by, SS 63
Great Chicago Fire (1871), print of, CD 82-83
Greatbach, Daniel, BB 57
Great Northern Railway, menu from, MN 34
Great Raymond, The, LM 101; props, LM 94, 101
Great Seal of the United States, AB 30
Greeley, Horace, caricatures of, BC 106, 108
Green, Anna Katharine, ·

"facsimile" letter from book by, CD *154*

Green, Seth, DF 158

Greenaway, Kate, SS 36; *Almanack*, CC 8, *9*; greeting cards, FH 70, *72, 73*

Green Hornet ring, PQ *113*

Greeting cards, FH 68-81; Japanese, IL *44-45*; silk pictures on, SS *25. See also* Valentines

Greiner, Ludwig, DF 39

Greiner-Schlotfeger, Louis, CC 36

Greyhounds, depictions of, BC *51*, DF *6, 10, 15*

Griffen, Smith and Hill, Phoenixville, Pa.: employees, LM *106;* majolica, LM *104-105, 107, 110, 112, 113, 116, 117, 120, 121;* marks, LM *115*

Griffith, D. W., memorabilia of, MN *60*

Grills (gridirons), IL 116, *118*

Groh, Heinie, AB *140*

Grose, Francis, art by, BC *107*

Grosvenor, J. M., Co., Boston, Mass., product of, OP *155*

Grueby, William E., pottery by, AB *75-76;* mark, AB *84*

Guidebooks, LM, 126, *149*

Guild, Curtis, Jr., caricature of, BC *109*

Guiteau, Charles, J., AB *89*

Gum machine, OP *118*

Guns, FH 82-99; bottles shaped like, BB *132*, PQ *60;* canes, BC *42, 44-45, 49;* Civil War, CC 73, *74-75*, FH *84, 86;* cowboys, CD *62, 67;* knife combined with, IL *139*

Günthermann, S., Nuremberg, Germany, toy by, TT *93*

Gutta-percha: eyeglass frames, DF *87, 90;* golf balls, FH 62, *63;* photos enclosed in, CC *85;* thimble case, MN *127*

Gwinnett, Button, autograph, AB *101*

Gyokuzan (Japanese artist), netsuke by, MN *147*

H

Hackbarth, Otto, putter by, FH *63*

Hadrian (Roman emperor), on coins, CC *125*

Hagen, Walter, golf club endorsed by, FH *65*

Hairpins, CC *144;* boxes, BB *159*, SS *56;* tray, BC *59*

Hair-tonic bottles, BB *142*

Hale, Nathan: autograph, AB 92, *96;* on stamp, SS *107*

Haley, Bill, record by, RS *52*

Half-dolls, DF *47*

Hall, Ralph, platter by, SS *85*

Hall, Thomas, clock by, CC *91*

Hallet, Davis & Co., Boston, Mass., piano by, TW 37, *47*

Halley's comet: cut-glass motif, CD *111;* postcard commemorating, PQ *85*

Hamilton, Alexander, SS 23; fake silhouette of, SS *9*

Hamilton & Biesinger, Philadelphia, Pa., box by, SS *56*

Hamlin, Samuel, pewter by, OP 137, *140*

Hammers, TT *82;* snuff tool, SS *68;* scrimshaw, RS *116*

Hammerstein, Oscar, OP 40

Hammett, Dashiell, books by, CD 155, *158*

Hammond, John, record by, CD *34*

Hammond, Turner & Sons, Birmingham, England, button by, BC *17*

Hammond typewriter, TW *12*

Hancock, John, AB *97;* autograph, AB 97

Hancock, Winfield, cartoon of, BC *105*

Handbags, AB *153*, FH 100-109

Handcar, model of, RS *24*

Hand coolers, DF *69*, MN *124*

Handcuffs, PQ *61*

Handel Company, Inc., Meriden, Conn., lamps by, LM 21, *32*

Hand puppets, PQ 135, *136-138*

Harding, Warren G.: campaign beanie, PQ *74;* on stamp, SS *107*

Hardy Boys books, CC 8

Harlequin and Columbine, bank portraying, AB *118*, 121

Harlequin ware, DF *134*

Harlow, Jean, MN 55, *56, 58*

Harmoniums, MN *84, 91*

Harold Lloyd glasses, DF *86*

Harper's (magazine), poster for, PQ *98*

Harper's Bazar (magazine), LM *86*

Harper's Weekly (magazine), LM *74;* art for, AB *99*, BB *83*, BC *98, 99, 104, 105,* 106, LM *74*

Harrison, Benjamin, PQ *cover*

Harrison, Rex, props used by, MN *62*

Harrison, Richard Edes, map by, LM *147*

Harrison, William Henry, BB *141;* autographs, AB *89-90, 95;* memorabilia, PQ 64, 66, *125;* print of, CD *91*

Harunobu (Japanese artist), prints by, IL *38*

Hassan cigarettes, SS *65;* cards from, AB *143*, SS *65*

Hastings, Fourth Marquess of, caricature of, BC *108*

Hasui (Japanese artist), print by, IL *51*

Hatpins, FH 110-117; holders, BC *58*, FH *114, 115*, OP *50*

Hats, FH 118-129; bush hat, TW *142;* cowboy, CD *63, 70;* French, buttons depicting, BC *9;* lace ties, IL *156;* movie-costume, MN *62;* political, PQ 66, *74, 75;* Presley, Elvis, memento, RS *55;* railroader's, RS *26;* stovepipe, DF *143*, FH *122. See also* Caps; Helmets

Hausser, O. & K., Neustadt, Germany, model soldiers by, MN 42, *53*

Hawkes, T. G., & Company, Corning, N.Y., cut glass by, CD *103;* marks, CD *103*

Hawthorne, Nathaniel, books by, BB *111;* art from, CC *15*

Hayes, Rutherford B.: cartoon of, BC *107;* on stamp, SS *107*

Hay knife, DF *116*

Hazan, Marcella, book by, CD *11*

Headdress, theatrical, TT *32*

Headlights, old-car, AB 102, *105*

Hearn, Lafcadio, book by, CD *13*

Hearses: horse-drawn, FH *158-159;* ornament for, FH *14*

Heart molds, IL *128*, OP *147*

Hearty Good Fellow Toby jug, SS *95*

Heath, William, art by, BC *103*

Hebrard, A. A., Foundry, France, cat by, BC *135*

Heeley, Desmond, art by, TT *16*

Heinlein, Robert, book by, RS *104*

Heinz, H. J., Company, advertising spoon from, SS *76*

Heisey, A. H., Company, Ohio, pressed glass by, PQ *133*

Heishi necklace, IL *100*

Heisler, John, decoy by, CD *130*

Helck, Peter, AB 110

Held, Anna, PQ *94*

Held, John, Jr., art by, TT *23*

Helen of Troy, on plate, LM *108*

Heller, J. H., music box by, MN *78-79*

Helmets: firemen's, DF *143;* movie-costume, MN *63;* policemen's, PQ *54, 60;* World War memorabilia, TW *140, 142*

Hemingray Glass Co., Covington, Ky., insulators by, IL 18, *19, 21, 22*

Hemingway, Ernest, CC 47, LM *75;* books by, BB 95, 105, *116, 117*

Hemming bird, MN *133*

Hempfield Railroad coverlet, CD 48, *57*

Henderson, Fletcher, IL *65;* record label, IL *72*

Hendrix, Jimi, poster, RS *62*

Henkels, George J., company, Philadelphia, Pa., furniture by, TW *48-51*

Henry, Tal, recording group, CD *37*

Henry VII, King (England), on coin, CC *129*

Henshall, Samuel, corkscrew invented by, CD *20,* 22

Henshall, Williams and

Company, Staffordshire, England, pitcher by, SS *87*

Henson, Josiah, autograph of, AB *96*

Hepburn, Audrey, costume used by, MN *62*

Hepburn, Katharine, LM *85*

Heppenheimer & Maurer, New York, N.Y., trade card by, TT *114-115*

Heralds (fliers): circus, CC *62, 70;* movie, MN *60*

Herbert, Henry William, BB 106

Herbert, Victor, opera score by, OP *42*

Herring Co., New York, N.Y., lock by, LM *70*

Herschell-Spillman Company, North Tonawanda, N.Y., carousel animals by, BC 68, *76*

Herwin record label, CD *35*

Herzog, Arthur, Jr., music by, IL *72*

Hess, Richard, art by, PQ *107*

Hetling, Francis (hoax), PQ *20*

Heyde, Georg, model soldiers by, MN 42, *47*

Heywood Brothers and Wakefield Company, wicker by, TW 96, *97, 100*

Hiatt Company, England, handcuffs by, PQ *61*

Hibbard, George, caricature of, BC *109*

Hicks, Andrew, IL *135*

Hicks, Edward, art by, FH *10-11*

Hideyoshi (Japanese artist), netsuke by, MN *136, 137*

High chairs, OP *12;* plate for, MN *159*

Highnight, Luke, record by, CD *33*

Hildesheimer, S., & Co., London, England, card by, FH *76*

Hill, Rowland, SS *99*

Hill, William. See Griffen, Smith and Hill

Hiller, Elizabeth O., book by, CD *18*

Hilpert, Johann Gottfried, MN *42*

Hindu items: bell, BB *54;* magic tricks, LM *90, 92*

Hinton, John, art from book by, BB *99*

Hippopotamuses: circus advertisement, CC *67;* postcard, PQ *83*

Hires root beer, advertising giveaways for, AB *9, 17*

Hiroshige (Japanese artist): prints by, IL 36, *48-49;* wife of, IL 36

Hirsch, Max, OP *34*

Hirschfeld, Al, art by, BC *110-111*, TT *21*

Historical Blue (Staffordshire china), SS *82, 83, 84-88*

Hitchcock, Edward, map by, LM *140*

Hitchcock, Lambert, chair style, OP 58, 60, 66

Hitchcock, Robert, lamp invented by, LM 20, 25

Hitchcock, W. H., print by, TW 116

Hitler, Adolf, on matchbook, MN 13

Hit of the Week record label, IL 73

Hoare, J., & Company, Corning, N.Y., CD 107; marks, CD 103

Hobbles, for horses, CD 66

Hobbs, Brockunier & Company, Wheeling, W. Va., glassware by, AB 58, 68

Hoboken school, MN 105; paintings by, MN 104, 105

Hoes: Aztec, miniature, CC 128; blade, DF 117

Hoffmann, Professor (Angelo Lewis), book by, LM 102

Hoffritz cutlery company, knife made for, IL 132-133

Hogan's Alley (comic strip), CC 149, 150

Hogarth, William, BC 100; engraving by, BC 102

Hokusai (Japanese artist), prints by, IL 34, 50-51

Holbein, Hans, the Younger, imitation of jewelry by, IL 88

Holbrook, John Edwards, art from book by, TW 119

Holden, Queen, OP 75

Holiday, Billie: autograph, AB 101; memorabilia, IL 72

Holland-American Line poster, OP 29

Holly, Buddy, record by, RS 52

Holmes, Benjamin, CD 131

Holmes, Sherlock, CD 152, 156, 157; pipe style, PQ 43

Holsters, cowboy, CD 60, 62, 67

Home New York Insurance Co. fire mark, DF 148

Homer, Winslow, art by, LM 74

Homer Laughlin China Company, Newell, W. Va. See Fiesta ware

Honey Brook Pottery, Pa., RS 46

Honeywell, Martha Anne, silhouettes by, SS 9, 14

Hood, C. I., Company, Lowell, Mass., calendars from, AB 6, 7

Hood, Phineas, iron by, IL 28

Hooked rugs, FH 130-143

Hooks, fishing, DF 152, 158

Hoop toy, TT 92

Hoover, Herbert, PQ cover

Hoover vacuum cleaner, prototype of, TT 68

Hopi: blankets, MN 118-119; jewelry, IL 99; kachina dolls, DF 36, OP 48

Hornet (ship), trade card, TT 110

Horns, old-car, AB 102, 105

Horoscopes, on beer cans, BB 33

Horse-drawn carriages, FH 144-

160; Currier & Ives print, CD 96; TT 113; toy, TT 101

Horse racing: bank, AB 121, 123; beer-can series, BB 33; Currier & Ives prints, CD 83, 84; ivory carvings, BC 50; periodicals, BB 106

Horses: bells for, BB 46, 52, 53; carousel, BC 66-68, 74, 76-81; on corkscrew, CD 26; Currier & Ives prints, CD 88, 89, 94-96, TT 113; on inro, MN 144; on pipe, PQ 36; plaster sculpture, RS 71; police, depictions of, PQ 62, 63; puppet, PQ 144; toys, PQ 63, TT 84-85, 100, 101; weather vanes, TW 72, 73

Horsley, John Calcott, greeting card by, FH 69, 70

Horst, H. P., photo by, LM 87

Houdini, Harry, LM 90, 92, 93, 97, 98-99; posters for, LM 98, 99

Hounds and Hunting through the Ages (book), BB 104

Houses: Christmas tree ornaments, CC 35, 38, 40; stein, SS 132. See also Dollhouses; Log cabins

Howard, J., Company, East Bridgewater, Mass., weather vanes by, TW 68, 70-71, 76

Howard the Duck (comic character), CC 158

Howdy Doody puppet, PQ 145

Howland, Esther, TW 17-18

Hubcaps, AB 103, 105-106

Hubley Manufacturing Company, Lancaster, Pa.: bank, AB 127; toy, TT 106

Hudson (car), BC 92

Hudson, Rock, paper doll, OP 86

Hudson River School, art of, TW 116-117

Hughes, Charles Evans, PQ 69

Hughes, Howard, car owned by, BC 92

Hughes-Stanton, Blair, woodcut by, BB 113

Hull, Charles, corkscrew invented by, CD 22, 23

Humidors, SS 60; in cane, BC 50; carnival-glass, BC 62; in radio, RS 18

Hummel figurines, RS 68, 69

Humphrey, Doris, CD 124

Humphreys' Homeopathic Medicine Company, cabinet from, OP 158

Hunneman, William C., fire pumps, DF 141; on buckle, DF 147

Hunter, Alberta, label from record by, IL 66

Hunting, Robert, lithograph of, CC 71

Huntley Boorne and Stevens tea caddy, TT 56

Hunzinger, George, Co., New York, chairs by, TW 37, 53

Hurd, Earl, AB 39

Huxley, Aldous, book by, RS 101, 104

I

IBM, gun by, FH 96-97

Icebox, oak, OP 9

Ice tongs, silver, SS 52

Ideal Cash Register Company, product of, BC 124

Ideal Novelty and Toy Co., dolls by, CC 153, DF 54

Ile de France (ship), magazine from, OP 28

Illingworth, Leslie, cartoons by, BC 104, 112

Illions, Marcus Charles, carousel animals by, BC 68, 77

Illuminated manuscripts, BB 74, 75

Ilsley, S. A. & Co., Brooklyn, N.Y., tobacco tin by, SS 62

Impalas (rock group), record by, RS 57

Imperial Glass Company, Bellaire, Ohio, BC 55, 57

Implement seats, DF 120

Incense holder, BC 130

Index of American Design, AB 24

Indian Head cent, CC 136

Indians, American: baskets, AB 150, 151, 153, 156, 157-159, 160; beads and beadwork, BB 7, 9, 16, 17, 19, DF 70; Bibles, BB 69; crèche, CD 72-73; decoy, CD 130; jewelry, IL 99-101; kachina dolls, DF 36, OP 48; peace medals for, MN 20, 29; pipes, PQ 36, 40; pottery, OP 48, RS 42, 43; tobacco use, SS 60; wampum, CC 128. See also Arrowheads; Navajo blankets; individual tribes

Indians, American, portrayals of: bottle, BB 140; Catlin plate, BB 103; chess set, BC 156; Christmas tree ornament, CC 41; cigar band, CC 50; cigarette package, SS 65; coins, CC 136-138; currency, OP cover, 94; doorstop, DF 56; fruit-crate label, FH 44; hatpins, FH 114; insignia, TW 138; postcard, PQ 85; radiator cap, AB 104; spoons, SS cover, 80; stamps, SS 107, 110; ticket, TW 124; trays, AB 11, 13; weather vane, TW 71

Ingersoll, Robert H., watch by, TW 61

Ingraham, Elias, clock design by, CC 92

Inhalers, OP 157; lamp, LM 27

Ink bottles, BB 133, 143

Inkwells, AB 54, IL 6-15, TT 46

Inros, MN 137, 144

Insulators, IL 16-23

Insurance companies, fire marks of, DF 148

International Harvester Company: medal, MN 22, 24; tractor, DF 114-115

International Mutoscope Company, coin machines by, OP 114, 119

International Silver Company, flatware by, SS 49, 50

Iowa Fox bag, MN 117

Irish, portrayals of, AB 121, 125, BC 105

Iron Cross, Prussian (medal), MN 30

Irons, IL 24-33, TT 63; curling iron, TT 68; trivets for, TT 153, 154, 155

Irons (golf clubs), FH 61, 62, 64, 65

Iroquois: egg, DF 70; sash, MN 117

Irving, Washington, art from book by, BB 111

Isotta-Fraschini (car), AB 107

Ives, James M., CD 85. See also Currier, Nathaniel

Ives, W. & S. B., Company, Salem, Mass., games by, FH 47, 48, 49

Ives Corp., Bridgeport, Conn., toys by, TT 86, 87, 88, 98, 100, 101, 124, 127, 129

Ivory: baton handle, PQ 54; buttons, BC 6, 9, 10; cane handles, BC 49-51; chess sets, BC 150, 152-154, 156, 157; chick in egg, DF 71; combs, CC 140, 144; etui, MN 135; fans, DF 97, 104, 106, 107; flute, MN 95; gun grip, FH 95; hatpin, FH 116; jewelry, IL 81, 94, 97, 98, 103; netsukes, FH 25, MN 136-138, 141-143, 145-147, 149; ojime, BB 14; on plane (tool), TT 79; razor handle, OP 55; sewing tools, CC 26, MN 126-128, 134, RS 120, 121; snuff tools, SS 68; sword hilt, SS 154; vegetable ivory, CC 144, MN 127. See also Scrimshaw

J

Jack, wagon, FH 156

Jack Armstrong premiums, PQ 113, 116

Jackets: Civil War uniform, CC 82; "Pierrot," CC 107; riding, CC 112

Jackie Coogan peanuts, advertising for, AB 17

Jack-in-the-box, TT cover

Jack-in-the-pulpit vases, CD 110, TT 49

Jackson, Andrew, FH 84; on stamps, SS 105, 106

Jackson, Stonewall, PQ 23

Jackson Napa soda, giveaways for, CD 25

Jacobsen, Antonio, paintings by, MN 104, 105

Jacquard loom, CD *49;* coverlets made on, CD *44,* 45-46, 47, 48, *50-59;* inventor, silk portrait of, SS *27. See also* Silk: pictures

Jacques, J., factory, chess sets by, BC 148, *149,* 150

Jade: Chinese, DF *69,* IL 102, *103, 104,* SS *69;* eggs, DF *69;* sphere, LM *160*

Jaguars (cars), BC 86; toy, TT *108*

Jaillot, Alexis Hubert, map published by, LM *128-129*

Japanned ware, OP 156. *See also* Tinware

Jarrett, Guy, LM 93

Jars, IL 52-61; art-glass, AB *59;* beater in, IL *122;* cut-glass, SS *56;* drug, OP *151;* Indian, RS *42, 43;* Lalique, LM *9;* redware, RS *34, 37;* Staffordshire lid, SS *89;* stoneware, SS *145;* tobacco, BC *62,* SS *60;* Wedgwood, TW *88*

Jarvis, Deming, PQ 122

Jasper ware, Wedgwood, BC 9, TW 84, 86, *88,* 89

Jazz, IL 108; memorabilia, IL 62-75

Jeannette Glass Company, Jeannette, Pa., wares by, CD *142*

Jeep (vehicle), TW *134-135*

Jefferson, Blind Lemon, label from record by, CD *30*

Jefferson, Joseph, PQ *23;* sculpture of, RS *74*

Jefferson, Thomas, AB 30; autograph, AB *92;* on stamp, SS *107*

Jeffries, James J., PQ *50*

Jelliff, John, TW 46

Jenner, Hans, Sr., decoys by, CD *134*

Jensen, Georg, FH 111

Jerome, Chauncey, clocks by, CC 90, *98*

Jewel boxes, BB *156, 157;* as dollhouse cupboard, DF *28;* egg-shaped, DF *68;* in foot warmer, FH *156;* tramp-art, TT *145*

Jewelry, AB 22, *108,* DF *69,* IL 76-105; beads for, BB 6-21; watches as, TW *66;* Wedgwood, TW *88. See also* Buttons; Combs; Hatpins; Netsuke

Jigsaw puzzles, LM *51,* RS *86*

Jig saws, in catalogue, TT *76*

Jiminy Cricket (cartoon character), AB *36*

Johnson, Andrew, impeachment resolution of, AB *88*

Johnson, Earl, and brothers, CD *33*

Johnson, James P., IL *64*

Johnson, Lyndon, buttons for, PQ *67, 69*

Johnson, Samuel, SS 69

Johnson, Thomas, LM 21

Jolivet, Pierre Jules, fan by, DF *96*

Jonah (Biblical character): bank portraying, AB *118,* 121; on medal, MN 26

Jones, Gershom, porringer by, OP *142*

Jones, Robert Meredith, TT 142

Jones, S. L., art by, FH *20*

Joplin, Scott, music by, IL *64*

Joyant, Maurice, book by, CD 7

Joyce, James, book by, BB 112, *113,* LM *75;* set design for dramatization of, TT *29*

Judge (magazine), BC 106, 110

Judge's Library (magazine), BC 105

Jugates, political, PQ 66, 68, 69, *72,* 74

Jug bands: record label, CD *40;* song list, CD *31*

Jugs: Chinese porcelain, CC *25;* cut-glass, CD *103;* Homer Laughlin pottery, DF *134, 135;* milk jug, SS *92;* redware, RS *39, 44-45;* royal souvenir, RS *79;* stoneware, SS *136-139, 142;* Toby jugs, SS 83, 85, *94, 95*

Jukeboxes, IL 106-115

Jumeau, Pierre François, dolls by, DF 34, 36, *50;* mark, DF *49*

Jung, Moriz, postcard by, PQ *86*

Jurgensen, Jules, watch by, TW *64*

K

Kachina dolls, DF *36,* OP *48*

Kämmer & Reinhardt, Waltershausen, Germany, doll bodies by, DF *35;* mark, DF *49*

Kander, Mrs. Simon, CD 8

Karsavina, Tamara, memorabilia of, CD *120, 121*

Katana sword, SS *156-157*

Katzenjammer Kid (comic character), CC *150*

Kaufman, George S., autograph of, TT *39*

Kay, John, art by, BC 100, *101*

Keaton, Buster, poster, PQ *109*

Kellar, Harry, shaving mug of, RS 140, *151*

Kellie, Edward (One-Arm), decoys by, CD *135*

Kellogg cereals, paper doll from, OP *81*

Kelly, Grace, paper doll, OP *86*

Kelly, Michael, AB 132

Kelly, Mike, AB *140*

Kelly, Walt, comic characters by, CC 148, *156*

Kelmscott Press, books published by, BB 78, 112

Kemble, Fanny, print of, TT *25*

Kendall, Marie, photo by, PQ *26*

Kennedy, John F., AB 101, RS 112; memorabilia, PQ 69, 75

Kennedy, Mrs. John F., PQ 123

Kenny, C. D., Coffee Company, giveaway from, CD 25

Kent, Rockwell, illustrations by, BB 97, *112*

Kenton Hardware Co., Kenton, Ohio, toy by, TT *101*

Kentucky Mountaineers (recording group), CD 28

Keppler, Joseph, art by, BC *107*

Kerr, William B., & Co., Newark, N.J.: buckle, IL *91;* perfume bottle, SS *56*

Kestner family, dolls by, DF 34, *35,* 36, *48;* mark, DF *49*

Ketoh, IL *101*

Kettles, IL *cover;* inkwell shaped like, IL *11;* milk, IL *117*

Kewpies, CC *151,* DF 39, *54*

Keys, LM 58-71; railroad, RS *24*

Keystone Manufacturing Co., toy by, TT *103*

Khosru II, King (Sassanian dynasty), on coin, CC *127*

Kickapoo Oil, OP 151, *158*

Kimball, C. B., FH 147

Kimball, Ward, railroad owned by, RS 30-31

Kincaid, Bradley, CD 32

King, Billie Jean, bank portraying, AB *124*

King, C. Daly, CD 152

King, Clyde, scrimshaw by, RS *115*

King James Bibles, BB *77;* modern, BB 68, 71

King Kong poster, MN 57

Kingsbury Manufacturing Co., Keene, N.H., toy by, TT *102*

Kinnear, Delamar, lamp designed by, LM 19, *24*

Kipling, Rudyard: book by, CC *18;* cigars, CC 49

Kirchner, Raphael, postcard by, PQ *87*

Kirk, Samuel, pitcher by, SS *46*

Kirkpatrick, W. Wallace and Cornwall, stoneware by, SS *142, 143*

Kirmse, Marguerite, DF 6, 8; etching by, DF *10*

Kissinger, Henry, caricature of, BC *113*

Kitchen equipment, IL *cover,* 116-131. *See also* Jars; Toasters; names of other individual pieces

Kitchen Kraft jug, DF *135*

Kite, TT *86*

Kleukens, Friedrich, poster by, PQ *99*

Knapsack, United States Army, CC *80*

Knight, Laura, mugs by, RS *83*

Knights, models of, MN *43*

Knights Templar, sword of, SS 155

Knitting needles, RS *121*

Knives, CD 25, IL 132-143; chamfer knife, TT *81;* Chinese, miniature, CC *128;*

chopping, IL *124;* Indian, AB 46, 48, *52;* ink knife, IL *13;* silver, MN *158,* SS 48, *49,* 50

Knockers, LM *66,* 67

Knowles, Taylor & Knowles Co., East Liverpool, Ohio, china by, BB 36, *41;* mark, BB *44*

Kodak cameras, BC 22, 23, 28

Koh-i-noor diamond, IL 85

Kolomoku, Walter, recording group, CD 37

Kookaburras: on carnival glass, BC *61;* stamp, SS 120

Kuchenreuter family, FH 90

Kuethe, William, tumbler designed by, BC 58

Kuniyoshi (Japanese artist), prints by, IL 36, *42-47*

Kuttner, Henry, art for story by, RS *106*

L

Labels: cigar, CC 46-59; food containers, FH 38; fruit-crate, FH 30-45; seed, RS *131;* silver-plated, for bottles, SS *45;* tea facing, CC *27;* tobacco, *63, 64*

La Branche, George, book by, BB 106

Lace, IL 144-160; on fan, DF *104;* on hat, FH *122;* paper, on greeting cards, FH *71;* on valentines, TW 24, 25, 29, 32

Lacy pressed glass, AB 26, 27, BC 10, PQ 121, *122-126,* 129

Lada, Josef, art by, stamp from, SS *121*

Ladies' Home Journal (magazine), art from, LM *78, 82*

Ladles, pewter, OP *141*

Lafayette, Marquis de, BC 30; on bottle, BB *134;* check awarded to, AB 90, *94;* on jar, IL *57;* stamp honoring, LM *56*

Lafayette Brewery, Lafayette, Ind., beer can from, BB *30*

LaFrance, Mitchell, decoy by, CD *136*

La Fresnaye, Roger de, painting by, on stamp, SS *119*

La Guardia, Fiorello, OP 112

Laing, Albert, CD 131

LaJoie, Napoleon, AB *143*

Lalique, René: glass, AB 107, BB *50,* BC 10, *136,* LM *cover,* 6-17, TW 127; hatpins, FH 111; jewelry, IL *94;* medal, TW *149*

Lamb, Dana S., book by, BB 106

Lambert, Frank, typewriter, TW *14*

Lambert pharmaceutical company, shaving mugs from, RS *143*

Lambs: chalkware, BC *147;* Paschal, on egg, DF *69;* toy, TT *91*

Lamotte, Bernard, art by, MN 38

Lamps, LM 18-35; Belleek, BB *45;* in canes, BC 48; carnival-glass, BC 63; carriage, FH *156;*

cars, early, AB 102, *105;* cat, BC *132;* cut-glass, CD *110;* Depression-glass, CD *151;* fire-engine, DF *145;* Lalique, LM *16;* nautical, MN *98, 101, 108;* pottery, AB *86,* BB *60;* railroad, RS 23, *25, 27;* Tiffany, LM 21, *30,* TT *42, 43, 44;* tramp-art, TT *149;* wicker, TW *99*

Lancaster, U.S.S., figurehead from, AB 24, 26

Lanceheads, AB *43, 48*

Landon, Alf, on necktie, PQ *74*

Landsberger, Julius, IL 52

Landseer, Sir Edwin, DF 6

Lane, John, DF 110

Lane, Theodore, print from art by, TT *24-25*

Lang, Andrew, books by, CC *14*

Lang, George, book by, CD *8, 11*

Lanterns: candle, BC *39;* conductor's, RS 23, *27;* paper, PQ *67;* ships', MN *98, 108*

Lantern-slide projector, PQ *22*

Lapel pins: advertising giveaways, AB *15;* car salesmen's, AB *108, 114-115;* world's fair souvenirs, TW *124, 131*

Lapel watch, TW *66*

Lapis lazuli: beads, BB *9;* hatpin head, FH *117;* pendant, IL *103*

Lappets, lace, IL *156*

Lap robe, PQ *157*

Lariat, CD 66

LaRocca, Nick, IL *63*

Lash's root beer, mug advertising, AB *17*

La Tourette, Sarah, coverlet woven by, CD *54*

Latta, Alexander, DF 141

Latticinio glass, AB *64,* LM *153*

Laughlin, Homer, China Company, Newell, W. Va. *See* Fiesta ware

Laurel, Stan, and Oliver Hardy, OP *28*

Laurençin, Marie, art by, CD *121*

Laurent, Claude, flute by, MN *95*

Lauscha Christmas tree ornaments, CC 36, *39-41*

Lavater, Johann Kaspar, SS 7, 11; machine by, SS *11*

Leaded glass, Tiffany, TT *40-43*

Lear, Edward, work of, CC *13*

Le Campion, Valentin, bookplate by, BB *96*

LeClercq, Tanaquil, book by, CD *16*

Lee, Ann, RS 124, 125

Lee, Robert E., AB *99;* autograph, AB *98;* on coin, CC *138*

Lee Arms Red Jacket gun, FH *95*

Leeds, Albert and Lodowick, iron patented by, IL 27

Legion of Honor, French (medal), MN *30*

Lehar, Franz, score by, OP *42*

Lehmann, Lilli, label from record by, OP 37

Leica cameras, BC 18, 22-23, *24*

Leisy Brewing Company, Peoria, Ill., mugs from, SS *128*

Lenci doll, DF *41*

Lenox, Inc., Trenton, N.J., Belleek by, BB 36, *42, 43;* marks, BB *44*

Leonard, Hiram, company, fishing rods by, DF 154

Le Page's glue, trade card for, TT *118*

Leslie, Eliza, book by, CD *9*

Lessore, Emile, TW *86*

Letter openers: giveaways, AB *15;* silver, SS *57;* trench art, TW *148*

Letter-writing cases, BB *153*

Levers-machine lace, IL *158*

Leviathan (ship), memorabilia of, OP *24, 28, 31*

Levine, David, caricatures by, BC *111, 113*

Levi Strauss & Co. trade card, TT *117*

Lewis, Angelo, book by, LM *102*

Lewis, McKee & Co., LM 59

Lewis, Meriwether, and William Clark, book by, BB *102*

Lewis, Sinclair, books by, BB 96, *115*

Lewis, Ted, record by, IL *70*

Leyendecker, J. C., art by, AB *109, 111,* LM *72, 82*

Lib (caricaturist), art by, FH *60*

Libbey Glass Company, Toledo, Ohio, TW *123;* cut glass, CD *102;* marks, CD *103*

Liberty & Co., London, England, button by, BC *17*

Liberty china, TW 86, *94*

Librettos, OP *40*

License plates, AB *106, 109;* attachment, political, PQ *72*

Liebig's extract of beef, trade cards for, OP *47,* TT *119*

Life (humor magazine), BC 110, FH *66,* LM *84*

Life (magazine), LM 75, *88*

Life preserver, ship's, OP *32*

Liggett drugstores, medicine spoon from, OP *157*

Light, Edward, lyre-guitar by, MN *85*

Light bulbs, LM *33;* Christmas tree ornaments, CC *38*

Lighters, cigarette, OP *130,* SS *70, 71*

Lightning (Colt gun), FH *93*

Lightning rods, LM *36-45;* weather vanes, TW 68, *77*

Lights. *See* Lamps

Li'l Abner (comic character), toy based on, CC *152*

Limberjack, PQ *139*

Limited Editions Club, The, book from, BB 112, *113*

Limoges eggs, DF *64-65*

Limousine, toy, TT *104-105*

Lincoln, Abraham, AB *100;* autographs, AB 92, 94, *100;* on currency, CC 117, OP *88, 89;* on knife, IL *142;* medal from administration, MN 20, *29;* memorabilia, AB 92-93, PQ *67;* mystery story by, CD *152;* playbill mentioning, TT 17, *19;* sculpture of, RS *73;* on stamps, SS *106, 107*

Lincoln, Mary Todd, PQ *23*

Lincoln Head cents, CC 117

Lincolns (cars): Continental, AB *105;* Sport Phaeton, BC 85-86, *90*

Lind, Jenny, PQ *20;* buggy named for, FH *150;* on flask, BB *135;* trivet, TT *158*

Lindbergh, Charles, CD *35;* memorabilia, CC *53,* LM *46-57*

Linnaeus, Carolus, BB 119

Lionel Corporation: founder, TT *126;* toy trains, TT 124, *125, 128, 129, 130-139*

Lions: bank, AB *126;* Bennington pottery, BB *66;* carousels, BC *71-73;* on coin, CC *121;* on currency, OP *93;* door knocker, LM *66;* furniture ornaments, OP *14, 15;* on insignia, TW *138;* Japanese ornament, IL *102;* silver finial, SS *37;* on stein, SS *125;* on stoneware, SS *144;* on sword hilt, SS *154;* tobacco tag, SS *64*

Lippincott's (magazine), poster for, PQ *98*

Litchfield Manufacturing Company, Conn., candlestand by, OP *68*

Lithography, use of, BC 100, 106, 110; cigar labels, CC *58*

Little Fanny doll, OP 76, *78*

Little Minxes, The (book), art from, CC *11*

Little Nemo (animated-film character), AB 39

Little Orphan Annie (comic character), CC *150, 151;* Christmas tree light, CC *38;* on marble, LM *157;* radio premiums, PQ *113, 118*

Little Red Riding Hood: bank, AB *119;* button, BC *13;* doorstop, DF *62;* fruit-crate label, FH *34*

Little Review, The (magazine), LM *75*

Little Richard, record by, RS *56-57*

Lloyd, Harold: bank portraying, AB *126;* eyeglass style, DF *86*

Loar, Lloyd, MN 86

Lobmeyr, J. & L., Vienna, Austria, platter by, CD *108*

Locke, Joseph, AB 57, 68

Locke and Company, New York, N.Y., car by, BC 85-96, *90*

Lockheed airplanes, LM *52, 53*

Locks and keys, LM *58-71;* railroads, RS 23, *24*

Locomobiles (cars): hubcap, AB *103;* Type E Tonneau, BC *84*

Log, ship's (instrument), MN *103*

Log Cabin quilts, PQ *154;* hooked rug copying, FH *137*

Log cabins: bottles shaped like, BB *141;* on button, PQ *66;* on cup plate, PQ *125;* dollhouse, DF *19;* on spoon, SS *76*

Lomasney, Martin, caricature of, BC *109*

London, Jack, book by, BB *115*

Lonely Eagles (recording group), record by, CD *36*

Lone Ranger premiums, PQ *112, 113*

Lonesome Ace record label, CD *35*

Long, "Germany," AB *140*

Longacre, James B., coins designed by, CC *136*

Longfellow, Henry Wadsworth: books by, BB 99, *111;* on cigar label, CC *50;* poetry on hatpin holder, FH *114*

Looff, Charles, carousel animals by, BC 68, *78*

Looms: Navajo, MN *112. See also* Jacquard loom

Lorgnettes, DF 85, *88, 89*

Lorraine-Dietrich (car), illustration of, AB *111*

Lost-wax process: glassmaking, LM *6;* medal making, MN *19*

Lotus Ware, BB 36, *41*

Louwelsa pottery, AB 73

Lovebirds, chalkware, BC *144*

Lovecraft, H. P., book by, RS *105*

Love spoon, SS *74*

Love tokens, TW 22, *23*

Loving cups: cut-glass, CD *102;* royal souvenir, RS *86;* silver-and-staghorn, AB *114*

Low, Daniel, & Co., Salem, Mass., spoons by, SS 75, *77*

Low, David, art by, BC 110, *112*

Loy, Myrna, on magazine, MN *66*

Lucotte company, Paris, France, products of, MN 42, *46-47*

Luna balloon (toy), TT *96*

Lunceford, Jimmie, IL *69*

Lunch boxes: model of, BB *145;* tinware, TT 55

Lund, William, corkscrew invented by, CD 20, 22

Lunt, Alfred, TT 35

Lusterware (Staffordshire china), SS *93*

Lutz, Nicholas, marbles named for, LM 152, *155*

Lyle, Rudy, CD *42*

Lyly, John, book by, BB *93*

Lyman, Fenton & Co., Bennington, Vt., BB 57, 63

Lynch, Lawrence L., book by, CD *155*

Lyon, Kathy, bronze by, DF *15*

Lyrebird, on fan, DF *106*

AB *Advertising Giveaways to Baskets;* BB *Beads to Boxes;* BC *Buttons to Chess Sets;* CC *Children's Books to Comics;* CD *Cookbooks to Detective Fiction;* DF *Dogs to Fishing Tackle;* FH *Folk Art to Horse-drawn Carriages;* IL *Inkwells to Lace;*

M

MacArthur, Douglas, PQ 43
Macbeth-Evans Glass Company, Charleroi, Pa., product of, CD 147
McBirney & Co., Belleek, Northern Ireland, products of, BB 36-37; marks, BB 36, 44
McCall's Magazine, LM 78
McCay, Winsor, AB 38, 39
McClellan, George: on coin, CD 138; print of, CD 91
McClure's Magazine, LM 75, 81
McCormack, John, OP 37
McCormick, Robert and Cyrus, DF 110
McCormick company equipment, DF 110, 112, 113, 122, 125; on medal, MN 24; toy, TT 102
MacDonald, Jeanette, MN 65
MacDonald, Pirie, photo by, PQ 25
McFaddin, H. G., Co., New York, N.Y., lamps by, LM 20, 34
McGraw, John, AB 140
McKearin, George S., collection, jug from, RS 45; label, RS 44
McKinley, William, TW 125; memorabilia, PQ 64, 68, 74; on stamp, SS 107
McLaughlin's coffee, paper doll from, OP 81
McLoughlin Brothers, New York, N.Y.: book, CC 6; dollhouse, DF 18; games, FH 46, 47-48, 50-51, 55, 56, 59; model soldiers, MN 43, 52; paper doll, OP 79
McPharlin, Paul, puppet by, PQ 144
MacWhirter, J. A., painting by, stamp from, SS 110
Madison, James: autograph, AB 92; on stamp, SS 106
Magazines, LM 72-89; automobilia, AB 109-110, 111, 112, 114; botanical, print from, BB 127; carriage-industry, FH 147; cartoons and caricatures, BC 99, 100, 104, 105, 106, 108, 110, 112, LM 85, OP 84; cigar band from, CC 47, 49; Civil War art for, AB 99, LM 74; detective fiction, CD 155, 158; golf, FH 66; jazz, IL 62, 75; movie, MN 55, 58, 66; paper dolls, OP 84, 85; photography, LM 75, 85, 87, 88, PQ 25; posters for, PQ 97, 98; rock and roll, RS 53, 54, 60; science fiction, RS 100, 101, 102, 103, 107-110; ship's, OP 28
Magicians, LM 90-103; canes, BC 47; sculpture of, RS 66; shaving mug, RS 140, 151
Magnifying glass, SS 57
Magny, Pierre, book by, CD 127
Majestic radio, RS 18
Majolica, LM 104-121

Makah Indian baskets, AB 156
Makeig-Jones, Daisy, TW 84, 86; vase designed by, TW 95
Maldonado, Alex, painting by, FH 16-17
Mallet, bone, RS 116
Manderson, Tom, vase design by, TT 49
Mandolins, MN 86, 88; measuring tape shaped like, MN 132
Mangling board, IL 26
Manoil Manufacturing Company, Waverly, N.J., model soldiers by, MN 43, 52
Mansell, Joseph, card by, TW 19, 24
Manship, Paul, MN 22
Mantle, Mickey, AB 144, 147
Manure spreader, DF 124
Maps, LM 122-149; Currier & Ives panorama, CD 99; on powder horn, FH 85; radio premium, PQ 119; sampler, RS 93; on scarf, TW 143; on stoneware pig, SS 143
Marbles, LM 150-160
Marble-topped table, TW 45
Marcasite pins, FH 112, IL 94
Marcus Ward & Co., England, cards by, FH 70, 72, 73
Marescotti, Antonio, medal designed by, MN 20
Margaret Rose, Princess (England), paper doll, OP 83
Marichal, Juan, AB 147
Marinaro, Vincent, BB 105
Marine Corps insignia, TW 138
Marionettes, PQ 134, 135-136, 142-145
Markham, Gervase, book by, CD 8
Markhardt, Simon and Peter, FH 90
Marks, J. L., London, England, booklet from, TW 28
Marlinespike, in knife, IL 138
Marlowe, Julia, memorabilia of, TT 18, 25, 32
Marmon automobile advertisement, LM 83
Marolin, MN 84
Marquand & Company, New York, sauceboat by, SS 41
Marquard, Richard, statistics about, on card, AB 143
Marquetry: cane, BC 42; cash registers, BC 119, 120
Marrow scoop, SS 50
Marseille, Armand, dolls by, DF 34, 36, 48; mark, DF 49
Marsh company, London, England, knife by, IL 140
Martha Gunn Toby jugs, SS 94
Martin, Billy, AB 144
Martin, C. F., & Co., N.Y., guitars by, MN 84, 86, 88-89
Martin, Jimmy, CD 42
Martin, Pepper, AB 145
Martinka & Co. catalogue,

LM 102
Marvel comics, CC 149, 158
Marx, Louis, & Company, N.Y., toys by, MN 43, TT 94-95, 124
Marxochime Colony autoharps, MN 84
Mary, Queen (England), souvenirs of, BB 155, RS 81
Mary Gregory glass, AB 54; buttons, BC 12
Maser, Jacob, desk of, OP 72
Maserati (car), toy, TT 108
Mason, George, AB 94
Mason, John Landis, IL 52
Masons: Knights Templar, sword of, SS 155; symbols, CC 25, CD 51, RS 146, TW 63
Massani, Pompeo, art by, TT 116
Master razor, RS 144
Masters, Edgar Lee, book by, BB 115
Matchbook covers, MN 13, OP 31
"Matchbox" series (toys), TT 108
Matchsafes and match holders, MN 6-17; giveaways, AB 10, 14; owls on, OP 50, 52; on Tiffany ashtray, TT 46
Mathews, Eddie, AB 144
Matisse, Henri, art by, BB 112, 113; on stamp, SS 119
Mattel Toys, DF 39
Matthews Decorative Glass Co., New York, N.Y., paperweight advertising, OP 103
Maugham, Somerset, caricature of, BC 113
Mauldin, Bill, art by, PQ 69
Maurer, Louis, art by, CD 84, 85
Maurer, Sasha, art by, PQ 101
Mauretania (ship), launch brochure for, OP 27
Maxim, Hiram, FH 86-87
Mayer, Louis B., MN 63
Mays, Willie, AB 147
Meacham, David, spinning wheel by, RS 128
Meader, Deborah, puppets by, PQ 135, 136
Measuring devices, TT 73-75; cup, CD 151; egg scale, IL 131; half pints, OP 136; on letter opener, SS 57; pharmacist's, OP 154; Shaker, RS 129; tapes, IL 31, MN 132
Mechanicals (cards), FH 70, 77, PQ 90, TT 112, 119
Medal of Honor, MN 30
Medals and medallions, MN 18-31; composers, OP 38; eagles, AB 27, MN 28; Holmes, Sherlock, on, CD 157; Lindbergh on, LM 49; post-World War I, TW 149; royal souvenir, RS 78; from ships, OP 31; Taft, William Howard, on, AB 89; Wedgwood, TW 82; world's fair souvenir, TW 122
Medical memorabilia: books, BB 107; knife, IL 138; medals,

MN 18, 19, 27; stamp, SS 98; trade cards, TT 120, 122. See also Pharmacists: equipment
Medicine bottles, BB 130, 131, 133, 136, 140, 141, OP 153, 158; lock, LM 71
Medinger, Jacob, pitcher by, RS 46
Meek, J. F. and B. F., DF 153
Meek (stationer), London, England, valentine, TW 29
Meeks, J. and J. W., chair by, TW 38
Megaphone, leather, MN 63
Meisselbach fishing reels, DF 154, 156-157
Meissen porcelain factory, Germany: bells, BB 46, 51; cats, BC 127; pipe tamper, SS 67; thimble, MN 124
Melba, Nellie, OP 37
Mellor, Venables and Company, Staffordshire, England, plate by, SS 88
Melotone records, IL 65, 73
Melrose Bros. sheet music, IL 67
Melville, Herman, book by, BB 109, 112
Memphis Jug Band, list of songs by, CD 31
Mennonite cookbook, CD 13
Menominee beadwork, BB 17
Menus, MN 32-39; Baker Street Irregulars, CD 157; circus banquet, CC 67; dinner honoring Dickens, CD 10; jukebox advertisement, IL 114; ocean liners, OP 22, 28; railroads, MN 34; RS 29
Mercedes (cars): hubcap, AB 103; lapel pins, AB 114; painting of, AB 109, 111
Mercer, Joe, bronze by, DF 14
Mercer, Johnny, IL 72
Mercer Raceabout (car), BC 82
Merchant's Exchange, New York, N.Y., print of, CD 85
Mercury (silvered) glass, AB 54, BC 35, LM 39, 42, 43
Meredith, James, button supporting, PQ 70
Meriden Britannia Company, Meriden, Conn., silver pieces by, SS 41, 44
Meriwether, W. H., AB 132
Merrill's Marauders, insignia of, TW 139
Merry-go-rounds. See Carousels
Merry Makers mouse band (toy), TT 94-95
Merton, Thomas, RS 123
Meteyard, Elizabeth, TW 84
Metford, Samuel, silhouette by, SS 15
Metro-Goldwyn-Mayer memorabilia, MN 56, 63, 67
Metropolitan Opera, New York, N.Y., memorabilia of, OP 40
Mettlachs (steins), SS 124, 125, 127, 129, 131

Meyer, William E., record label of, CD 35

Meyers, S. F. & Co., matchsafe by, MN 8

M-G-M: records, CD 42, MN 67. See also Metro-Goldwyn-Mayer

MGs (cars): TC, BC 86, 95; toy, TT 108

Mice: bone, IL 92; in children's book, CC 12; print of, TW 109; toy, TT 94-95

Michigan Cash Register Company, products of, BC 121

Mickey Mouse (cartoon character), AB 32-33, CC 151, 156; toy handcar, TT 138; watches, LM 50, TW 67

Microphones, RS 12

Middle Lane Pottery, East Hampton, N.Y., products of, AB 75, 77; marks, AB 84

Mielziner, Jo, stage designs by, TT 18, 29

Mignon typewriter, TW 15

Mignot, Henry, model soldiers by, MN 42, 46, 47

Mikiphone phonograph, PQ 14

Milam, Benjamin, DF 153

Miles, John, lamp by, LM 19, 21

Military items, AB 30; decorations, MN 30; entanglement wire, AB 133; maps, LM 124, 146, 147, TW 143. See also names of wars

Milk bottles, BB 139; opener for, AB 15

Milk glass: creamer, OP 50; lightning-rod balls, LM 38, 39, 41; needlecase, MN 126; pharmaceutical equipment, OP 151, 157

Milk jug, SS 92

Milk kettle, IL 117

Milk pan, redware, RS 49

Millais, Sir John Everett, illustration by, BB 110

Millay, Edna St. Vincent, BB 93

Millefiori: beads, BB 6, 7, 9; bell, BB 50; paperweights, OP 100, 101, 106; vase, AB 64

Miller, Arthur, play by: book, TT 38; set design, TT 18

Millersburg Glass Company, Millersburg, Ohio, products of, BC 55, 56, 57, 59, 60, 62

Millette, Jean, silhouettes ascribed to, SS 9

Million Guiet, Paris, France, carriage by, FH 154-155

Mills, William, & Son, catalogue from, DF 160

Millville Atmospheric fruit jars, IL 52, 56

Milne, A. A., books by, CC 7, 19

Milton, John, bust of, SS 96

Milton Bradley Co., games by, FH 47, 53, 57

Miner's lamp, LM 20

Minerva (car) lapel pin, AB 108

Miniatures, DF 29; Bennington pottery, BB 61; Bible, BB 77; Depression-glass, CD 150; jug, SS 136; lamps, LM 26; portraits in jewelry, IL 80, 81, 83; scrimshaw, RS 119; tramp-art, TT 146; trivet, TT 153. See also Dollhouses; Soldiers, model; Toys; Trains

Minneapolis Threshing Machine Company, tractor by, DF 110

Minox cameras, BC 23, 28

Minton & Company, Stoke-on-Trent, England, majolica by, LM 104, 113; marks, LM 114, 115

Miró, Joan, poster by, CD 116

Mirrors: pocket, AB 8, 9, 10, 17; silver-plated, SS 54; tramp-art frames, TT 140, 142

Misprints, BB 95; Bibles, BB 77; children's books, CC 7, 8; paper money, OP 97; stamps, SS 100, 101, 105

Mission-style furniture, OP 16, 17

Mission tray, AB 159

Mississippi 'Possum Hunters (recording group), record by, CD 40

Mr. Natural (comic character), CC 160

Mitchell, Edward H., company, postcards by, PQ 79, 82

Mitchell, John, map by, LM 136-137

Mithradates II, King (Parthian), on coin, CC 127

Mix, Tom, radio premiums, PQ 110, 112, 113

Moccasins, beaded, BB 16

Mockel, Henry, art by, BB 129

Model A Ford, BC 82, 85, 87

Model soldiers. See Soldiers, model

Model T Ford, AB 106, BC 84; as tractor, DF 110

Modox (beverage) tray, AB 11

Mogul (tractor), DF 114-115

Molds: basketmaker's, AB 152; Christmas tree ornament, CC 39; cigar, SS 72; kitchenware, AB 28, 29, IL 126-128, OP 147; suppository, OP 156

Molinari company, Brooklyn, N.Y., product of, MN 82-83

Moline Plow Company, tractor by, DF 113

Molnar, Ferenc, scene from play by, TT 35

Money. See Coins; Paper money

Money clip, AB 15

Monkeys: automatons, DF 53, TT 95; on corkscrew, CD 26; doorstop, DF 59; on Lalique bowl, LM 9; pitcher, LM 119

Monopoly (game), FH 54

Monroe, Bill, CD 42

Monroe, C. F., & Company, box decorated by, BB 156

Monroe, James, on stamp, SS 107

Monroe, Marilyn, LM 89; dolls, LM 50

Montana, Patsy, songbook, CD 41

"Montana peak" hat, CD 70

Montanari family, DF 37

Montaut, Edouard, prints by, AB 109, 111

Montgomery Ward, records sold by, CD 34, 39

Moonglows (rock group), label from record by, RS 52

Moon-landing memorabilia: button, LM 50; matchbook, MN 13; stamp, SS 113

Moonstones: hatpin, FH 117; jewelry, IL 86, 105

Moore, C. L., art for story by, RS 106

Moravian plate, RS 47

Morgan, Matt, BC 106

Morgan Belleek China Co., Canton, Ohio, products of, BB 36, 45; mark, BB 44

Morgan Litho Co., Cleveland, Ohio, posters by, MN 54, 56

Moriarity, George, AB 143

Morley, George and William H., art by, BB 36, 38, 42

Morley & Co., Wellsville, Ohio, majolica by, LM 118; mark, LM 115

Morris, William, AB 71, BB 78, 112, IL 90, OP 7

Morris and Willmore, Trenton, N.J., Belleek by, BB 35, 41, 43; mark, BB 44

Morris chairs, OP 7, 13

Morris Minor (car), toy, TT 108

Morse, E., OP 58

Morse, Samuel, F. B., IL 16

Mortar-and-pestle sets, OP 148, 150, 154

Morton, Ferdinand (Jelly Roll), IL 64, 68; record by, IL 69

Mosaic pins, FH 112, IL 86

Moser, Koloman, art by, LM 76, PQ 87

Mosher Folding Dollhouse, DF 19

Mother Goose. See Nursery rhymes

Mother-of-pearl: buttons, BC 8, 9, 16; corkscrew handles, CD 25, MN 125; egg, DF 68; eyeglass cases, DF 91; fan sticks, DF 104; gun grip, FH 93; knife handle, IL 132-133; longnette, DF 89; sewing accessories, MN 125; typewriter inlaid with, TW 7

Motion Picture (magazine), MN 66

Moto-Meters, AB 104, 106

Motorcycles: depictions of, PQ 83, 101; on rock album, RS 57

Motorcycle van, toy, TT 106

Mottoes, needlework, RS 88, 98

Moulin Rouge poster, PQ 96

Moulton, J., spoon by, SS 51

Mount Vernon Glass Works,

Mount Vernon, N.Y., IL 7

Mt. Washington Glass Works, New Bedford, Mass., AB 57, 68

Mountz, Aaron, AB 26

Mouron, Adolphe (A. M. Cassandre), posters by, PQ 95, 101

Movie memorabilia, MN 54-67; books, MN 66, OP 47, 86; cartoons, AB 32-41; paper dolls, LM 50, OP 85-87; playing cards, PQ 50; posters, AB 38, MN 54, 56-59, PQ 109, RS 51, 103, 110, 111; rock and roll, RS 51, 53, 55; science-fiction, RS 103, 110, 111

Movie simulations: mechanical peep shows, LM 51, OP 111, 112; toy, TT 88

Mowers, DF 122; blade, watch fob shaped like, TW 65

Moxie (beverage) trays, AB 11, 14

Mozart, Wolfgang Amadeus, AB 99, OP 34

Mucha, Alphonse: jewelry, IL 91, 93; posters, PQ 95, 97

Mudge Patent processor, IL 58

Mugs, AB 113; advertising giveaways, AB 17, SS 128; Belleek, BB 43, 45; frogs in, FH 22, 25; opera scenes, OP 43; pewter, OP 137; radio premiums, PQ 118; redware, RS 35; royal souvenirs, RS 83. See also Shaving mugs; Steins

Muller, Daniel Carl, carousel animals by, BC 67, 74

Munnings, Sir Alfred, art by, BB 104

Musical comedy, posters, TT 17, 22

Musical instruments, MN 84-97; in cane, BC 46; mechanical, MN 82-83; toy, TT cover

Musical memorabilia: movie-related, MN 67, RS 51, 53, 55; Shahn poster, PQ 108. See also Country music; Jazz; Jukeboxes; Opera mementos; Phonographs; Rock and roll; Sheet music

Music boxes, MN 68-83

Music stands: in cane, BC 46; tramp art, TT 147

Musket accessories, Civil War, CC 76, 77

Muskets, FH 84, 86-87; Civil War, CC 73, 74-75

Mustard pot, silver, SS 40

Mutoscopes, LM 51, OP 111, 112

Mutual Assurance Co. fire mark, DF 148

Mutual Litho Company, San Francisco, Calif., fruit-crate labels by, FH 31, 32

Myers, Ella, book by, CD 9

Myrick, Frederick, RS 114

Mystery stories. See Detective

Fiction
Mysto magic tricks, LM *103;* catalogue, LM *102*

N

Nadeau, R., sign by, RS *155*
Nails, date, RS 23, *25*
Nall & Williams Tobacco Co., Louisville, Ky., tin from, SS *62*
Name plates, cars', AB *103,* 104
Nancy Drew books, CC 8
Nanking ware, CC 22, *24*
Nansen, Fridtjof, spoon honoring, SS *79*
Napkin, world's fair, TW *130*
Napkin rings, silver, OP *30, 53,* SS *36, 43*
Napoleon: chess set, BC 150, *157;* eagles, AB 29, *30;* family crest, CC *25;* medals, MN 19-20, *23;* profile on cane, BC *49;* on snuffbox, SS *69*
Napoli glass, AB *59*
Nash, Leslie H., technique developed by, TT *44*
Nasser, Gamal Abdel, cartoon of, BC *112*
Nast, Thomas: cartoons by, BC *104,* 106, *108;* jug inspired by, SS *142;* print from art by, CD *98*
National-bank notes, OP 90, *95*
National Cash Register Company, products of, BC 114-125
National-parks commemorative stamps, SS 105, *111*
National Silk Manufacturing Company, Paterson, N.J., picture by, SS *29*
Nativity scenes, BB 76, CD 72-81
Nautical gear, MN 98-109; OP *32*
Navajo: blankets, MN *cover,* 110-123; jewelry, IL 99, *101*
Naval swords, SS *151, 154, 158*
Navy, United States: cap, Civil War, CC *82;* dog tag, TW *143;* ship, depiction of, TT *110;* stamps honoring, SS *113, 114*
Nazi relics, TW 136, *137, 142*
Nechansky, Arnold, postcard by, PQ *86*
Neckerchief ring, DF *144*
Necklaces, IL *76, 82, 88, 90, 95, 96, 101;* bead, BB 7, 10, *11, 13, 15, 18, 19,* IL 99, *100, 103, 104;* Wedgwood, TW 88. See *also* Pendants
Neckties, political, PQ *74*
Needlecases, CC 26, DF 28, MN *126, 127, 135*
Needlepoint cane, BC *47*
Needlework tools. See Sewing tools
Nellis, Sanders, SS 9
Nelson, Horatio, Viscount, ring commemorating, IL *83*
Nelson, Jack, AB *140*
Nemtchinova, Vera, depiction of, CD *118*

Neon signs, RS 154, *160*
Nester, J. P., record by, CD 37
Nets, fishing, DF *159*
Netsukes, FH *25,* IL 102, MN 136-149
Nevada Central Railroad locomotive, RS *30*
Newcastle, Duke of, caricature of, BC *101*
Newcomb College and Newcomb Pottery, New Orleans, La., products of, AB *76;* marks, AB *84*
New England Glass Company, Boston, Mass., AB 57, 68, BC 30; paperweights, AB *58;* salt dish, PQ *123*
New England Watch Company, products of, TW *61, 63*
New Haven railroad line, memorabilia of, RS *21-24,* 23, *26, 27*
Newman, Edwin, PQ 76
Newspapers: Army, TW *147;* caricatures in, BC *109;* comics, CC *149-151;* Lindbergh memorabilia, LM 46, *47;* paper dolls in, OP *77*
Newton, Richard, BC 100; art by, BC *101*
New York, Westchester & Boston railroad, memorabilia of, RS *24, 26*
New Yorker, The (magazine), LM 75
New York Yankees (baseball team), autographs of, AB 95
Neyret Frères, France, silk pictures by, SS *27*
Niagara Falls, United States-Canada: ambrotype, PQ *20;* color plate, BB *99;* paperweight, OP *105;* poster, TW *125;* spoon, SS *80;* stamp, SS *107*
Nichols, Red, IL 64
Nicholson, Francis and John, TT 72
Nicklaus, Jack, FH 62
Nicole, François, music box by, MN *76*
Nieder, John, autograph of, MN *36*
Niello technique, MN 9
Nifty Co., Germany, toy by, CC *153*
Nightstand, OP *60*
Nignon, Edouard, book by, CD *10*
Nijinsky, Vaslav, costume worn by, CD *121*
Nipper (RCA trademark dog), DF 8, PQ 8, *12*
Niven, David, movie scene featuring, MN *64*
Nixon, Richard M., caricature of, BC *113;* memorabilia of, PQ *cover*
Nizzoli, Marcello, poster by, PQ *101*

Noah's ark, toy, TT *91*
Nō costumes, netsuke depicting, MN *141, 142*
Nodders (figurines), BC 139, *143, 146;* bells, BB 46, *51*
Noisemakers: cricket, AB *16;* policemen's rattles, DF 140, PQ *61*
Noll, William and John, coverlet woven by, CD *59*
Nonesuch Press Bible, BB *68*
Norcross valentine, TW *33*
Nordica, Lillian, OP *35*
Nordskog Phonograph Record Company, IL *64*
Normandie (ship), OP *22;* memorabilia, OP *24-25*
Norris, Frank, book by, BB *114*
Norris Manufacturing Co., gum machine by, OP *118*
Northwest Airlines playing card, PQ *53*
Northwood Glass Company, Wheeling, W. Va., products of, BC 55, *56, 57, 58-61, 64, 65*
Norton, F. B., SS *138*
Norton, John, BB 57
Nosek, Hans and J., china decoration by, BB 36, *42*
Notgeld (money), OP *91, 99*
Nureyev, Rudolf, memorabilia of, CD *116,* 119
Nursery rhymes: on bookmarks, SS *26;* illustrations, CC *13;* matchsafe depicting, MN *8;* Wrigley's version, AB 18, *19*
Nursing bottles, MN 150-160
Nutcracker, IL *cover*
Nut dishes: Harlequin-ware, DF *134;* silver, SS *41*
Nutmeg graters, IL 119, *125;* on corkscrew, CD *25*

O

Oak (wood): furniture, OP 6-21, TW *100;* medicine cabinet, OP *158;* phonograph horn, PQ *11*
Obsidian marble, LM *159*
Oceanic Chemical Company, New York, N.Y., medicines by, OP *153*
Ocean liner memorabilia, OP 22-33; silk picture, SS *25*
Odeon record label, OP *37*
O'Hara Dial Company, watch face by, TW *61*
Ohr, George E., pottery by, AB 75, *77*
Oilcans, RS *25*
Ojibway beadwork, BB *16*
Ojimes, BB *14,* IL 102, MN *144*
Okatomo (Japanese), netsuke by, MN *149*
OKeh records, CD 29, *32, 33,* IL 64, *66, 70*
Okito (magician), tricks made by, LM 92, *94, 95*
Old Colony railroad line, Mass., key from, RS *24*
Oldfield, Barney, tires, sign for,

AB *110*
Old Honesty tobacco premium, TW *60*
Old Maid card game, PQ *51*
Oliver, King, IL 64; record label, IL *65*
Oliver, Thomas, typewriters, TW 9, *10*
Olivier, Laurence, movie scene featuring, MN *64*
Olmstead, Frederick Law, book by, BB *102*
Olympic (ship), OP *24;* deck plan, OP *25*
Olympics: medals, MN 22, *25;* playing cards, PQ *50*
O'Neill, Rose, DF 39, *54,* OP *75*
One-Eleven cigarette package, SS *65*
Opal glass, AB 54, *65*
Opal jewelry, IL 85, *86, 89*
Opera mementos, OP 34-47
Opium pipe, PQ *42*
Opper, Frederick, cartoon by, BC *105*
Optical toys, TT *88*
Oregon Trail, coin commemorating, CC *138*
Organs: mechanical, MN 69, *82-83;* portable, MN 84, *91*
Original Dixieland Jazz Band, IL *63;* record label, IL *62*
Ornaments. See Christmas decorations; Finials
Orwell, George, book by, RS 101, *104*
Ory, Kid, records by, IL 64, *65, 69*
O'Ryan, John Francis, TW *142*
Osiris, amulet of, BB *14*
Osmundo cigars, advertising giveaway for, SS *67*
Osterwalder, Ute, art by, RS *104*
Ostriches: carousel, BC *69;* eggs, DF 65, *67;* on matchsafe, AB *10*
Ostrich feathers: brass, RS *83;* fans, DF 96, *105;* handbag, FH *100;* hats, FH *123, 126*
Ott and Brewer, Trenton, N.J., Belleek by, BB *34, 35, 38;* marks, BB *44*
Outcault, Richard, comic characters by, CC *49,* 149, *150;* doll based on, CC *152*
Ovaltine, mugs for, PQ *118*
Overland Narratives, BB 101, *102*
Owens Pottery, Zanesville, Ohio, products of, AB 73, 74, 76, *80*
Owls, OP 48-57; decoys, CD *139,* OP 48; on inkwell, IL *15;* majolica, LM *118;* on pipe, PQ *40*

P

Pabst beer: cans, BB 24, *28;* mug, SS *128*
Packards (cars): Custom-Eight, BC *91;* hubcap, AB *103;*

paperweight, AB *115;* Twin Six, BC *82*
Packer, Asa, parlor of, TW *34-35*
Paget, Sidney, art by, CD *156*
Pagliacci (opera character), depictions of, BC *99,* PQ *88*
Painted furniture, OP 58-73
Pairpoint Manufacturing Company, New Bedford, Mass.: box, BB *156;* lamps, LM 21, *32*
Palethorp and Connell, Philadelphia, Pa., teapot by, OP *145*
Palissy, Bernard, LM 104, 112
Palmer, Arnold, score card signed by, FH *63*
Palmer, Fanny, prints from art by, CD 84, *97*
Panama hat, FH *125*
Pan American World Airways Inc. poster, PQ *107*
Pan Electric Manufacturing Company, toaster by, TT *64*
Paper dolls, LM *50,* OP 74-87
Paper embosser, FH *27*
Paper money, OP *cover,* 88-89
Paperweight-glass vases, OP *108,* TT *48*
Paperweights, OP 100-109; advertising giveaways, AB *8, 14, 114, 115,* OP *103;* frogs, FH *24;* fruit-shaped, AB *58;* inkwell, IL *10*
Papier-mâché: ballet props, CD *120;* buttons, BC *12;* candlestand top, OP *68;* dolls, DF 39, *43, 45, 53;* eggs, DF *68, 69;* eyeglass cases, DF *91;* matchsafes, MN *14;* music-box picture, MN *72-73;* puppets, PQ *139;* snuffbox, SS *69;* toy dog, TT *cover*
Parade flier, BB *53*
Paramount Pictures sign, RS *159*
Paramount records, CD *30,* IL *69*
Parasol, from movie, MN *62*
Parian ware, BB *35;* Bennington, 57-58, *59, 64;* Rogers-group duplicates, RS *67*
Park drag (carriage), FH *154-155*
Parker, C. W., Company, Abilene, Kans., carousel animals by, BC 68, *76*
Parker Brothers games, FH 52-*53, 54, 57, 58*
Parker pens and pencils, OP 124, *125, 127, 128, 131, 132*
Parloa, Maria, book by, CD *15*
Parrish, Maxfield, illustrations by, LM *83*
Parrots: cane head, BC *51;* chalkware, BC 139, *144;* movie prop, MN *62;* on playing card, PQ *53*
Partridge, Bernard, cartoon by, BC *112*
Paschal Lamb, on egg, DF *69*
Paste (glass) jewelry, IL 80, *82*
Pasteur, Louis, MN 151

Pastry trimmers, IL *117*
Patch box, BB *159*
Patent drawings: bank, AB *120;* barbed wire, AB *130, 131;* cash register, BC *117;* lock, LM *65;* silhouette machine, SS *11*
Patent furniture, TW 37, *53-55*
Patent medicines, OP 151; bottles, BB *130, 131, 136,* OP *158;* tins, OP *159;* trade card, TT *120*
Patent model, RS *24*
Patent Steel Whip Company, Springfield, Ohio, BC *43*
Pattern glass, AB *65,* PQ *120, 121, 122-123, 127-130, 133*
Patterson, John, BC 115
Patterson Mfg. Co., Philadelphia, Pa., giveaway from, AB *9*
Paul, Frank R., art by, RS *107*
Paul Revere Pottery, Boston, Mass., AB 86; bowl, AB *82;* marks, AB *84,* 86
Pavlova, Anna, CD 119, *124;* toe slipper, CD *120*
Pawnee Bill's Wild West Show, pamphlet for, CC *66*
Peach Blow glass, AB *54, 58, 61*
Peaches: glass, AB *58;* redware, RS *49*
Peacocks: in button display, BC *12;* on carnival glass, BC *58;* on jukebox, IL *111;* on Lalique vase, LM *11*
Peal & Co., London, England, puttees by, TW *141*
Peale, Charles Willson, IL *80;* silhouette by, SS *8*
Peanut machine, OP *118*
Pearls: hatpin, FH *112;* jewelry, AB *108,* IL *76, 82, 83, 86, 87, 89, 92, 94;* watches, TW *64, 66*
Pearl Satin glass, AB *60, 67*
Pears: glass, AB *58;* redware, RS *49*
Peart, Mary, print by, TW *118*
Peary, Robert, menu honoring, MN 34, *37*
Peddler's wagon, FH *158*
Pedometer, PA *116*
Peer, Ralph, CD 29, 32
Pegasus, CC *15;* on coin, CC *116*
Peking glass: beads, BB *15;* snuff-bottle stoppers, SS *69*
Pelé, on stamp, SS *120*
Pellegrini, Carlo, caricatures by, BC 106, *108*
Peltier Company, Ottawa, Ill., marbles by, LM *157*
Pencil box, BB *154*
Pencils. *See* Pens and pencils
Pendants, BB *19,* IL *76, 78, 81, 88, 92, 103, 104;* for Tiffany lamp shade, TT *43. See also* Necklaces
Penfield, Edward, art by, PQ *98*
Penguin, carved-wood, FH *14*
Pennant, auto-race, AB *114*
Pennsylvania Dutch: baskets, AB *153,* 156; boxes, BB 146, *148,*

152; chalkware, BC 139; china made for, SS *92;* desk, OP *72;* Easter eggs, DF *70;* eyeglasses, DF *85;* kitchenware designs, AB 28, 29, IL *121, 124, 128;* locks, LM 59, *64;* nurser, MN *153;* quilts, PQ 147, 149, *159;* silhouette, SS *12;* valentines, TW 17, *20-21*
Pennsylvania Railroad memorabilia, RS *28, 32*
Penny arcade machines, LM *50, 51,* OP 110-123
Pens and pencils, OP 124-133; Civil War, CC *86;* display facsimile, RS *157;* seamstress's, MN *135*
Penwipers, IL *12, 15,* TT *46*
Pepper grinder, silver, SS *43*
Pepper shakers. *See* Salt-and-pepper shakers
Pepys, Samuel, TW 17
Perchin, Michael, egg by, DF *66*
Percolator, CD *151*
Perfect record label, CD *39*
Perfume and cologne bottles, BB *158,* MN *135,* OP *108;* corkscrews for, CD *25,* MN *125;* cut-glass, CD *112;* inside egg, DF *69;* Lalique, LM *6, 17;* parian, BB *64;* royal souvenir, RS *78;* silver, SS *56*
Perkins, Carl, record by, RS *52*
Perlee, Incorporated, Trenton, N.J., Belleek by, BB 36, *45;* mark, BB *44*
Perry, Matthew C., IL *34;* on stamp, SS *112*
Petticoat, CC *109*
Pewabic Pottery, Detroit, Mich., AB 86
Pewter, OP 134-147; button, BC *17;* nursing bottle, MN *153*
Phaetons, FH *145, 151*
Phair, Charles, BB *105*
Pharmacists: equipment, OP 148-160; trade card, TT *122*
Philadelphia style of carousel animals, BC *66-75, 67*
Philadelphia Toboggan Company, Pa., products of, BC 67, *68, 70, 71, 74, 75*
Philco radios, RS 7, *9, 10*
Philip, Prince (England), on box, LM 50
Philippines: beads, BB *18;* iron, IL *26*
Phillips, Ammi, art by, FH *8*
Phillips, Coles, art by, LM *79, 83*
Philo Vance books, CD 155
Philp, Hugh, FH 60
Phonographs, PQ 6-15; records *(see* Records); on trade card, TT *116. See also* Jukeboxes
Photoengraving, use of, BC 110
Photographs, PQ 16-31; circus, CC *68, 69;* Civil War, CC *85,* PQ *22;* of fireman, DF *140;* Lindbergh memorabilia, LM *54, 55;* magazines, LM *75, 85,*

87, 88, PQ *25;* movie publicity, MN 54, 56, *64, 65,* RS *110;* of policeman, PQ *56;* political buttons, PQ *64, 66, 67;* postcards, AB *112,* CD *114, 120,* PQ *71, 77, 80-85,* RS *125;* theatrical, TT 17, *34-37;* World War I, TW *146, 147;* world's fair souvenirs, TW *126-127. See also* Cameras
Photolithography, use of, CC 58
Pianos: mechanical, MN *82;* music for, OP *39, 42;* traveling, MN *90;* Victorian, TW 37, *47*
Piano stool, wicker, TW *104*
Picasso, Pablo: art by, CD *116;* caricature of, LM *85;* quoted, TW 68
Pickford, Mary, menu honoring, OP *28*
Pickwick card game, PQ *51*
Picture frames, OP *61;* Flint Enamel, BB *67;* silver, SS *55;* Tiffany, TT *46;* tramp-art, TT *142*
Picture Play (magazine), MN *66*
Pie dishes: Flint Enamel, BB *61;* Wedgwood, TW *90*
Pierce-Arrows (cars), AB 104, *105,* BC *89*
Pierrotti family, DF 37
Pie trimmer, IL *cover*
Pigeons: print, TW *112-113;* tureen, LM *109*
Pigs, PQ *26;* automaton, MN *74;* bottle shaped like, BB *132;* carousel, BC *76;* chalkware, BC *146;* folk-art sculpture, FH *18;* ice-cream mold, IL *128;* measuring tape, MN *132;* stoneware, SS *143;* weather vane, TW *77*
Pillbox, BB *159*
Pillmaking devices, OP 150, *155*
"Pillow" book, Japanese print from, IL *39*
Pillowcase, World War I, TW *149*
Pillow-cats, BC 127, *132*
Pin-back buttons: advertising, AB *8, 10;* astronauts, LM *50;* comic character, CC *148;* Lindbergh, LM *49;* policeman, PQ *56;* political, PQ *cover,* 66, *67, 68-70;* rock and roll, RS *50, 58, 63;* royal souvenirs, RS *83,* 87
Pinball machines, OP 111, 112, *116, 117*
Pin box, Wedgwood, TW *89*
Pince-nez spectacles, DF *85, 90*
Pinchbeck: eyeglass, DF *87;* in paperweights, OP 101, *109*
Pincushions, MN *129, 133*
Ping-Pong, FH *57*
Pin holder, AB *17*
Pinocchio (character), AB *36*
Pins, AB 22, IL *76, 80, 85, 86, 93, 94, 98, 100;* automobilia, AB *108, 114-115;* hairpins, CC *144;* lapel pins, AB *15, 108,*

114-115, TW *124, 131;* political, PQ *68;* stickpins, AB *15,* IL *86. See also* Hatpins
Pin tray, royal-souvenir, RS *80*
Pipes, PQ 32-43; accessories, SS *67, 70;* Civil War, CC *79;* holder, netsuke, MN *140;* rack, RS *18;* tobacco for *(see* Tobacco)
Piqué-work earrings, IL *89*
Pirate, on label, FH *44*
Pisanello (Italian craftsman), MN 19; medal honoring, MN *20*
Pistols: bottles shaped like, BB *132,* PQ *60;* in canes, BC 45, *49;* on knife, IL *139;* pocket-sized, FH *95;* presentation pieces, FH *90-91;* semiautomatic, FH 87, *96;* World War II, FH *97. See also* Guns; Revolvers
Pitchers: art-glass, AB *cover, 54, 66;* beer, BB *43,* SS *128;* Belleek, BB *37, 38, 43;* Bennington pottery, BB 57, *58, 59, 61-65;* carnival-glass, BC *56, 57;* child's, MN *158;* cut-glass, CD *100;* Depression-glass, CD *140, 142-144, 147, 148;* Fiesta-ware, DF *132-133, 136;* majolica, LM *111, 117-119;* pewter, OP *146;* pressed glass, PQ *130, 132;* redware, RS *38, 46;* silver, SS *46, 47;* Staffordshire, SS 87, *92, 93;* Wedgwood, TW *89, 90. See also* Creamers; Jugs
Pitchfork, bentwood, DF *116-117*
Place cards, SS *18*
Plains Indians, illustration of, BB *103*
Planes (tools), TT *73, 74, 78-79;* bone, RS *116*
Plank, Eddie, AB *141*
Plant stands, OP *63,* TT *150;* pedestal, wicker, TW 98, *103*
Plaster of paris. *See* Chalkware
Plates: art-pottery, AB *74;* automobilia, AB *113;* Belleek, BB 36, 38, *42, 45;* calendars on, AB *113,* OP *51;* carnival-glass, BC *54, 59;* children's, CD *143,* MN *159;* Chinese porcelain, CC *20-25, 28, 31;* Depression-glass, CD *143, 144, 149;* dining-car, RS *29;* Fiesta-ware, DF *126, 130, 137;* Flint Enamel, BB *61;* Lalique, LM *8;* majolica, LM *104-105,* 107, *108, 110, 113;* opera scenes on, OP *44-45;* pewter, OP *139;* pressed-glass, AB *27,* PQ *120, 124-127;* redware, RS *40, 41, 47, 48;* royal souvenirs, RS *76, 81;* Staffordshire, SS *82, 84, 88, 92;* Tiffany, TT *51;* tin, Civil War, CC *78;* Wedgwood, TW *89, 91, 92;* world's fair souvenirs, TW *130, 132*
Platters: art-pottery, AB *72;*

Depression-glass, detail of, CD *145;* engraved glass, CD *108;* Homer Laughlin pottery, DF *126, 135, 136;* Palissy-style, LM *112;* redware, RS *41;* silver-plated, SS *38;* Staffordshire, SS *85*
Platters (rock group), label from record by, RS *52*
Playbills, CD *115,* TT 17, *19*
Playboy (magazine), LM *75, 89*
Player pianos, MN *82*
Playing cards, PQ 44-53; in magic tricks, LM *96, 97;* from ship, OP *31*
Plique-à-jour enamel, BC *15,* FH *112*
Plows, walking, DF 110, *123;* on cup plate, PQ *125*
Plug tobacco: box of, SS *63;* cutter, SS *73;* tags from, SS *62, 63, 64*
Pluto (cartoon character), AB *32-33*
Pocahontas, on stamp, SS *110*
Pocket watches. *See* Watches
Poe, Edgar Allan, CD *152*
Pogány, Willy, art by, CD *117*
Pogo (comic character), CC *cover, 148, 156*
Pointer, The (film), scene from, AB *32-33*
Police memorabilia, PQ 54-63; board game, FH *59*
Political souvenirs, BC *42,* MN 13, PQ *cover,* 64-75
Pomander, silver, SS *56*
Pontiacs (cars): on matchbook, MN *13;* radiator cap, AB *104*
Pony Express, stamps commemorating, SS *115*
Pony-sailor wagon, FH *148-149*
Poole, Charlie, CD *42*
Pop bottles, stoneware, SS *141*
Pope Hartford bus, AB *112*
Popeye (comic character), CC *cover, 154;* toys of, CC *152, 153*
Porcelain: art-pottery, AB *81, 82;* bells, BB *41, 46, 51;* box, BB *156;* buttons, BC *14;* candleholders, BC *30;* cats, BC 127, *129-132;* Chinese, AB 22, 26, BC 127, *129;* clock case, CC *95;* dolls, DF 34, *35, 36-37, 46-48,* 49, *50-52, 54, 55;* eggs, DF *64-65;* frog, FH *23;* hatpin holders, FH *115,* OP *50;* Hummel figurines, MN 68, *69;* inkwell, IL *14;* insulators, IL *16-17, 23;* lightning-rod ball, LM *44;* match holders, MN *16;* netsuke, MN *148;* owls, OP 48, *50;* pharmacist's equipment, OP *151, 154, 157;* pipes, PQ *34, 41;* pipe tamper, SS *67;* royal souvenirs, RS *78, 81;* signs, RS 154, *158, 159;* spheres, LM *158, 159;* steins, SS *129, 133;* thimbles, MN *127;* toasters, TT *64;*

Wedgwood, TW 86, *94, 95. See also* Belleek; Chinese export porcelain; Parian; Satsuma
Porky Pig (cartoon), AB *40*
Porringers, OP 138, *142, 143*
Portland Glass Company, Me., goblet by, PQ *129*
Portland vase, reproductions of, TW *83, 84*
Porto-Products radio, RS *18*
Port tongs, CD *27*
Post, Wiley, airplane of, LM *53*
Postcards, PQ 76-91; automotive, AB *112;* dancers, CD 114, *120;* political, PQ *71;* railroadiana, PQ *85,* RS *32;* Shaker, RS *125;* silk pictures on, SS *25;* valentines, TW 18-19; World War I, TW *146*
Posters, PQ 92-109; ballet, CD *116, 117,* PQ *109;* for barbed wire, AB *135;* circus, CC *60-66, 71;* Citizens' Food Committee, AB *23;* comic-character, CC *148;* magicians, LM *90-91, 93, 98, 99;* movie, AB *38,* MN 54, *56-59,* PQ *109,* RS *51, 103, 110, 111;* ocean-liner, OP *29;* opera, OP 36, *46;* political, PQ *65;* rock and roll, RS *51, 53, 62;* theatrical, PQ *94, 97,* TT 17, *22, 23;* world's fair souvenirs, TW *125;* World Wars, PQ 95, *104-105,* TW 136-137, *144, 145*
Potato slicer, IL *125*
Pot de crème, porcelain, CC *23*
Pots: chocolate pot, BB *39;* Dutch oven, IL *120;* hot-water pot, TW *94;* redware, RS *36, 46;* stoneware, SS *134, 145, 146. See also* Coffeepots; Teapots
Pottery: advertising giveaways, AB *17;* automobilia, AB *113;* bells, BB 46, *51;* buttons, BC 6, *16;* candleholders, BC *30;* cats, BC 127, *129-132, 136;* chess set, BC *157;* Chinese, AB 22, 26, BC 127, *129;* crèche, CD *78-79;* dolls, DF 36-37, 46, 47, *55;* frogs, FH 24, *25;* Indian, RS 42, *43;* mess basin, MN *99;* nursing bottles, MN *150-152;* pharmacist's equipment, OP *151, 157;* railroadiana, RS *29;* royal souvenirs, RS *83. See also* Art pottery; Bennington; Chalkware; Faïence; Fiesta ware; Majolica; Porcelain; Redware; Satsuma; Shaving mugs; Staffordshire; Steins; Stoneware; Wedgwood
Potts, Mary Florence, sadiron inventions of, IL 26-27, *28*
Poulenc, Francis, CD *121*
Powder box, LM *8*
Powder horns, FH *85*
Powder jar, SS *56*
Prairie Ramblers (recording group), record by, CD *40*

Prang, Louis, company, cards by, FH *68, 69, 70, 78, 79,* TT 112, *113*
Pratt, F. & R., firm, Staffordshire, England, container lids by, SS *89*
Pratt & Letchworth, Buffalo, N.Y., toys by, TT *86*
Pratt-type Staffordshire figures, SS *95, 97*
Prayer books, BB *74, 76*
Prayer rug, DF *80*
Premiums, PQ 110-119; cake box, TT *54;* watch, TW *60. See also* Cigarettes: premiums
Preserving. *See* Canning
Presidents, United States: autographs, AB 89-93, *94, 95, 100,* 101; cartoons, BC *107, 113;* cigar bands, CC 49, *55;* on flasks, AB 26, BB 131, 133, 134; medals, MN 20, *21,* 22; on stamps, SS *104-107;* wives, paper dolls of, OP 75, *83. See also* Political souvenirs; individual names
Presley, Elvis, memorabilia of, RS *53, 54, 55*
Press books, BB *112, 113;* Bibles, BB *68, 69, 78, 79*
Pressed glass, PQ 120-133; Amberina, AB *55;* candleholders, BC 30, 32, 39, *40;* eagle motif, AB 26, 27, PQ *125;* inkwells, IL *6, 8-10, 12;* lamp shade, TT *44;* owls on, OP *50;* royal souvenir, RS *80;* steins, SS *126. See also* Carnival glass
"Princess and the Pea, The," illustration from, CC *17*
Prints: automobile art, AB 109, *111;* botanical, BB 118-129; cats, BC *128,* CD *98;* comic, BC 98-113, DF *85,* FH *60;* Currier & Ives, CD 82-99; dogs, DF *10;* Japanese, IL *34-51;* nautical, CB *87,* MN *98;* theatrical, TT *24-25;* wildlife, CD *97,* TW 108-119; world's fair souvenirs, TW *121, 122, 127. See also* Maps
Prior, William Matthew, FH *7*
Prisms, glass, BB *60,* BC *37*
Programs: ballet, CD *116,* 119; circus, CC *66, 70;* movie, MN *60, 61;* opera, OP *40, 41;* theatrical, TT 17, *20, 21*
Psst . . .! (magazine), BC *105*
Puccini, Giacomo, memorabilia of, OP 34, *36, 38*
Puck (magazine), BC *105,* 106, 110
Pullman Company memorabilia, RS 22, *29, 32*
Pump, hand-cranked, DF *118*
Pumps, fire, DF 140-141, *149-151;* on belt buckle, DF *147;* steam-driven, DF *138-139,* 141
Punch (character): matchsafe,

MN 10; puppet, PQ 138
Punch (magazine), cartoons from, BC 100, 104, 112
Punch bowls, BC 57, 60, CD 106
Pungs-Finch Limited (car), BC 82
Puppets, PQ 134-145
Purina company, knife from, IL 142
Purrington General Store, Dover, N.H., model of, DF 24
Purses: Chinese, embroidered, DF 82; world's fair souvenirs, TW 122. See also Handbags
Pushkin, Alexander, set design for play by, TT 28
Puss-in-Boots, portrayals of, BC 13, 135
Putnam, Grace Storey, doll patented by, DF 44
Putnam, Henry W., IL 52
Puzzles: Lindbergh, LM 51; political, PQ 72; royal souvenir, RS 86

Q

Quack box, OP 153
Quaker sampler, RS 88, 92
Quartz: bead, BB 9; eggs, DF 66, 68; hatpin head, FH 112; marbles, LM 152, 159, 160; pendants, BB 19, IL 92
Quassia cups, OP 157
Queen, Ellery (pseud.), book by, CD 158
Queen Anne style: chandelier, BC 34; teapot, OP 144
Queen Elizabeth (ship), candy container from, OP 31
Queen Mary (ship), memorabilia of, OP 26, 31
Queen's ware (Wedgwood), TW 84, 86; marks, TW 85; plate, TW 92
Quezal Art Glass and Decorating Company, Brooklyn, N.Y., lamps by, LM 21, 31
Quillen, Nate, decoy by, CD 135
Quilts, PQ 146-160
Quimper, Henri, bell by, BB 51
Quirts, CD 66

R

Rabbits: in children's books, CC 10; doorstop, DF 62; foot bones, SS 68; gold, in egg, DF 69; netsuke, MN 149; pottery design, AB 74; on spoon handle, SS 50; on tableware, MN 159
Raccoons, illustrations of, BB 98, TW 116
Race records, CD 29, 30; listings of, CD 31
Races: automobile, memorabilia of, AB 103, 107, 108, 109, 110, 111, 114, 148, FH 57; bicycle, medal for, MN 25. See also Horse racing
Radiator emblems, old-car, AB 103, 104

Radiator ornaments, car, AB 104, 106-107, LM 8, 16
Radio premiums, PQ 110-119
Radios, RS 6-19
Rag dolls, DF 37, 39, 40
Raggedy Ann: cartoons, AB 34; doll, DF 40
Railroadiana, MN 34, PQ 53, 85; RS 20-33
Railroads: coverlet honoring, CD 57; purveyor for, IL 99; route map, on stoneware, SS 143; stamp, SS 112; watch, TW 59. See also Trains
Rake, wooden, DF 116-117
Raleigh, Sir Walter, SS 60
Ramirez, Martin, art by, FH 17
Rams: in children's book, CC 10; weather vane, TW 74-75
Rams' horns: snuff container, SS 68; vase shape, BB 38
Rand, Sally, TW 123, 129
Rand McNally atlas, LM 148
Ravenna Glass Works, Ravenna, Ohio, jar by, IL 54
Raymond, Alex, art by, CD 158
Raymond, The Great (magician), LM 101; props, LM 94, 101
Razors: safety, RS 143, 145; straight, OP 55, RS 144
RCA Victor: phonographs, PQ 8, 9, 11; radios, RS 8, 16; record lists, CD 31; recording artists, CD 41, OP 34, 37; records, CD 32, 34, 37, 39, 40, IL 64, 69, OP 34; trademark (Nipper), DF 8, PQ 8, 12
Reade, Charles, book by, BB 95
Reapers, DF 110, 113, 125; on medal, MN 24
Rebecca (Biblical character), doorstop portraying, DF 61
Rebuses: Bible, BB 77; on spoon handle, SS 80
Record players. See Jukeboxes; Phonographs
Records: comic-related, CC 148; cylinders, PQ 6, 7, 8-9; movie sound tracks, MN 67, RS 55; opera, OP 34, 36, 37; rock and roll, RS 50, 52, 53, 55-57, 59, 61, 63. See also Country music; Jazz
Red Kamel cigarettes and lighter, SS 71
Redouté, Pierre-Joseph, prints by, BB 120, 128
Redware, RS 34-49
Reed, Long Cleve, label from record by, CD 30
Reed. See Wicker
Reed, Thomas, caricature of, BC 112
Reed & Barton silver tableware, SS 37, 48
Regimentals (steins), SS 124, 126, 130
Relish dishes, BC 58, LM 112
Remington, E., & Sons, typewriters, TW 6, 8, 9, 11

Remington, Frederick, LM 74
Remington Arms Company: gun cane, BC 49; guns, FH 86, 95; knives, IL 135, 141, 143
Renaissance Revival: furniture, TW 36, 38, 44-46, 48-51, 54-55; jewelry, IL 88
Renault (car), serial-number plate from, AB 102
Repoussé work, SS 35, 41
Revere, Paul, BB 97; spoon honoring, SS 78; teapot by, SS 32
Revere Pottery, Boston, Mass. See Paul Revere Pottery
Revolutionary War, MN 21; Currier & Ives print, CD 91; maps, LM 124, 146; money, OP 90, 91; muskets, FH 84, 86-87; stamps commemorating, SS 113, 115; swords, SS 149, 150-153
Revolvers, CC 74, FH 94, 95; bottle shaped like, PQ 60. See also Guns
Rexsoma (drink), cup for, AB 17
Reynard the Fox, illustration of, CC 10
Reynolds, Charles, Trenton, N.J., majolica by, LM 107, 112; mark, LM 115
Reynolds, Milton, pens by, OP 126, 132
Rhead, Frederick H., AB 76-78, 83
Rheims-Douay Bible, BB 69, 70, 72
Rhinoceros, on corkscrew, CD 26
Rhodes, Alan, bottle by, MN 160
Rhythm and blues recordings, RS 50, 52, 53, 57
Ribbons, political, PQ 67, 68
Rice, Elmer, scene from play by, TT 36-37
Richard, J. H., art by, TW 119
Rifles, CC 73, 74-75, CD 67; accessories, CC 76, 77; canes, BC 49. See also Guns
Riggs, Bobby, bank portraying, AB 124
Ring holder, egg-shaped, DF 68
Ringling Brothers circus, CC 61-62; posters, CC 64, 65
Rings, IL 76, 83, 94, 98, 101; Chinese (magic trick), LM 93; keys worn as, LM 62; pipe tamper, SS 67; radio premiums, PQ 112-113, 117, 118; on valentine, TW 24; watch in, TW 66
Rip Van Winkle (character): actor as, PQ 23; puppet, PQ 145
Ritchie, William Norman, caricatures by, BC 109
Rittenhouse, Evans and Company, Trenton, N.J., BB 35; mark, BB 44
Ritty, James and John, cash register by, BC 115, 117

Riviera ware, DF 135
Road signs, AB 109, 110, RS 158, 159
Robb, Samuel, carving by, RS 154-155
Robbins, Carrie, art by, TT 26
Robert, Nicolas, BB 119
Robert-Houdin (magician), LM 92
Robertson, Hugh C., pottery by, AB 74-75
"Robes," English (dresses), CC 102, 104, 105, IL 147, 157
Robineau, Adelaide Alsop, pottery by, AB 81, 82; marks, AB 84
Robinson, Edwin Arlington, BB 99
Robinson, Jackie, bank, LM 50
Robinson, Sugar Ray, AB 148
Robots: movie scene, RS 110; toy, TT 95
Rock and roll memorabilia, RS 50-63
Rock crystal: egg, DF 68; goblet, CD 109
Rockefeller, Abby Aldrich, folk art center, AB 22, FH 7
Rocking chairs, OP 16, 59; Shaker, RS 122, 125, 135; Victorian, TW 52; wicker, TW 105
Rockingham ware, BB 56, 57, 59, 65, 66, 67
Rock Island Plow Company: corn planter, DF 108-109; implement seat, DF 120
Rockne, Knute, AB 148
Rock-Ola Manufacturing Company jukeboxes, IL 108-109; brochure, IL 114
Rockwell, Norman, art by, LM 73, 78, 81, PQ 104-105
Rockwell Silver Co., overlay work by, BB 38, 43
Rococo Revival furniture, TW 36, 38-41
Rodgers, Jimmie, CD 29, 32, 34, 37
Rodgers, Joseph, & Sons, Sheffield, England, knife by, IL 140
Rods, fishing, DF 154-155; in cane, BC 48
Rogers, John, sculpture by, RS 64-75
Rogers, William D., carriages by, FH 147, 154
Rogers Bros. trademark, silverware with, SS 48, 49, 50, 53
Rohmer, Sax, book by, CD 160
Rolling pins, RS 119
Rolling Stones (rock group), memorabilia of, RS 63
Rolls Royces (cars), AB 105, 106; toy, TT 108
Roly-poly (tobacco tin), SS 61
Rombauer, Irma, book by, CD 6
Ronson Penciliter, OP 130

Rookwood Pottery, Cincinnati, Ohio, AB 72-73, 76, 78; marks, AB *84*; vase, AB *73*

Roosevelt, Franklin D., SS 105; memorabilia of, PQ 66, *69, 72-74*; on scrip note, OP *93*

Roosevelt, Theodore, DF 32, TW 56; memorabilia of, AB *125*, MN *21, 22*, PQ *cover, 69, 71, 74*; on stamp, SS *107*

Roosevelt Stock Farm (toy), DF *32*

Roosters: chalkware, BC *138*; on iron, IL *24*; netsuke, MN *149*; weather vanes, TW 68, *76*; whirligig, TW *78*

Roover Brothers Company, Brooklyn, N.Y., coin machines by, OP *113, 114*

Rose, Rufus, puppet by, PQ *134*

Rose bowls, BC *64*

Rose Canton (style of Chinese porcelain), CC *29, 31*

Rose Medallion (style of Chinese porcelain), CC *21, 23, 24, 28, 29, 31*

Rosenbaum, W. S., art by, FH *18*

Rose palette (in Chinese porcelain), CC *21, 23, 24*

Roseville Pottery, Zanesville, Ohio, products of, AB 73, 74, 76, 77, *87*

Ross, Diana, record by, RS *61*

Ross, E., & Company, Toledo, Ohio, FH *131*

Roth, John, decoys by, CD *135*

Roulette wheel, AB *16*

Routledge, George, books published by, CC 9, *10*

Rouveyre, André, art by, BC *111*

Rowing toys, TT *98-99*

Rowlandson, Thomas, art by, BC *100, 103*

Royal Bayreuth owl, OP *50*

Royal Club corkscrew, CD *22, 23*

Royal Copenhagen Porcelain Manufactory, Denmark, BC 127

Royal Doulton china, AB *113*, RS *81*

Royal Flemish glass, AB *59*

Royal souvenirs, RS 76-87; paper dolls, OP *82, 83*

Royal Worcester Porcelain Company, England, perfume bottle by, RS *78*

Rubies: on Easter eggs, DF *66*; jewelry, IL *83, 86, 88, 94, 105*

Rugs: hooked, FH 130-143; "marrying" rug, ship's, OP *24*; Navajo blankets as, MN 113, *122, 123*; prayer rug, DF *80*

Runabout (carriage), FH *144-145*

Ruskin, John, IL *90*

Russell, Bill, AB *148*

Russell, John, IL *133*

Russell, Lillian, PQ *51*

Rust Craft Greeting Cards, Inc., products, FH 71, *80, 81*, TW *32*

Ruth, George Herman (Babe), AB *141*

Ruttman, Troy, AB *148*

S

Saalburg, Leslie, AB 110

Saalfield Publishing Company, Akron, Ohio, book from, OP *83*

Sabers. *See* Swords

Sabu (actor), MN 65

Saddlebags, OP 153

Saddles, CD 60, 62, *64, 65*

Sadirons, IL 26-27, *28, 29, 31*; trivet for, TT *154*

Sailors: chest, MN *109*; knives, IL *135, 138*; models of, MN *41, 42*; as whirligig, TW *79*. *See also* Scrimshaw

St. Denis, Ruth, CD 119, *124, 125*

Saint-Gaudens, Augustus, designs by, CC *137*, MN *21, 22*

St. Louis Cash Register Company, product of, BC *124*

St. Louis company, France, OP 101; vase, OP *108*

Salamander (kitchen tool), IL *118*

Salomon, Erich, BC 23

Salt-and-pepper shakers: Depression-glass, CD *144, 145*; Fiesta-ware, DF *133*; musical, MN *71*; redware, RS *46*

Salt dishes: glass, AB *54*, PQ *123*; pewter, OP *141*; scrimshaw, RS *119*; silver, SS *43*

Samplers, RS 88-89. *See also* Embroidery

Samurai: depictions of, IL *44-45*, MN *145*; swords, SS 149, *156-157*

Sandoz, Edouard Marcel, cat by, BC *131*

Sandwich Glass Company. *See* Boston & Sandwich

Santa Clara pueblo bowl, RS *42*

Santa Claus: buttons, AB *8*; Christmas card, FH *79*; Christmas tree ornaments, CC *38, 41*; currency, OP *92*. *See also* Father Christmas

Sargent & Greenleaf, Rochester, N.Y., lock by, LM *70*

Sarony, Napoleon, photo by, PQ *23*

Sashes: Civil War officer's, CC *83*; Iroquois, MN *117*

Sasieni of London, Inc., England, pipe by, PQ *39*

Satin glass, AB 60, *67*, DF *68*

Satin stitching, DF 73, 76, 78, *79*

Satsuma pottery, BC 8, *14, 130*, FH *112*

Saturday Evening Girls pottery, AB 86-87; bowl, AB *82*; marks, AB *84, 86*

Saturday Evening Post (magazine), LM *72, 75, 81*

Sauceboats: Fiesta-ware, DF *133*; silver, SS *41*

Saucers: Belleek, BB *35, 37*; Chinese porcelain, CC *20, 25*; dining-car, RS *29*; Fiesta-ware, DF *129, 130*; glass, AB *59*, CD *143, 145, 147*; majolica, LM *104, 105, 110*; political souvenir, PQ *66*; Staffordshire, SS *88*

Savitsky, Jack, art by, FH *17*

Savoy, The (magazine), LM 73, 77

Sawin, John, clock by, CC *94*

Saws, TT *77*; in catalogue, TT *76*; in knife, IL *132*

Sax, Adolphe, MN 87

Scales: for eggs, IL *131*; pharmacist's, OP *154*

Scarabs: belt-buckle design, IL *98*; hatpins, FH *113, 116*

Scarves: map on, TW *143*; world's fair souvenirs, TW *124, 130*

Schacht, Al, AB *141*

Scharff, Anton, medal by, MN *21*

Schiaparelli, Elsa, FH 119

Schick razor, RS *145*

Schiffli lace, IL *158*

Schimmel, Wilhelm, AB 26

Schmidt, Benjamin, decoys by, CD *128-129*

Schmidt, Oscar, International, Inc., autoharps by, MN *84*

Schneider, Gebrüder, Germany, model soldiers by, MN *45*

Schoenhut, A., & Co., Philadelphia, Pa., toys by, DF *16, 22, 28, 39, 45*, TT *91*

Schoenner, Jean, toy by, TT *12*

Schrever & Co. toy car, TT *107*

Schuco convertible (toy), TT *107*

Schumann, Robert, stamp honoring, SS *123*

Schumann-Heink, Ernestine, OP *37*

Science fiction, RS 100-111; comic characters, CC *cover, 158, 159*

Scientific American (magazine), matchsafe promoting, MN *12*

Scissors: in knife, IL *132*; royal souvenir, RS *81*; sewing, MN *124, 125, 126, 135*; sign depicting, RS *154-155*

Sconces, BC *35, 38*

Scott, Peter, book by, BB *105*

Scott, Robert Falcon, LM 134, *135*

Scott, Sir Walter: armorial plate, CC *25*; books, BB *108*

Scott, Winfield, CD *91*

Scott radios, RS 10, *19*

Scottsboro Boys, button supporting, PQ *70*

Scrapers, Indian, AB *46, 52*

Scrimshaw, RS 112-121

Scrip notes, OP *93*

Scroddled ware, BB 57, *58-59, 65, 67*

Scythe, cradle, DF *117*

Seals (animals): on button, PQ *70*; on stamp, SS *98*

Sears, Roebuck & Company: catalogue, furniture in, OP 7, *10*; Silvertone radio, RS *14*

Secessionist-style art, PQ *99*

Secor, Jerome, bank by, AB *119, 120-121*

Seeburg, J. P., Corporation, jukeboxes by, IL *107*, 109

Sells Brothers circus, memorabilia of, CC *67-71*

Sells-Floto Circus clowns, CC *68*

Sem (Georges Goursat), illustration by, MN *32-33*

Serapes, MN *111, 115, 118-120*

Serial-number plates, old-car, AB *102, 104-105*

Serpent (musical instrument), MN *94*

Serpents. *See* Snakes

Servers, silver, SS *53*

Set designs, art for, CD *122-123*, TT *17-18, 28-31*

Settees: Victorian, TW *46*; wicker, TW *102*

Sewer-pipe sculptures, FH 22, *29*

Sewing desk, RS *122*

Sewing machines, MN *130, 131*

Sewing tools, MN 124-135; basket for, AB *150*; in cane, BC *47*; of Civil War soldiers, CC *76, 79*; needlecases, CC *26*, DF *28*, MN *126, 127, 135*; painted boxes for, OP *58*; in piano, MN *90*; scrimshaw, RS *120, 121*

Seymour, Horatio, souvenir of, PQ *64*

Seymour, Robert, art by, BC *103*

Sgraffito technique, RS 36, *48*

Shadow box, magician's, LM *101*

Shadow, The, rings, PQ *113*

Shahn, Ben, poster by, PQ *108*

Shaker crafts, AB *157*, FH 38, RS 122-139

Shakers (tableware), OP *141*, RS *29*. *See also* Salt-and-pepper shakers

Shakespeare, William, plays by: memorabilia of, TT *19, 27, 32-34*; in sculpture, RS *74*

Sharaku (Japanese artist), IL 36

Shaving basin, OP *140*

Shaving mugs, RS *cover*, 140-151

Shaw, George Bernard, BB 94, CC *47*; autograph, AB *101*

Shawls, paisley, CC *111*, DF *81*

Shawn, Ted, CD 125

Shay (carriage), FH *146*

Sheaffer company: pen, OP *131*; pencil, OP *130*

Sheep: chalkware, BC *147*; in children's book, CC *10*; on egg, DF *69*; toy, TT *91*; weather vane, TW *74-75*

Sheet music, CD 119; country, CD 28, 38, 41, *43*; jazz, IL *63, 64, 67, 69, 72*; Lindbergh-related, LM *48*; for movie, MN *67*; operatic, OP *39, 42*; police-related, PQ *55*; World War II, TW *147*

Sheffield knives, IL *134*, 135, *139*, *140*

Sheffield plate, BC 35, SS 32, *38*

Sheldrake, Timothy, book produced by, BB *123*

Shell: beads, BB *11*, *12*; buttons, BC 8, 9, *11*, *12*, *16*; eggshell, in jewelry, IL *97*, *98*; Indian jewelry, IL *99*, *100*; money, CC *128*; in picture frame, TT *46*; Victorian curio, TW *42*; walnut, netsuke from, MN *140*. See also Mother-of-pearl; Tortoise shell

Shell casing, vase from, TW *148*

Shelley, Mary, book by, RS *103*

Shell motif: carnival glass, BC *56*; Chinese porcelain, CC *30*, *32*; majolica, LM *104-105*, *112*, *113*, *116*; netsukes, MN *146*, *148*; radio receiver, RS *10*; silver, SS *43*, *51*

Shepard, E. H., art by, CC *19*

Shepp's Shredded Cocoanut, New York, N.Y., premium from, TT *54*

Sheraton, Thomas, clock style, CC *91*

Sheridan, Philip, CC 81

Sherman, William Tecumseh: on card, PQ *51*; on stamp, SS *106*

Sherwood, Robert, quoted, TT 17

Shiebler, Geo. W., & Co., spoon by, SS *81*

Shiloh, Battle of, map of, LM *146*

Shinn, W. C., Neb., lightning-rod ball by, LM *41*

Ships and boats: bell, BB *48*; on chair back, TW *105*; on cup plate, PQ *125*; on currency, OP cover, *92*; Currier & Ives prints, CD *87*, *97*; doorstop, DF *58*; eagle ornaments, AB *24*, *25*, *26*, *29*; on love token, TW *23*; scrimshaw, RS *112-113*, *115*; on stamp, SS *98*; toy, TT *98-99*; trade cards for, TT *110*; on watch, TW *61*. See also Ocean liner memorabilia; Nautical gear

Shirley Temple dolls, DF *54*, OP 75, 86

Shirts: cowboy, CD *68*; Indian, BB *17*, MN *117*; world's fair memorabilia, TW *130*

Shock machines, OP *113*, *153*

Shoe buttons, BC *12*

Shoehorn, AB *14*

Shoes, CC *107*, *114*, *115*; Belleek, BB *38*; Christmas tree ornaments, CC *36*; Civil War, CC *83*; cowboy boots, CD *63*; moccasins, BB *16*; performers' slippers, CD 119, *120*, TT *33*; pincushion, MN *133*; sneakers, RS *58*

Sholes & Glidden Type Writer, TW 6, *8*

Shooting break (carriage),

FH *157*

Shovel, power (toy), TT *103*

Shrine, chalkware, BC *140*

Shute, S. A. and R. W., FH 7

Siamese twins, PQ *23*

Sicard, Jacques, pottery by (Sicardo), AB *80*

Sideboards, oak, OP 6, *14*

Sidewheeler, toy, TT *99*

Siercke, Hans, cat by, BC *135*

Sifter, IL cover

Signet-ring pipe tamper, SS 67

Signs, AB 109, *110*, RS 152-160

Silhouettes, OP 61, SS 6-19; iron weather vanes, TW 68, 70, 76

Silk pictures, SS 20-29

"Silk" (tobacco premium), SS *64*

Silver, SS 30-59; beads, BB *12*, *20*; belt buckle, IL *91*; Bible binding, BB *76*; boxes, BB *156*, *159*, CC *26*, SS *40*, *56*, TW *122*; bracelets, IL *97*, *105*; brooches, AB *22*, IL *86*, *98*, *104*; buttons, BC *16*, *17*; candleholders, BC 30, *35*, *36*, *40*; cane handles, BC *42*, *50*; chess set, BC *151*; children's tableware, MN *158*; cigar cutter, SS 67; cigarette cases, AB *108*, BC *42*; cigarette holder, SS *66*; coins, AB *21*, 22, CC *117*, *119*, *121-125*, *127*, *129*, *133-138*; comb, CC *143*; compact, BC *133*; corkscrews, CD *25*, *26*; dining-car ware, RS *29*; earrings, IL *82*; eggs, DF *67*; eyeglass case, DF *91*; eyeglasses, DF *87*, *88*; on flutes, MN *95*; on guns, FH *90-91*; hairpins, CC *144*; hatpin heads, FH *110*, *114*, *116*, *117*; Indian jewelry, IL *99*, *100*, *101*; Japanese fasteners, BB *14*, IL *102*, MN *142*; knives, IL *134*, *140*, MN *158*, SS 48, 49, 50; matchsafes, MN 6, 8, 9, *10*, *12*; medals and plaques, MN *18*, *22*, *26*, *27*, *29*; napkin rings, OP 30, *53*, SS 36, *43*; necklaces, BB *19*, IL *90*, 95, *101*; overlay, on Belleek, BB 38, *43*; papboat, MN *153*; pens, OP *128*; sewing tools, MN *126-128*, *132*, *133*; speaking trumpet, DF *144*; spoons, MN *158*, OP *157*, SS 42, 48, *49-51*, 74-81, TW *130*; stein lid, SS *129*; sword hilt, SS *148*; tea service, miniature, DF *29*; trophy, AB *114*; world's fair souvenirs, TW *122*, *130*

Silver, Horace, IL 75

Silvered (mercury) glass, AB *54*, BC 35, LM 39, *42*, *43*

Silver Screen (magazine), MN 55, 58

Simmons, Amelia, book by, CD 6

Simon, Andre, book by, CD 17

Simon & Halbig, Gräfenhain, Germany, doll heads by, DF *35*, *48*; mark, DF *49*

Simonson, Lee, stage set designed by, TT *36-37*

Simplex (car): hubcap, AB *103*; Moto-Meter, AB *104*

Simplex Electric Heating Company, curling iron by, TT 68

Sinbad the Sailor (book), CC 18

Singer, J. H., company, N.Y., card game by, PQ *51*

Singer Manufacturing Company, sewing machine by, MN *131*

Sinsei Toy Company, Japan, product of, TT *107*

Sioux: moccasins, BB *16*; necklace, IL *99*; pipes, PQ *40*

Skeleton, in book, BB *107*

Skeleton clock, CC 96

Skeleton watch, TW *63*

Skewers, IL *119*; silver, SS *50*

Skirt panel, Chinese, DF *79*

Skittles, pins for, TT cover

Skulls: on badge, TW *142*; padlock, LM 60, *68*; stein, SS *133*; watch, TW *64*

Skunk, illustration of, BB *98*

Sky King ring, PQ *113*

Skylab, stamp honoring, SS *113*

Slag glass, lightning-rod balls made of, LM 39, *44*

Slag marbles, LM *154*

Sled, TT *87*

Sleighs, FH *160*; bells, BB *53*; mold shaped like, OP *147*; print of, CD 95

Slices (servers), silver, SS *53*

Slide projector, PQ *22*

Slot machines, OP 112-113, *120*, *121*

Smart Set, The (magazine), LM *84*

Smith, Al, memorabilia of, PQ cover, 66, 72

Smith, Bessie, CD 29, IL 66

Smith, David. See Griffen, Smith and Hill

Smith, Mamie, CD 29, 30; label of record by, IL *66*

Smith, Oliver, painting by, CD *122-123*

Smoking paraphernalia, BB *155*, BC *62*; SS 60-73; canes, BC *42*, *50*; netsuke, MN *140*; radio, RS *18*; from ships, OP 30, *31*; Tiffany, TT *46*; tinware, TT *58*; world's fair souvenirs, TW 130. See also Cigarettes; Cigars; Matchsafes; Pipes; Snuff

Snakes: on bowl, RS *42*; folk-art sculpture, FH *19*; on insignia, TW *138*; jewelry, IL 77, *85*, *86*, *88*, *92*; on jug, SS *142*; medal, MN *28*; on pen, OP *128*; print of, TW *119*; on vase, LM *11*

"Snowbird," AB 27

Snowplow, on toy train, TT *139*

Snow White and the Seven Dwarfs (film), AB 33, 35, 37

Snuff: containers, BB *155*, CD *25*, MN *70*, SS *68*, *69*, TW *122*; tools, SS *68*; trade

card, TT *121*

Snuffers. See Candles

Snyder, George, DF 153

Soap, royal souvenir, RS *87*

Soap dish, majolica, LM *121*

Soapstone: chess set, BC *155*; inkwell, IL *15*; iron, IL *28*

Société Française de Fabrication de Bébés et Jouets (S.F.B.J.), dolls by, DF 36, *52*; mark, DF 49

Sofas: dollhouse, DF *28*; Victorian, TW *40-41*, *46*; wicker, TW 96, *106*

Soldiers, model, MN 40-53

Songbooks, CD 28, *38*, *41*, *43*, TW *147*. See also Sheet music

Sons of the Pioneers (recording group), CD *41*

Soup bowls, CD *145*, DF *128*

Soup tureens. See Tureens

Southern Broadcasters (recording group), CD 35

Southern Grocery Company, Pine Bluff, Ark., cigar band from, CC *49*

Southern Pacific Lines playing card, PQ *53*

Sowerby, James, art by, BB *124*

Sowerby, Kole, bronze by, DF *15*

Space-program memorabilia, LM *50*, MN *13*, SS *98*, *113*

Spades (servers), silver, SS *53*

Spades (tools), DF *116-117*; miniature, CC *128*

Spalding, A. G., Bros.: golf book, FH *62*, *66*; golf clubs, FH *62*, *65*

Spangled glass, AB *54*, *60*, *67*

Spanish-American War: game inspired by, FH *58*; Gatling gun, FH *98-99*; sword, SS *160*

Speaking trumpets, fire chiefs', DF 139, *140*, *144*

Spear points, AB *42*, *53*

Specialty Manufacturing Company, St. Paul, Minn., egg scale by, IL *131*

Speke, John, book by, LM *135*

Spencerian handwriting, FH 8

Spense, Thomas, MN 19

Spices: boxes for, OP *63*, RS *139*, TT *54*, *57*; cookbook, CD 15

Spikes, Reb and John, label from record by, IL 64, *65*

Spinning wheel, Shaker, RS *128*

Spirit of St. Louis (airplane), LM 46; cigar label honoring, CC *53*; memorabilia, LM 48, *49*, *51*, 56

Spittoons: cane, BC *44*; carnival-glass, BC *63*; cut-glass, CD *111*; Flint Enamel, BB 58, *60*; majolica, LM *121*

Splitdorf radio, RS *10*

Spode china: marks, SS *91*; nursing bottle, MN *150*; willowware, SS 85, *88*

Spool holders, MN 125, *128*, *129*

Spool turning, TW *36*

AB *Advertising Giveaways to Baskets;* BB *Beads to Boxes;* BC *Buttons to Chess Sets;* CC *Children's Books to Comics;* CD *Cookbooks to Detective Fiction;* DF *Dogs to Fishing Tackle;* FH *Folk Art to Horse-drawn Carriages;* IL *Inkwells to Lace;*

Spoons, SS *cover*, 74-81; medicine, OP *157*; mixing, IL *123*; pewter ladles, OP *141*; silver, MN *158*, OP *157*, SS *42, 48, 49-51*, TW *130*; for snuff, SS *68*; valentine motif, TW *29*
Spoon warmer, SS *43*
Sports: doorstops, DF *61*; literature, BB *104-106*; steins, SS *131. See also* individual names
Sports cars, BC *86, 95, 97*
Spreaders (machines), DF *124*
Sprigging, SS *92*
Springfield Armory, Mass., products of: ammunition pouch for, CC *76*; rifled muskets, CC *73, 74-75*, FH *84, 86-87*; sword, SS *160*
Spurs, CC *84*, CD *62-63*
Squares (tools), RS *129*, TT *73*
Squash, redware, RS *49*
Squash-blossom necklace, IL *101*
Squier, Ephraim George, books by, LM *134*
Squirrels: chalkware, BC *145*; on Lalique vase, LM *11*
Staffordshire, SS *82-97*; bell, BB *51*; cats, BC *127, 129*; dogs, DF *8, 9*; frog mugs, FH *22, 25*; imitation, BC *143. See also* Wedgwood
Staghorn: corkscrew, CD *24*; netsuke, MN *142*; trophy handles, AB *114*
Stained glass, AB *59*; lampshade inserts, AB *86. See also* Leaded glass
Stamp box, Tiffany, TT *46*
Stamp case, giveaway, AB *14*
Stamps, LM *56*, SS *98-123*; collage, PQ *89*
Standard plumbing fixtures, bookmark advertising, AB *15*
Standard ware, AB *73*
Standish, Burt, BB *106*
Stanesby, Thomas, Sr. and Jr., instruments by, MN *87, 95*
Stanley, F. T., Co., New Britain, Conn., lock by, LM *59, 64*
Stanley, Henry M., LM *135*
Stanley Rule & Level Company, New Britain, Conn., TT *74*
Stanley Steamer Runabout (car), BC *82*
Stanton, Edwin, sculpture of, RS *73*
Stark, Dolly, AB *141*
Stationery, CC *86*, OP *130*; holder, TT *46*
Station wagon (1937), BC *87*
Statue of Liberty: in paperweight, OP *105*; on shaving mug, RS *147*; silk picture, SS *28*; spoon handle, SS *80*; stamp, SS *107*; on ticket, TW *124*
Staunton, Howard, chess sets, BC *149, 150*
Steadfast, Thomas L., MN *30*

Steam engines, DF *110*, TW *121*
Steam roller, toy, TT *103*
Steichen, Edward, photos by, LM *85, 87*
Steiff company, Germany: puppets, PQ *135, 137*; teddy bear, TT *90*
Stein, Solomon, carousel animals by, BC *68, 78-81*
Steinbeck, John, books by, BB *112, 115*
Steiner Company, Paris, France, dolls by, DF *46*; mark, DF *49*
Steinlen, Theophile-Alexandre, cat by, BC *135*
Steins, SS *124-133. See also* Beer
Steinway, Theodore E., SS *100*
Stephenson, D., coverlet woven by, CD *56*
Stephenson, George, SS *22*
Stepstool, Shaker, RS *132*
Stereo photos, CC *85*, PQ *24*
Sterling Brothers brewery, Evansville, Ind., beer cans from, BB *33*
Sterling record label, CD *43*
Stern board, from yacht, AB *25*
Stevens, J & E, Manufacturing Company, Cromwell, Conn., bank by, AB *116*
Stevens, Thomas, silk pictures by: bookmarks, SS *26*; Stevengraphs, SS *20, 21, 22-25, 23*
Stevens-Duryea (car), serial-number plate from, AB *102*
Stevenson, Adlai, button, PQ *69*
Stevenson, Ralph, pottery, Staffordshire, England, teapot by, SS *87*
Stevenson, Robert Louis, CC *8*, MN *40*
Stewart Warner radio, RS *18*
Stickley, Gustav, and brothers, furniture by, OP *16, 17*
Stickney engine, DF *111*
Stickpins, AB *15*, IL *86*
Stiegele, Carl, rifle by, FH *90-91*
Stieglitz, Alfred, magazine published by, LM *75*, PQ *25*
Stilettos, MN *125, 135*
Stingray (car), BC *86, 97*
Stirrup cup, Wedgwood, TW *86*
Stirrups, Civil War, CC *84*
Stock certificate, RS *33*
Stocking purse, FH *103*
Stockings: silk, CC *106, 107*; world's fair souvenirs, TW *124*
Stomacher, IL *87*
Stoneware, SS *134-147*; beer bottle, BB *138*; mugs, AB *17*, SS *128*; royal souvenirs, RS *78, 79*; Wedgwood, TW *82, 86-88*
Stoop, Dirck, etching by, DF *10*
Storer, Maria Longworth Nichols, AB *72*
Storks: bell, BB *55*; scissors, MN *124*; vase, AB *55*
Storr, Paul, silver pieces by, SS *30-31*; hallmarks, SS *34*

Stovepipe hats, DF *143*, FH *122*
Stoves, TT *70-71*; dollhouse, DF *30*; iron doubling as, IL *33*; laundry, IL *29*; lid-lifter trivet, TT *154*; potbellied, RS *31*
Stowe, Harriet Beecher, books by, AB *96*; art from, CD *17*; figures from, SS *97*
Straight Arrow rings, PQ *113*
Stratton Brothers & Co., Greenfield, Mass., level by, TT *75*
Straw: baskets, AB *153, 156*; handbag, FH *108*; hats, FH *118, 120, 123-125, 127, 129*; spreader for, DF *124*
Strawberries: cigar label, CC *52*; dish for, LM *111*; emery cushions, MN *127*
Strength testers, OP *110, 112*
Stringfield, Clarence, carvings by, FH *20*
Strobridge Lithographing Company, Cincinnati, Ohio, posters, CC *60-65, 71*, LM *93*
Stroller, wicker, TW *107*
Stromberg-Carlson Telephone Manufacturing Company, products of, TT *9, 14*
Strothmann, Fred, poster by, TW *144*
Structo Mfg. Co., toy by, TT *103*
Struwelpeter (book), art from, CC *11*
Stubbs, Joseph, pottery, Staffordshire, England, plate by, SS *82*
Studebaker (car), toy, TT *107*
Studebaker Brothers, South Bend, Ind., wagons by, FH *147*
Studio, The (magazine), LM *77*
Stutz (car), BC *85*; radiator emblem, AB *103*
Stuyvesant, Peter, DF *140*; on currency, OP *92*
Suffragette buttons, PQ *70*
Sugar bowls: art-glass, AB *58*; Belleek, BB *35, 37*; Chinese porcelain, CC *29*; Depression-glass, CD *143, 144, 147*; Flint Enamel, BB *59*; Liberty china, TW *94*; majolica, LM *111*; pressed-glass, PQ *130, 132*; silver, SS *35*
Sugar tongs, silver, SS *48, 52*
Sukenobu (Japanese artist), print by, IL *37*
Sulkies, FH *157*; Currier & Ives print of, CD *89*
Sullivan, Arthur, memorabilia of, OP *43*
Sullivan, John L., PQ *50*
Sulphides: doorknob, OP *108*; marbles, LM *152, 157*; paperweights, OP *101, 109*
Sunglasses, DF *92, 93*
Sunkist seal, FH *32, 33, 34, 40, 42, 44, 45*
Sunshine record label, IL *64, 65*
Superman (comic character), CC

151, 154, *155*; toy, CC *153*
Supremes (rock group), record by, RS *61*
Surrey, FH *149*
Surtees, Robert Smith, BB *106*
Susse Frères foundry, France, cat by, BC *135*
Sutherland, Samuel, FH *86*
Sutlers, CC *79*
Swans: button, BC *16*; on corkscrew, CD *26*; Depression-glass, CD *150*; on vase, BB *64*
Swanson, Gloria, OP *28*
Sweeper, suction, TT *68*
Swift (yarn winder), RS *120*
Swift & Company giveaways, AB *8*, CD *15*
Switch stand, railroad, RS *25*
Sword canes, BC *44, 45, 49*
Swords, CC *74-75*, SS *148-160*
Sykes, Charles, AB *106*

T

Tables: billiard, miniature, TT *146*; end table, tramp-art, TT *151*; oak, OP *6, 15, 17*; painted, OP *60, 62, 67, 68*; sewing, MN *134*; Shaker, RS *131, 133, 137-139*; Victorian, TW *34-35, 45, 48, 100*; wicker, TW *100*
Table tennis, FH *57*
Tachi sword, SS *156-157*
Taft, William Howard, memorabilia of, AB *89*, PQ *cover, 71*
Taglioni, Marie, on cigar cases, CD *118*
Tags, tobacco, SS *62, 63, 64*
Taine, John, art for story by, RS *107*
Tait, A. F., prints from art by, CD *85, 97*
Tankards: cut-glass, CD *100*; pewter, OP *134, 135*
Tape measures, IL *31*, MN *132*
Target balls, glass, BB *133, 144*
Target brand cigarette-rolling equipment, SS *65*
Tarot cards, PQ *49*
Tarzan books, CC *8*
Tassies, IL *80*
Taylor, Deems, autograph of, TT *39*
Taylor, Elizabeth, paper doll of, OP *87*
Taylor, James, RS *116*
Tea bowl, CC *20*
Tea caddies, BB *146, 147, 150*; Chinese porcelain, CC *25*; silver, CC *26*; tinware, TT *56, 58*
Teacart, wicker, TW *101*
Teapots: Belleek, BB *35, 37, 41, 45*; cat, BC *132*; pewter, OP *144, 145*; silver, SS *32, 35*; Staffordshire, SS *87*
Tea sets: Belleek, BB *37*; miniature, DF *29*; silver, SS *35-36*

Teco Pottery, Ill., vase by, AB *86*
Teddy bears, TT *cover, 90;* bank, AB *126;* food pusher, MN *158*
Teenage Rock and Roll Review (magazine), RS *54*
Teenie Weenies (comic characters), CC *151*
Teeth, animal: chess set, BC *155;* hatpin heads, FH *116. See also* Scrimshaw
Telegraph equipment, TT *13*
Telephones, TT *6-15. See also* Insulators
Telescopes, CC *80,* MN *103*
Temple, Shirley, MN *66;* dolls, DF *54,* OP *75, 86*
Templier, Raymond, brooch designed by, IL *98*
Temptations (rock group), record by, RS *61*
Tenniel, Sir John, art by, BC *100, 103, 104,* CC *16*
Tennis motif: bank, AB *124;* postcard, PQ *91*
Tennyson, Alfred, Lord, book by, BB *110*
Terra cotta: cats, BC *136;* doll, DF *34;* nursing bottle, MN *152*
Terriers: doorstops, DF *59;* painting of, DF *12-13*
Terry, Eli, clocks by, CC *89-90;* label, CC *89*
Testaphones, AB *102, 105*
Thayer Magic Manufacturing Co., Los Angeles, Calif., tricks by, LM *92, 95;* catalogue, LM *102*
Theatre, The (magazine), LM *77*
Theatrical memorabilia, TT *16-39;* playing cards, PQ *51;* posters, PQ *94, 97,* TT *17, 22, 23*
Theorem paintings, FH *8, 12,* TW *17, 20*
Thermometer, in baby bottle, MN *152, 157*
Thimbles and thimble holders, AB *150,* MN *124, 126, 127, 135*
Thomas, Bert, art by, BC *110*
Thomas, Chauncey, & Co., Boston, Mass., carriage by, FH *144-145, 147*
Thomas, Seth, clocks by, CC *88, 89-90, 91*
Thomas Flyer (car), AB *106;* radiator emblem, AB *103*
Thomason, Edward, corkscrew invented by, CD *20*
Thompson, George E., Company, Minn., products of, LM *43*
Thomson, E. Gertrude, art by, CC *16*
Thonet, Michael, TW *37, 52*
Thor (comic character), CC *cover*
Thornton, Robert John, BB *119*
Thread waxers and winders, MN *125, 128*
Threshers, DF *112;* toy, TT *102*

Thrilling Wonder Stories (magazine), art for, RS *100*
Thunderbird (car), BC *97*
Thurston, Howard, posters for, LM *90-91*
Ticket punches, railroad, RS *21, 27*
Tiebacks, curtain: Flint Enamel, BB *67;* glass, PQ *122*
Tiffany, Louis Comfort, artware by, TT *40-51;* hatpins, FH *111;* inkwells, IL *7,* TT *46;* lamps, LM *21, 30,* TT *42, 43, 44;* mark, AB *84;* pottery, AB *78, 82*
Tiffany & Co., New York, N.Y., TT *41;* inkwell, IL *7, 11;* matchsafes, MN *8, 12;* medal, MN *21;* plate, TW *130;* playing cards, PQ *47, 48;* silver tray, SS *39;* spoons, SS *78*
Tigers: carousel, BC *71;* claw, as pendant, IL *103;* fruit-crate label, FH *32-33;* insignia, TW *139*
Tilden, Samuel J., cartoon of, BC *105*
Tiles, decorative, AB *75,* BC *131*
Time, BC *110*
Timely Tunes records, CD *34, 39*
Timetables, railroad, RS *20-21, 32*
Tin Decorating Co., Baltimore, Md., tobacco tin by, SS *61*
Tin Goose (airplane), LM *52*
Tinsel print, TT *25*
Tintypes, PQ *19, 21, 67*
Tinware, TT *52-61;* candleholders, BC *38;* lamps, FH *156,* LM *22;* lanterns, BC *39;* molds, BC *32,* IL *128;* nursing bottle, MN *153;* oil cans, RS *125;* plate, RS *77. See also* Pewter; Tin
Tip trays, AB *11, 14*
Tirtoff, Romain de (Erté), art by, LM *86,* TT *30-31*
Titanic (ship), memorabilia of, OP *24, 25*
Tlingit capes, MN *117*
Toads. *See* Frogs
Toasters, TT *62-71*
Toast rack, OP *30*
Tobacco: for cigarette rolling, SS *65;* containers, BB *155,* BC *62,* MN *140,* RS *18,* SS *60-63,* TT *58;* Indians' use of, SS *60;* label for crate, SS *64;* plug cutter, SS *73;* premiums, TW *60 (see also* Cigarettes: premiums); tags, SS *62, 63, 64*
Toby jugs, SS *83, 85, 94, 95*
Toilet case, BB *157*
Toklas, Alice B., book by, CD *16*
Tole ware, TT *53, 58*
Tolson, Edgar, carving by, FH *21*
Tom Swift books, CC *8*
Tom Thumb, PQ *23*
Tongs: pipe smoker's, SS *70;* for port, CD *27;* silver, SS *48, 52*

Tonics, BB *131*
Toolboxes, BB *152,* TT *73*
Tools, TT *72-83;* scrimshaw, RS *116;* Shaker, RS *129*
Toothpicks: folding, AB *14;* holders, OP *50*
Tootsietoy company, DF *18*
Tops, spinning, AB *16,* RS *122,* TT *cover*
Tortoise shell: chess set, BC *155;* cigarette holder, SS *66;* combs, CC *140, 141, 147;* combs imitating, CC *142, 146, 147;* earrings, IL *89;* fan sticks, DF *100, 105;* lorgnettes, DF *89;* razor handle, RS *144;* snuffboxes, BB *155*
Toth (Egyptian god), amulet of, BB *14*
Totteridge Kennel, England, dogs from, in art, DF *12-13*
Touch marks, in pewter, OP *137, 140, 142, 143*
Touchstone, use of, IL *77*
Toulouse-Lautrec, Henri de: book by, CD *7;* posters by, PQ *92, 95, 96*
Tower of London, silk picture of, SS *25*
Towle Maple Syrup Co., spoon advertising, SS *76*
Townshend, George, print by, BC *101*
Toyokazu (Japanese artist), netsuke by, MN *146*
Toyokuni I (Japanese artist), prints by, IL *39, 42*
Toys, TT *cover, 84-109;* advertising giveaways, AB *16;* cats, BC *127, 128;* comic-character, CC *152, 153,* DF *54,* LM *157;* coronation coach, RS *84-85;* dishes, CD *150,* RS *119;* fluting iron, IL *31;* frogs, FH *27;* police wagon, PQ *63;* scrimshaw, RS *118, 119;* Shaker, RS *122;* whirligigs, TW *78, 79;* world's fair souvenirs, TW *132. See also* Banks; Dollhouses; Dolls; Games; Marbles; Puppets; Soldiers; Trains
Tractors, DF *110, 113-115;* toy, TT *102*
Tracy, Spencer, MN *65*
Trade cards, BC *107, 128,* CD *85,* OP *47,* TT *110-123*
Trade stimulators (machines), OP *122, 123*
Trains, board-game motif, FH *52-53;* on button, BC *16;* Christmas tree ornament, CC *37;* Currier & Ives print, CD *86;* glass portrayals of, BB *135, 145;* on shaving mug, RS *147;* silk picture, SS *22;* toy, TT *124-139. See also* Railroadiana
Tramp art, DF *26,* TT *140-151*
Transformation cards, PQ *47, 48*
Trans-Mississippi Exposition

(1898), stamp from, SS *110*
Traymore, Hotel, Atlantic City, N.J., menus from, MN *35, 36*
Trays: advertising giveaways, AB *11-13,* 14, 16; Belleek, BB *45;* Chinese porcelain, CC *29;* cut-glass, CD *111;* Depression-glass, CD *144;* Indian, coiled, AB *158, 159;* majolica, LM *113;* pin, BC *59,* RS *80;* silver, SS *30-31, 38, 39, 42, 47;* tinware, TT *58, 60, 61*
Trench art, TW *148*
Tricycles, BB *85-86, 88,* TT *84-85;* frog riding (toy), FH *27*
Trilby (novel), SS *cover*
Trinket boxes, BB *64,* BC *130;* egg-shaped, DF *68*
Trivets, BC *131,* TT *152-160*
Trollope, Anthony, book by, BB *110*
Trompe l'oeil: oyster plate, LM *113;* painting, BC *128,* OP *71,* PQ *88*
Trophy, auto-race, AB *114*
Troutbeck, William, clock by, CC *90*
Trowels (servers), SS *53*
Trucks, toy, TT *102, 106, 108*
Truman, Harry, PQ *cover*
Trumbull, John, art by: print from, CD *91;* silk picture from, SS *23;* stamp from, SS *113*
Trumpets, Christmas tree ornament, CC *42;* speaking, fire chiefs', DF *139, 140, 144;* toy, TT *cover*
Trunks. *See* Chests
Tsuba (sword guards), SS *156, 157*
Tuareg amulets, BB *7, 12*
Tuck, Raphael, & Sons, London, England: cards, FH *74;* paper dolls, OP *74, 82*
Tucker, Sophie, pen from, OP *132*
Tumblers: art-glass, AB *54, 64, 65;* carnival-glass, BC *56, 57, 58;* Depression-glass, CD *145, 148;* Homer Laughlin pottery, DF *130, 134, 136;* pewter, OP *138;* Tiffany, TT *50*
Tureens: Chinese porcelain, CC *23, 29;* faïence pigeon, LM *109;* silver, SS *30-31*
Turkeys: bell for, BB *52;* print of, TW *114;* on stein, SS *131*
"Turkish" furniture, TW *34-35, 36, 38*
Turquoise: jewelry, IL *88, 94, 99, 100, 101, 104;* thimble, MN *127*
Turtle bottle, MN 152, *156*
Turtledoves, Lalique, LM *9*
Tuscarora Advertising Company, Coshocton, Ohio, trays by, AB *13,* 14, 16
Tuthill Cut Glass Company, Middletown, N.Y.: bowl, CD *104;* marks, CD *103*

Twain, Mark: books by, BB 92-93, 114, CC 7-8; quoted, BC 139, OP 124, TW 8
Tweed, William M. (Boss): bank portraying, AB 117, 120; cartoons attacking, BC 104, 106; on jug, SS 142
Twentieth Century-Fox movie prop, MN 62
Tyler, Elman, coverlet by, CD 50
Tyler, Harry, coverlet by, CD 51
Tynietoy company, Providence, R.I., DF 16, 18; products of, DF 18, 23
Typewriters, TW 6-15

U

Ulanova, Galina, on plaque, CD 118
Ulrich, Hans, book by, RS 104
Umbrella handle, BC 50. See also Parasols
Uncle Sam: posters, PQ 95, 105, TW 137; strength tester, OP 110
Uncle Scrooge (comic character), CC 157
Underwood's High Chair Baby Plate, MN 159
Underwood typewriter, TW 11
Ungerer, Tomi, art by, PQ 106
Union Cutlery Company, knives by, IL 136, 139, 141
United Firemen's Insurance Co. fire mark, DF 148
United States Playing Card Co., Bicycle cards by, PQ 47, 52
United States Pottery Company, Bennington, Vt., BB 57, 63
Universal tractor, DF 113
University City Pottery, University City, Mo., AB 82; marks, AB 84; vase, AB 81
Unwin & Rodgers, Sheffield, England, knife by, IL 139
Upton, Florence Kate, MN 158
Urn, glass, AB 62
Utamaro (Japanese artist), prints by, IL 34, 39
Utensil currency, CC 128

V

Vacuum cleaner, prototype of, TT 68
Valentines, TW 16-33
Valentino, Rudolph, AB 107, LM 85, MN 66
Van Briggle, Artus, pottery by, AB 78, 79; marks, AB 84
Vanderbilt Cup Race pennant, AB 114
Van Deventer, Emma Murdoch, book by, CD 155
Van Dine, S. S. (pseud.), CD 154-155
Van Doren, Abram William, coverlet by, CD 56
van Gulik, Robert H., book translation by, CD 160
Van Houten cocoa, poster, PQ 97

Vanity box, BB 157
Vanity Fair (American magazine), LM 75; caricatures from, BC 110, 113, LM 85, OP 84
Vanity Fair (English magazine), caricatures from, BC 106, 108
Van Lansing Company, coin machine by, OP 119
Van Ness, James, coverlet by, CD 44
Van Vleck, Jay A., coverlet by, CD 52-53
Vaseline glass: inkwell, IL 10; marble, LM 156
Vases: art-glass, AB cover, 54, 55, 59-65, OP 108; art-pottery, AB 70, 72-74, 76-82, 86, 87; Belleek, BB 37-42, 45; Bennington-porcelain, BB 64; carnival-glass, BC 63-65; chalkware, BC 140; cloisonné miniature, DF 28; cut-glass, CD 110, 112; Fiesta-ware, DF 128; Lalique, LM 9-13; majolica, LM 120; on napkin holder, SS 43; pressed-glass, PQ 121; from shell casing, TW 148; silver-plated, SS 55; Tiffany, AB 78, TT 48-50; Wedgwood, TW 83, 87, 95
Vauxhall Victor (car), toy, TT 108
Vegetable ivory, CC 144, MN 127
Velez, Lupe, MN 60
Velocipede (tricycle), TT 84-85
Vending machines, OP 118, 119
Verdi, Giuseppe, memorabilia of, OP 38
Verne, Jules, RS 101
Ver Sacrum (magazine), LM 76
Vesalius, Andreas, book by, BB 107
Vests. See Waistcoats
Victor, RCA. See RCA Victor
Victoria, Queen (England): jewelry, IL 85; on medal, TW 122; as paper doll, OP 82; souvenirs of, RS 76, 77, 78, 79; table from, TW 34-35; underwear, DF 74
Victorian furniture, TW 34-57, 100, 106
Victorias (carriages), FH 147, 154
Victrola phonographs, PQ 9, 11
Vietnam War protests: button, PQ 70; poster, PQ 106
Vigoral (drink), cup for, AB 17
Villeroy & Boch company, Mettlach, Germany, steins by, SS 124, 125, 127, 129, 131
Vinaigrette, BB 159
Vincent, Gene, record by, RS 56
Violins, MN 86-87, 92-93; cane, BC 46
Vis-à-vis (carriages), FH 152-153, 160
Visiting cards. See Cartes de visite
Vocalion records, CD 33, 42, IL 65, 72
Vogue (magazine), LM 75, 87

Volstead, Andrew, caricature of, CD 27
Vonnegut, Kurt, Jr., book by, RS 104
von Sternberg, Josef, MN 58

W

Waffle irons, IL 121
Wager cup, silver, SS 58
Wagner, Honus, AB 141
Wagner, Richard, memorabilia of, OP 34, 38, 39, 44-45
Wagon jack, FH 156
Wagons, horse-drawn, FH 148-150, 158; police (toy), PQ 63
Wahl pen and pencil, OP 128
Waistcoats, CC 104, 111, DF 78; buttons for, BC 12; child's, CC 108; cowboy, CD 68
Wakefield, Cyrus, TW 96
Wallace, Lew, book by, BB 95
Waller, Thomas (Fats), IL 62, 69
Waller, William Oden, art by, TT 28
Walt Disney Productions. See Disney, Walt
Walton, Izaak, book by, BB 105, 106
Wampum, CC 128
Wanamaker's (store), Philadelphia, Pa., trade card from, TT 123
Wannopee Pottery Company, New Milford, Conn., LM 107
Wansey, Henry, art from book by, BB 98
Ward, F., silhouettes by, SS 18
Ward, Lem and Steve, CD 130
Ward, Marcus, & Co., England, cards by, FH 70, 72, 73, TW 18, 27
Ward, Montgomery, catalogue, records sold through, CD 34, 39
Wardle, Arthur, painting by, DF 12-13
War Eagle (riverboat), ornament from, AB 24
Warner Brothers cartoon characters, AB 39, 40
Washburn musical instruments, MN 86
Washington, Booker T.: on button, PQ 69; on coin, CC 138; on stamp, SS 112
Washington, George, AB 29, IL 80; autographs, AB 90, 91, 93; on cigar band, CC 55; on currency, OP cover; figurine, BC 143; inaugural buttons, BC 8; on medal, MN 21; on medallion, TW 82; in paperweight, OP 109; on plate, SS 84; poster, PQ 107; print of, CD 90; on speaking trumpet, DF 144; on spoon, SS 79; on stamps, LM 56, SS 104, 106, 107
Washington, Martha: letter from, AB 90; on spoon, SS 79; on

stamps, SS 106, 107
Washstands: oak, in catalogue, OP 10; painted, OP 64, 70, 71; Shaker, RS 133
Waste bowl, from tea set, SS 35
Watches, TW cover, 58-67; camera resembling, BC 29; in cane, BC 42; fireman's, DF 147; fobs, MN 70, TW 58, 65; holders, BC 140, FH 27; Mickey Mouse, LM 50, TW 67; musical, MN 69, 70; railroad, RS 27, TW 59; sign, RS 155; world's fair souvenirs, TW 131
Water cooler, stoneware, SS 144
Waterford glass, CD 108, 109
Waterman House, Warren, R.I., miniature of room in, DF 29
Waterman pens, LM 48, OP 124, 127-129, 131; display facsimile, RS 157
Watermarks, SS 102-103
Watkins, Carleton W., PQ 19
Watling Manufacturing Company, coin machine by, OP 114
Waud, Alfred, art by, AB 99
Waverly road wagon (car), BC 85
Wax: Christmas tree ornaments, CC 45; dolls, DF 37, 42, 43, 47, 53
Wayne, John, on poster, MN 59
Weather vanes, TW 68-81; eagles, AB 29; for lightning rods, LM 38, TW 68, 77
Weaving: beadwork, BB 16. See also Baskets; Blankets; Coverlets; Silk pictures
Webb, Thomas & Sons, Stourbridge, England, CD 109; ewer, AB 66
Weber, Karl Maria von, trade cards honoring, OP 47
Weber reproducing piano, MN 82
Webster, Daniel, autograph of, AB 90, 95
Webster, Noah, BB 70, BC 30
Wedding cup, silver, SS 58
Wedgwood, TW 82-95; buttons, BC 9; majolica, LM 110, 111, 116, 117; mark, LM 115; type of mortar and pestle, OP 154
Weed tire chains, advertising for, AB 110, LM 98-99
Weinmann, Johann, print by, BB 128
Weller Pottery, Zanesville, Ohio, products of, AB 73, 74, 76, 77, 80, 83, 87, SS 129
Welles, Orson, MN 64
Wellington, Duke of, in paperweight, OP 109
Wells, H. G., books by, RS 101; art from, RS 103; poster for movie of, RS 110
Wells & Co., Ltd., London, England, toy by, TT 106
Welsbach gas mantles, advertising giveaways for,

AB 15
Welty, Eudora, CD 12
Wermuth, Christian, MN 19
West, Mae, MN 57
West, Nathanael, book by, BB 116
Western Americana (books), BB 101, 102, 103; LM 134
Whale brand tobacco, SS 63
Whale ivory and bone: cane, BC 53. See also Scrimshaw
Whalen, Grover, BC 110
Wharton, Edith, BB 96
Wheaties bowl, PQ 116
Wheelbarrow, DF 119
Wheel covers, car, AB 105
Wheeled chair, TW 107
Wheeler, Charles (Shang), CD 130
Wheelmaking tools, TT 74, 82
Wheelmen (bicyclists' organization), AB 81, 87, 89; stein, SS 131
Whieldon, Thomas, TW 91
Whippets, bronze, DF 14
Whipple, Mark, decoy by, CD 136
Whirligig of Life toy, TT 88
Whirligigs, TW 78, 79
Whiskbrooms, Shaker, RS 127
Whiskey flasks. See Flasks
Whiskey jug, cut-glass, CD 103
Whiskey set, Depression-glass, CD 150
Whistles: giveaways, AB 16; in matchsafe, MN 11; stoneware, SS 146; train, RS 23
Whitall Tatum insulator, IL 17
White (car), hubcap, AB 103
White, E. B., books by, CC 8
White, O. C., Company, Worcester, Mass., lamp, LM 34
White, Peregrine, TW 96
Whitehead & Hoag Company, Newark, N.J., products of, AB 9, 10
Whiteman, Paul, record by, IL 70
White's Pottery, Utica, N.Y., SS 138
Whitman, Walt: book, BB 111; on cigar label, CC 50
Whitney, Eli, guns by, FH 84
Whitney, Gertrude Vanderbilt, FH 7
Whitney-Reed Chair Co., Leominster, Mass., dollhouse by, DF 22
Wicker, TW 96-107; basketry, AB 151, 153-155, 156, 157, 160; phonograph case, PQ 13
Wick trimmer, LM 23
Wick-Werke, Germany, stein by, SS 127
Wiener Werkstætte postcards, PQ 86

Wig, Beatles, RS 59
Wilcox, Archie, AB 148
Wildlife prints, CD 97, TW 108-119
Wild West show memorabilia, CC 66, PQ 94
Wiles, Irving R., art by, TT 25
Wilhelm, Kaiser (Germany), on stein, SS 130
Will, George F., quoted, TT 124
Will, William, pewter by, OP 137, 139
Willard, Simon and Aaron, clocks by, CC 89, 91, 94
Willets Manufacturing Company, Trenton, N.J., Belleek by, BB 35, 43; mark, BB 44
Willette, Adolphe, poster by, PQ 97
Williams, A. S., PQ 56
Williams, Hank, CD 34; memorabilia, CD 43
Williams, Ted, AB 141
Williams typewriter, TW 8, 9
Willimantic Linen Co. trade card, TT 118
Willington Glass Company, flask by, AB 28
Willkie, Wendell, on matchbook, MN 13
Willow baskets, AB 151, 153, 155, 156, 160
Willowware, blue, SS 83, 85, 88
Wills, Bob, record by, CD 42
Willys jeep, TW 134-135
Wilson, Alexander, art by, TW 108, 110, 112-113
Wilson, Woodrow, OP 24; campaign postcard, PQ 71; on cigar band, CC 55
Wilson's Photographic Magazine, PQ 25
Winchester rifles, CD 67, FH 82, 86, 88-89
Wind chime, BB 54
Window, Tiffany, TT 40-41
Windsor chairs, OP 59, 69
Wine accessories, silver, SS 44, 45
Wine cooler, Belleek, BB 37
Winnie Mae (airplane), LM 53
Winnie-the-Pooh books, CC 7, 19
Witches: puppet, PQ 134; on spoons, SS cover, 75
Withers, Jane, MN 63
Wittstein, Ed, art by, TT 29
Wolfers, Philippe, pendant by, IL 92
Wollheim, Donald A., book edited by, RS 104
Woltz, Da Costa, CD 35
Woman's Christian Temperance Union float, AB 112
Woman's Home Companion (magazine), paper doll from, OP 85

Women's Political Union postcard, PQ 84
Wonder Stories (magazine), art for, RS 100, 107
Wonder Woman (comic character), CC 155
Wood, David, clock by, CC 92
Wood, Enoch, and Sons, Staffordshire, England, china by, SS 84, 85, 86
Wood, L., knife by, IL 136
Wood, Ralph, bust by, SS 96
Wood and Son, England, teapot by, BC 132
Wood-block prints, IL 34-51
Woodstock festival, RS 50; souvenirs of, RS 63
Woodward, George, art by, BC 100
Woolworth, Frank, CC 36
Wooton, William S., company, desks by, TW 37, 54-55
Works Progress Administration (WPA), AB 24; Federal Theatre memorabilia, PQ 145, TT 22
World War I: board game based on, FH 58; china, TW 86, 94; cigarette box, BB 155; cookbooks, CD 8, 12; knife, IL 136; memorabilia of, AB 30, MN 28, 29, TW 134, 136, 137, 138, 140-143, 146-149; posters, PQ 95, TW 136-137, 144; razors, RS 145; soldiers, models of, MN 42, 44-45, 52, 53; sword, SS 160; valentines, TW 19; watches, TW 59
World War II: air-raid bell, BB 47; camouflaged beer cans, BB 24, 28; cigarette lighter, SS 70; fruit-crate label, FH 43; guns, FH 87, 96-97; jukebox brochure, IL 114; jukeboxes, IL 108, 112, 113; knife, IL 135, 136; maps, LM 147, TW 143; matchbook, MN 13; memorabilia of, TW 134-135, 136, 137, 139, 141-143, 147; posters, PQ 104-105, TW 145; radio premiums, influence on, PQ 110-111, 116; stamps commemorating, SS 113, 118; typewriters, TW 9; valentine, TW 33
World's Columbian Exposition. See Columbian Exposition
World's fair souvenirs, TW 120-133; Chicago (1933), PQ 144, TW 123, 129; New York (1964), LM 143, TW 132; Panama-Pacific (1915), AB 15, CD 104, SS 102, TW 123; Paris, AB 15, CD 103, FH 147, TW 122, 123, 126-127; St.

Louis (1904), SS 29, TW 123; Trans-Mississippi (1898), SS 110. See also Centennial Exhibition; Columbian Exposition
Worth, Thomas, CD 84
Wostenholm, George, & Son, Sheffield, England, knives by, IL 134, 140
Wragg, F. C., knife by, IL 134
Wreath, Victorian, TW 43
Wreck truck, toy, TT 108
Wrestler, print of, IL 46
Wrigglework, OP 138
Wright, Willard Huntington, CD 154-155
Wurlitzer, Rudolph, Company, jukeboxes by, IL 106, 107, 108, 110-113, 115; promotional material, IL 114
Wyeth, N. C., art by, CC 8, 18, LM 82

Y

Yale, Linus, Jr., locks by, LM 59-60, 65
Yardstick, Shaker, RS 129
Yarn winder, RS 120
Yei rug, MN 123
Yellow cabs: cigar label, CC 53; toy, TT 106
Yellow Kid (comic character), CC 149, 150; doll, CC 152
Yoshiiku (Japanese artist), print by, IL 47
Yoshitoshi (Japanese artist), prints by, IL 41, 45
Young, Roland, TT 39

Z

Zalar, John, carousel animals by, BC 67, 68, 70, 71
Zap comic book, CC 160
Zebras, on stoneware, SS 134
Zenith radios, RS 8, 10, 15
Zeppelins: cigar label, CC 53; stamp, SS 108; toy, TT 96-97
Zia pueblo, jar from, RS 43
Ziegfeld, Florenz, PQ 94
Zim Lines ashtray, OP 30
Zimmerman, Eugene, cartoons by, BC 105, CC 59
Zira cigarette premium, SS 64
Zither (Ukelin), MN 86
Zodiac: on beer cans, BB 33; on Wedgwood, TW 88
Zola, Emile, cartoon of, BC 105
Zouave-design handbag, FH 106
Zsolnay pottery, Pécs, Hungary, products of, FH 22, 23
Zuñi: jar, RS 42; jewelry, IL 99, 100, 101

AB *Advertising Giveaways to Baskets;* BB *Beads to Boxes;* BC *Buttons to Chess Sets;* CC *Children's Books to Comics;* CD *Cookbooks to Detective Fiction;* DF *Dogs to Fishing Tackle;* FH *Folk Art to Horse-drawn Carriages;* IL *Inkwells to Lace;* LM *Lalique to Marbles;* MN *Matchsafes to Nursing Bottles;* OP *Oak Furniture to Pharmacist's Equipment;* PQ *Phonographs to Quilts;* RS *Radios to Signs;* SS *Silhouettes to Swords;* TT *Telephones to Trivets;* TW *Typewriters to World War Memorabilia*